PEDRITO U.
MAYNARD-REID

Diverse
Worship

African-American, Caribbean
& Hispanic Perspectives

InterVarsity Press
Downers Grove, Illinois

InterVarsity Press
P.O. Box 1400, Downers Grove, IL 60515
World Wide Web: www.ivpress.com
E-mail: mail@ivpress.com

InterVarsity Press® is the book-publishing division of InterVarsity Christian Fellowship/USA®, a student movement active on campus at hundreds of universities, colleges and schools of nursing in the United States of America, and a member movement of the International Fellowship of Evangelical Students. For information about local and regional activities, write Public Relations Dept., InterVarsity Christian Fellowship/USA, 6400 Schroeder Rd., P.O. Box 7895, Madison, WI 53707-7895.

Cover illustration: Roberta Polfus

ISBN 0-8308-1579-1

Printed in the United States of America ∞

Library of Congress Cataloging-in-Publication Data

Maynard-Reid, Pedrito U.
  Diverse worship : African-American, Caribbean & Hispanic perspectives / Pedrito U. Maynard-Reid.
    p. cm.
  Includes bibliographical references.
  ISBN 0-8308-1579-1 (pkb. : alk. paper)
    1. Afro-American public worship. 2. Public worship—Caribbean area. 3. Public worship—Mexico. 4. Hispanic Americans—Religion. I. Title.
BR563.N4 M297 2000
264'.0089—dc21

                                                                              00-024894

---

17 16 15 14 13 12 11 10 9 8 7 6 5 4 3 2 1

13 12 11 10 09 08 07 06 05 04 03 02 01 00

To Lorraine Renee Jacobs
whose passion
for vibrant wholistic worship
inspires me

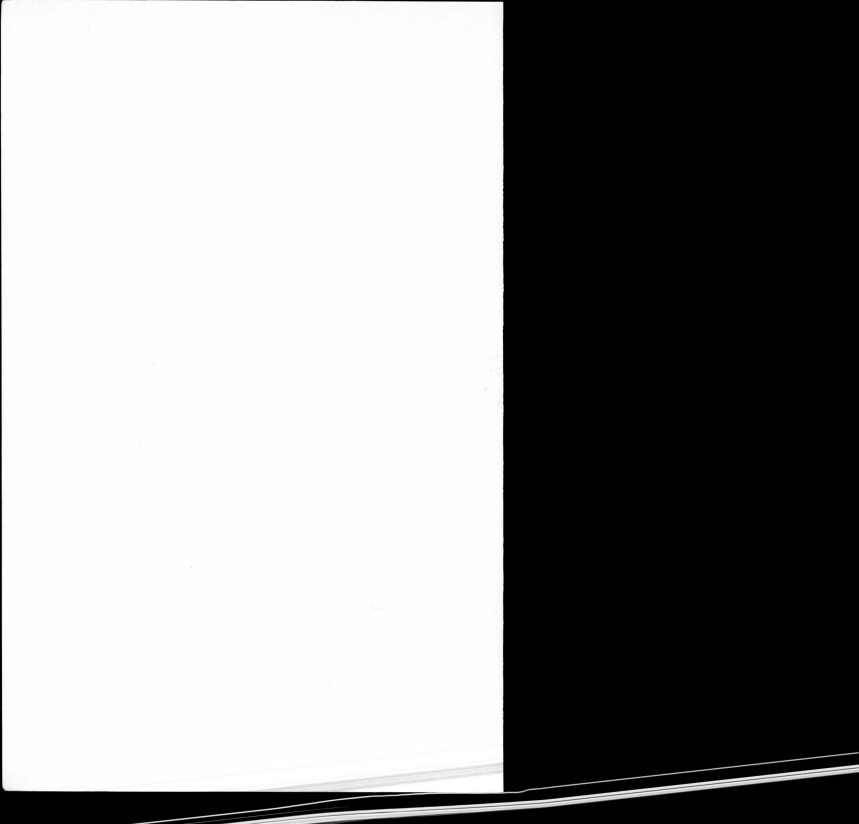

Contents

Preface ——————————————————————— 11

1 **Introduction** ——————————————————— 13
   Culture and Worship
   A Biblical Paradigm

Part 1: Historical Perspectives

2 **Worship Through the Ages** ——————————— 29
   The Early Church and the Middle Ages
   The Reformation Through the Eighteenth Century
   The Nineteenth Century and Beyond

3 **Constancy & Diversity** ———————————————— 41

Part 2: African-American Worship

4 **"We Had Church Today!"** ——————————— 53
   The African Roots
   A Wholistic View of Life and Worship
   Worship as Liberation
   Worship as Celebration

5 **African-American Music** ——————————— 69
   Vocal Music
   Instrumental Music
   Metered Hymns
   Spirituals
   Gospel

6 **The Spoken Word** ——————————————— 86
   The Preacher
   Cerebral Versus Emotive
   Prophetic Elements

Drama and Musicality

Dialogical Style

The Prayer

7   The Response —————————————————————— *99*

The Dance

The Shout

The Testimony

Other Responses

Part 3: Caribbean Worship

8   An Adventure of the Spirit ——————————————— *111*

A Historical Survey

Afrocentric Worship Communities

   Orisha

   Revival

   Spiritual Baptists

   Other semi-Christian groups

   Pentecostalism

An Indigenous Worship

9   Caribbean Music —————————————————————— *138*

Instrumental Distinctives

Song

10   The Word & the Response ——————————————— *150*

The Word

The Response

Part 4: Hispanic Worship

11   In the Spirit of a Fiesta ————————————————— *161*

History and Demographics

   Mexican-Americans

    Other Hispanic groups

   Religiosidad Popular

     Amerindian

     African

     Roman Catholic

     Pentecostal

     Other Protestants

     Summary characteristics

   Fiesta

     Fiesta as celebration

     Fiesta as liberation

12 Hispanic Music ———————————————— *187*

   Hymnody

   Instrumentation

13 Preaching, Prayer & Response ———————————— *194*

   Preaching

   Prayer

   Response

   Dance

   Other Senses

Part 5: Conclusion

14 Rational & Physical ———————————————— *203*

   Control of the Body

   Recapturing the Use of the Body

   Elevation of the Rational

   Recapturing the Emotive

   Dance

Notes ——————————————————————— *214*

Bibliography ————————————————————— *247*

Preface

This work had its genesis in 1991, when I presented the presidential address to the Andrews Society for Religious Studies at the annual meeting of the Society of Biblical Literature and American Academy of Religion in Kansas City. At that time my illustrative focus was on African-American and Caribbean worship. A couple of years later I was invited to give a plenary address to the Second International Adventist Worship Conference at La Sierra University, California. Then I added the Hispanic component.

The immediate result of the later presentation was an invitation from Robert Webber of Wheaton College to publish sections in volume seven of the Complete Library of Christian Worship (Star Song, 1994). An ongoing result has been an insistence by my students, my colleagues and many involved in the contemporary liturgical debate that I develop more extensively my wholistic thesis of worship—that a number of indigenous groups exhibit modes of worship that involve the whole person in praise to God within community.

The project was brought to fruition through the willingness of the fabulous folks at InterVarsity Press, particularly the most marvelous editor Cynthia Bunch-Hotaling. Her insights and attention to detail as well as to the broad picture are much appreciated.

Special acknowledgment must be given to certain foot soldiers who helped this project see the light of day. To my indomitable wife, Violet, who not only encouraged me during long, tiresome hours but also traveled with me and assisted in the research process, I am eternally indebted. As a reference librarian she was able to gain quick access to many difficult-to-obtain sources. To my sister Audrey and her husband Lee, who opened up all the resources of their home in California so I could spend a sabbatical researching and writing, I am most grateful. Warm thanks also go to others who housed and fed me and assisted in my research: Marisol Araujo and

Samuel Zita in Chicago; Pastor Errol and Monica Mitchell, Mother Monica Randoo, and Dr. Rawle Gibbons in Trinidad; my mother, Edith Maynard-Reid; my in-laws John and Iva Thompson; and my ever-there friend Erma Hutton in Jamaica.

Walla Walla College and in particular my colleagues in the School of Theology have been most supportive; not only did they grant me sabbatical time to produce this work, but they served as cheerleaders to spur me on. My student research assistants Leanne Veverka and Ronn Kakazu should be given medals. Their attention to detail and their insightful suggestions, along with their willingness to address the mundane necessities of research, typing and double-checking, were absolutely invaluable.

Words fail to fully express my feelings regarding the incomparable work Lorraine Jacobs has put into the production of this volume. She oversaw the project from beginning to end, giving pertinent advice and steering it in the right direction. As a Caucasian with a multicultural soul, she brought a unique perspective to the work. I thank her for her passion for wholistic worship, which gives the book a human face, as well as her dedication and tenacity in seeing the volume to completion. For these gifts and more, I dedicate this book to her.

It is my desire that this study not be another implement in the liturgical wars that have dominated the latter decades of the twentieth century. Instead I hope the reader will gain a bigger picture of God and ways God can be worshiped beyond the narrow confines of our comfort zones. And thus may we all be more united in praise and adoration of the mighty yet intimate God we serve.

Introduction

I*n a foreword to* Brenda Eatman Aghaowa's *Praising in Black and White*,[1] Martin E. Marty, the famous church historian and insightful student of the debates within modern Christianity, highlights the tension between today's opposing worship parties and how each perceives the other. The "aesthetic cultural warriors" oppose worship with praise songs. They grumble, "If the only way to get to heaven, Martha, is by worshiping with *that* in our ears, we just aren't going!" Or, "Praise songs. They are all about one word, God—sung in two syllables—lasting three hours." On the other side are the high-church liturgiologists, traditionalists who insist on preserving their versions of ancient Christian worship. These traditionalists are perceived as dogmatic. You might hear their opponents jesting: "What's the difference between a liturgiologist and a terrorist?" Answer: "You can negotiate with a terrorist."

In today's heated world of worship discussion, whether one is a high-church liturgiologist or contemporary celebration-church liturgiologist, there seems to be no room for negotiation or coming together. Yet I believe that a coming together, or at least a mutual appreciation, is possible if we will make the attempt to better understand our diversity.

At the heart of the contemporary liturgical debate is the question of what are appropriate and inappropriate practices and expressions within the worship service. The issue would lose some of its perplexity if we could grasp the notion that what we perceive as appropriate worship is culturally conditioned and has little to do with biblical orthodoxy or soteriological morality.

For many within the dominant Caucasian culture in the United States and Canada, cultural conditioning does not seem obvious, particularly not in worship and religious expression. Yet I'm convinced that worship practices are as culturally conditioned as any other aspect of the human experience. And this is the case within as well as between ethnic groups. When the cultural nature is affirmed and worship is thus celebrated wholistically, God is truly glorified and members of the worshiping community go forth richly blessed.

This volume aims to be an illustrative piece that demonstrates the cultural dimensions of the mechanics of worship. But my focus will be ethnic, non-Caucasian. There are geographical limitations as well. I have chosen the United States, Canada, Mexico and the Caribbean to illustrate my thesis partly because in these territories multiethnicity, or exposure to multiethnic practices and ideas, is generally in vogue. Thus the need to view worship as culturally conditioned is vital for Christians in this region.

The choice of my illustrations is also due in part to who I am and where my journey has led me. I am Jamaican by birth. I completed my undergraduate studies in Jamaica and taught there at the tertiary level for fifteen years. I then spent approximately five years teaching at a university in Puerto Rico, during which time I had the opportunity to visit, lecture and study throughout Hispanic America. My graduate work was done in the United States, and I have been on the faculty of a university in northwestern United States since 1990.

Worship activities have dominated my life since my early teenage years. Trained as an instrumental performer, I have served as pianist and organist, as well as choral director and minister of music in worship settings of all three cultures. In addition I have functioned as senior pastor of a university church and of a small rural worship community. For the past thirty years I have been principally an academician, with a terminal degree in biblical studies and a postdoctoral degree in missiology. As in my ministerial training classes on worship, I hope in this volume to draw on my varied experiences to present what I perceive as truly wholistic worship.

Issues surrounding the mechanics of worship have been very intense for churches in all cultures, and particularly in the North American and Caribbean regions. This is true of my present worshiping community, which is in a mostly Caucasian university setting. The debate here is not centered on ethnic issues. (We are allotted one annual black-history worship service, in which some African-American worship styles are by and large accepted.) The debate centers on contemporary versus traditional versus a more convergent or "blended" style of worship. This volume is not intended to systematically address all the specific points that are raised by all sides in that discussion. There are many good volumes on liturgy that attempt to focus on these concerns with a white audience in mind. Yet I'm convinced that the principles and illustrations contained in this work can and will enhance discussions in mostly Caucasian settings.

Within the African-American, Caribbean and Hispanic communities, the debate is as intense as it is in the dominant culture of North America. In these cases, however, the issue is not simply traditional versus contemporary. Rather, the focus of interest is how to incorporate one's traditional "native" culture and cultural practices into the praise and glory of God within community worship.

The difficulty of the debate in these cultures lies in the persistence of the powerful influence of the dominant Western or European culture or colonial teachings. Many blacks and Hispanics in North America, Mexico and the Caribbean firmly believe that non-European Western indigenous practices are evil and satanic. Any attempt to reintroduce the primal practices is heterodoxy as far as they are concerned. I hope that within these ethnic-dominant communities, this book will work to alleviate the tensions. Indigenous worship practices that are wholistic and christocentric are more acceptable to God than worship that is narrow, fragmented, compartmentalized and self-centered.

Although the volume focuses on ethnic-specific settings and sets forth principles that are relevant to white-dominated communities, in a special way it can be of significant value for multiethnic worship communities.[2] As music director and organist at a multiethnic church in the American Midwest in the late 1970s and early 1980s, I struggled to help some of my fellow parishioners appreciate the diversity within the community and the reasons for such diversity. Incorporating African-American, Hispanic, Caribbean, traditional European and at times East Indian elements in the service served to educate us. But the experience was more than educational: it was enriching. It produced a greater sense of community and empathy for what seems alien yet clearly ministers to one's worshiping neighbor.

My research and experience have shown that the liturgy incorporating indigenous elements produces a more wholistic worship than liturgy with a cognitive focus alone. Much of traditional Western worship has been one-dimensional, with emphasis on the rational. Eastern cultures—Middle Eastern (biblical world), African, Indian and others—do not dichotomize the human person the way Western thought does. For them, the human is a whole, one complete being—body, mind and soul, the physical, the rational, the emotional. All three dimensions of the person are interrelated and equally vital to existence.

Cultures that affirm their Eastern roots and worldview will invariably express worship in ways that involve the whole person. The rational and cerebral is not dispensed with, but it is not elevated over the emotive and physical. People of these cultures draw on all the ingredients of the human personality in worship and praise to God. In the liturgical construct there is an integral relation between the mind, body and spirit.

Culture and Worship

Because this volume focuses on cultures dominated by ethnic and racial groups that are non-European, it is especially important to clarify what culture is and how it relates to worship.

We are creatures of culture. As Cyprian Rowe notes, "Culture is what people are. We cannot talk about human beings in the abstract. We do not exist in the abstract."[3] Culture is therefore not something "out there,"[4] quite apart from one's social existence. We cannot run away from it. It is inextricably bound up with who we are.

Yet culture is not innate but learned. It is "learned in a process of socialization",[5] it is human achievement that is acquired through learning. Thus we distinguish nature and culture. To illustrate: "A river is nature, a canal culture; a raw piece of quartz is nature, an arrowhead culture; a moan is natural, a word cultural. Culture is the work of men's minds and hands."[6]

Culture is not biological or racial. These are natural and inherited. The color of one's skin, the texture of one's hair and the shape of one's nose are determined by genetic codes. Not so with culture. Culture is socially learned and assimilated. A number of writers have illustrated this difference by noting that, for example, an African-American child raised in Germany by Caucasian parents would be culturally German though racially black. Or an Irish boy who was adopted by a Chinese family at birth and brought up in Beijing would at the age of twenty-one be culturally Chinese. Even though his features would be very Irish, his language, mannerisms, ways of thinking and doing things, and reactions to situations would be very Chinese and not Irish.[7]

Because culture is not biological and innate, it is dynamic, fluid and open. "As people migrate from one neighbourhood to another, or from country to country, their identity, like their experiences, changes, taking on different meanings and expressions."[8] People adapt to their new cultural environment, learn new languages, accents and ways of doing things. They learn to maneuver their way through life with a different set of cultural values.

Culture includes these plus much more. Joseph Fitzpatrick says it "is the way of life of a people. It is the sum total of all those ways of doing things, of thinking about things, of feeling about things, of believing, that make up the life of a group of people."[9] It is the sum total of the actions and experiences of a people and a person. It is the means by which individuals or a set of human beings orient, organize and conduct themselves cognitively, affectively and behaviorally in a given time and place.[10]

Culture therefore goes beyond language, dialect and speech. It includes everything that is passed on, experienced and practiced. It involves information, education, techniques and inventions. It comprises customs, habits, aesthetic choices,[11] beliefs, rites, traditions, myths, legends, superstitions, stories, songs, dances, jokes, tastes, inherited artifacts, prejudices, attitudes and values—in short, everything that is part of one's social heritage and environment.[12]

Just as we cannot live without earth's atmosphere, we cannot live apart from culture. It influences everything we do, think and feel, whether we are aware of it or not. In a sense, it is our essential selves. The Caribbean theologian Iris Hamid is absolutely correct: "Man and his cultural milieu are not two separate realities, rather man is part and parcel of the cultural historical milieu so that a rejection of the latter inescapably involves rejection of man himself. In other words you cannot throw cold water on a man's culture and historical life without giving him the chills."[13]

In creating a "cosmos of meaning"[14] for the individual and members of society, culture provides a life that is safe, secure and comfortable. It allows the individual and community to survive. We can hardly argue with the observation that at the core of various definitions of culture is the motif of survival, for as Karen Ward states, "it is a system for navigating one's way through life."[15] Culture, therefore, is not optional. It is life itself.

Worship, as used in this volume, refers to the self-expression of a particular church community in a public celebration of its faith. It has both vertical and horizontal dimensions: one's relation to God and one's relationships with fellow worshipers. It involves both the transcendent and the immanent. It is an expression of adoration and praise to God in community.

If worship is the self-expression of a particular community, liturgy and culture must coexist "in a state of symbiosis."[16] In worship, people's cultural self-expressions are authenticated in the presence of God. If worship does not have its grounding in people's lives and cultural experiences, it will remain foreign, imposed and irrelevant. Another way of expressing this is to say that worship needs to be incarnational or "culturally specific," in Alison Siewert's words.[17] "God comes to us as we are and makes himself accessible to us according to our experience and background."[18]

Because culture is dynamic, worship cannot be static.[19] The liturgy must adapt itself to the changing cultural needs and environment of the worshipers. It is in worship that the changing felt needs of a community are best met, addressed and celebrated. In worship the light of the gospel is brought to bear on everyday living and existence. When people go to church they bring their culture with them, for culture is their essential selves—the sum total of their experience. Thus for worship to be relevant it has to be an integral part of people's lives and culture. This I have found to be true in cultures with African or Hispanic roots.

A Biblical Paradigm

It is tempting to go to Scripture to discover the ideal paradigm for liturgical practices. The fact is, however, Scripture prescribes no one monolithic form or language of worship. Biblical worship practice was diverse, reflecting the various cultural and apologetic environments of those gathered. We do not find any liturgical order or obligatory form for Christian worship in the teachings of Christ or the writings of the New Testament. It was a matter of course for each group to worship in a style and environment that met their felt needs. We must therefore be careful not to simply reach back to the worship of the primitive early church or Old Testament Hebraic practices and appropriate it for today.

Yet though the models presented in Scripture are diverse and may not be normative, they offer insights that can assist us in attaining an enhanced wholistic worship in our own local settings. First, let's briefly look at the Old Testament.

Nowhere in the Hebrew Scriptures do we find a worship format that precisely matches any practiced in Christian worship today. The concept of worship was varied and diverse. In the early nomadic life of the Hebrew people as recorded in Genesis, worship included family altars and sacrifices, and we find occasional theophanies, or special appearances of Yahweh, the Lord. It was not until the exodus that worship took on a larger corporate meaning. From then on, worship in Israelite culture was grounded in the exodus experience (just as in the New Testament it is grounded in the Christ event); in fact, that event shaped the life and worship of the Hebrews for millennia.[20]

The book of Exodus details the formalization of worship for the first time in Israelite history. The Mosaic instructions and regulations define where and how worship should take place. The erection of the tabernacle and the distinctive elements of sacrifices and feasts provided a unique cultural place and form for worship.

Feasts and festivals played a prominent role in the liturgical life of the Hebrew people. These (as well as sacrifices) were also staples in the liturgical life of the other peoples of the ancient Near East. The Israelites endeavored to keep their worship and celebration different from those of the surrounding nations, yet in some ways they were similar. For example, in the ancient Near East an important feature of religious life was one's relation to nature.[21] The Israelites did not discard this basic worldview, but instead of following the rituals of their neighbors, they established nature festivals (such as the Barley Harvest, the Wheat Harvest, and the General Yearly Harvest) in which Yahweh was central.

Not much seems to have changed in the worship patterns of

Israel even after their settlement in Palestine. It was left to David to make the most important changes and contributions to worship in the history of the Hebrews. He is credited as being the primary one who organized Israel as a worshiping community, and as "the example par excellence of a true worshiper."[22]

David's contribution was basically twofold. First, he erected a tent for worship in Jerusalem. It became the precursor of the temple of Solomon. Second, while continuing the ancient practice of animal sacrifices, David restructured the Mosaic worship service into an event of praise, thanksgiving and prayer, with song, musical instruments and dance. It seems that by the Davidic era, music, particularly instrumental music, had become part of the Israelites' cultural self-expression. The king therefore incorporated this feature into worship to the glory and praise of God.

The practice of worship took a significant turn during and after the Babylonian captivity. The intensity of noncultic aspects of worship in the temple was lost in this postexilic community. These aspects of worship were taken over by the synagogue, an institution that developed during the Babylonian exile.[23] The synagogue grew out of the exiles' need for a substitute place to worship God. "A motivating concern was the preservation and propagation of the Word of the Lord in the context of the Jewish community."[24] Synagogue life thus expanded beyond worship events to make the synagogue a religious, educational and social (even judicial[25]) center of Jewish life. The synagogue thus became a cultural artifact in Judaism.

The synagogue became the center of noncultic worship—the *ekklēsia*, (assembly or congregation). A distinctive worship pattern developed that included the reading and exposition of the Torah, prayer, the recitation of Deuteronomy 6:4 (the Shema) and recitations of psalms.[26] Thus a new form of worship was created in reaction to new circumstances.

The study of worship in the New Testament is difficult, mostly because of the fragmentary nature of the material that deals with worship. New Testament texts include individual elements derived from worship, but no extended liturgical discussions. We must remember that the authors of the New Testament were writing as theologians and not as historians or liturgiologists.[27] Their primary concern was addressing a theological problem in their community. Historical, biographical and liturgical concerns were only incidental to the tasks at hand. Thus every New Testament document reflects the concerns and circumstances of quite different communities— issues that in most instances were not related to liturgical practices.

There are no liturgical books or "order of worship" documents in the New Testament. But we can read between the lines in order to tentatively sketch the "cultural and liturgical ferment" [28] that was taking place during the first century of the Christian era. For "pluralism and controversy [were] part of the identity or essence of Christianity itself."[29] And the snippets of information we possess certainly confirm the cultural pluralism and tensions over worship at that time.

During the period of the Jesus movement and the apostolic era, clearly distinguishable lines were drawn between Jewish and Christian worship. "Christian worship, like Christian literature, was continuous with, and yet in marked contrast to, Jewish worship,"[30] says C. F. D. Moule. Christian worship bears the same kind of relationship to Jewish worship as the New Testament writings bear to the Hebrew Scriptures. The temple and the synagogue continued to play a significant role in the worship practices of Jesus and the early Christians, yet a unique Christian culture was developing, necessitating some new liturgical expressions.

An illustration of this cultural development is the addition of a third liturgical place for gathering. Acts 5:42 says, "And every day in the temple and at home [or from house church (*kat' oikon*) to house church] they did not cease to teach and proclaim Jesus as the Messiah." As early as immediately after the Pentecost experience we read of the new believers gathering in homes to hear the teachings of the apostles and to pray, fellowship and "break bread"—share a meal or love feast, possibly involving Communion[31] (Acts 2:42-47).

These Christian meetings, though synagogal in nature, seemed to have developed some new forms, or at least incorporated some liturgical practices foreign to traditional Jewish synagogue worship. For one, the gathering was not in a building dedicated to activities of a synagogue but in a private home. There is no mention of the reading of Scripture. But we should assume that the "teachings of the apostles" involved the presentation of the Word. The breaking of bread or common meal, fellowship, and signs and wonders are additions that may have been unique to the early believers.

What we have seen so far is that there was a diversity of worship patterns in the very early church, including patterns that were traditional and culturally Jewish and new forms created to meet the needs of an emerging pluralistic community. All this imposed severe strain on the church, but the Jerusalem community was stronger in the end.

Not only do Christians use the Bible as grounding for their liturgical practices, but historical traditions play a significant role in shaping expectations of the worship experience. And just as culture influenced worship practices in biblical times, it has influenced all Christian worship through the ages. Chapter two will explore this influence and demonstrate the diversity of worship both spatially and temporally.

In any discussion regarding diversity, relevance and contextualization in worship, whether in history or on the contemporary scene, one question invariably arises: What are worship's unchangeable constants? Are there some essential historical and theological truths and practices that take precedence over local cultural practices and forms? If so, what are they? Chapter three attempts to address this issue, calling for a healthy tension between constancy and diversity in worship.

The three sections that follow chapter three constitute the heart of the volume. Here I illustrate my thesis by taking the reader on a survey of African-American, Caribbean and Hispanic worship. These three cultures are chosen to demonstrate the wholistic nature of true worship: worship that involves the triune God and community, a worship involving mind, heart and body—the whole being.

African-American, Caribbean and Hispanic worship patterns are not monolithic. Each culture includes a diverse spectrum. I will be focusing on worship patterns that utilize indigenous cultural elements and attempt to incorporate them into traditional, orthodox Christian worship to produce a wholistic and meaningful worship experience.

Much has been written on African-American worship. This community's mode of worship has contributed a great deal to American art, music and religious life. Chapter four shows how African-Americans have built on a traditional European liturgical base and infused it with expressions that are deeply African. The spirituals and gospel music, the rhythmic instrumentation, the creativity and expressiveness of the presentation of the Word, and the highly physical response all have their roots in the celebrative primal culture of the motherland.

Celebration in the African-American church is best expressed in its music. This is naturally so because music permeates African-American life. Here wholism dominates. African-Americans utilizes every musical idiom to worship. In effect, they demolish the thought that the devil holds copyright on particular forms and idioms of musical expression. Chapter five paints a picture of the richness and wholeness of African-American liturgical music.

The jury is out on whether music or preaching is more central in the African-American church. Black preaching has been honed to an art form. In chapter six I will demonstrate how in this part of the service content and musicality, the cognitive and the emotive, the artistic and the dramatic lift the congregation to a spiritual high that is difficult to duplicate in any other setting.

Worship in the black church in the United States is not a spectator sport. Members of the congregation not only listen and sing but respond with their whole being. Chapter seven explores how African-Americans, like their African ancestors, turn themselves loose in responsive celebration with one another. Full worship is communal, vocal and physical.

Part two surveys the Caribbean scene. It is virtually impossible to find any broad, systematic treatment of Caribbean worship as a whole. The difficulty of writing such a study is possibly due to the enormous diversity that exists throughout the English-speaking Caribbean.[32] However, from the research done in this area as seen in chapter eight, it is clear that worship in the Caribbean is an adventure of the Spirit. Though Christians in the West Indies are firm believers in the triune God and their worship demonstrates such, one cannot leave a Caribbean service and not feel a perceptible movement of the Spirit which in turn moves the worshiper's spirit.

This movement of the Spirit is expressed in the vibrancy of the music (chapter nine) and the power of the preaching and the response of the congregation (chapter ten). As in the black North American scene, the whole person is involved in this liberating and celebrative experience.

If there is hardly any broad systematic treatment of Caribbean worship, such an approach to Hispanic worship is even harder to find. Here part of the problem is the difficulty in identifying or defining this cultural group of people, also referred to as Latinos and Latinas. Chapter eleven attempts to paint a definition with some broad strokes, focusing on Hispanics found in Mexico, the United States and the Caribbean region.

Unlike most of the people who accept themselves as African-Americans or as English-speaking Caribbean persons with roots in Africa, most Hispanic persons have European roots from Spain. However, the Hispanics in the Caribbean and North America are for the most part an amalgam that includes Amerindian or African. When the undertones of these two cultures are mixed with traditions of the culture of the Iberian peninsula, a new spirit is born. It is a fiesta spirit. The passion of this fiesta spirit is expressed in both religious and nonreligious events. In worship this spirit is probably best expressed in music (chapter twelve).

Worship for Hispanics is communication. The final chapter of the section shows how preaching, prayer and response achieve this goal. Oral communication is vital, as in the proclamation of the Word. But just as important is communication with God and with one's worshiping neighbors via all one's senses and bodily movement.

Among a number of Hispanics as well as significant segments of the other cultures addressed here, and among many (possibly most) persons in the dominant North American culture, this aspect of worshiping with one's body is anathema. Yet I'm convinced that worship that is whole of necessity needs to involve the whole person. The book's concluding chapter lays out my viewpoints on this issue.

The three cultures discussed, I believe, offer paradigms of what wholistic worship should be. The discussion, of course, demonstrates that there is no one set pattern of worship. I am not proposing that Caucasian churches or Asian congregations adopt the exact mechanics of worship of African- or Hispanic-based cultures. I hope, however, that those who worship differently—whether they be black, brown or white—will come to appreciate these other cultural forms. And more than that, it is my desire to see all worship experiences in every culture call upon all aspects of the worshiper's being and living in wholistic adoration and praise to God in community, as these three cultures model for us.

Part 1

Historical
Perspectives

Part Two

Historical
Perspectives

Worship
Through the Ages

C hristians, *for the most part, take the Bible and historical liturgi-*
cal tradition as the grounding for their liturgical practices. In
debates over worship we hear not only a call for a return to the biblical way of worship but an insistence that worship forms developed
in earlier centuries of Christendom are as valid today as they were
then. What this argument fails to take into account, as the previous
chapter began to demonstrate, is that neither Scripture nor the subsequent history of Christendom offer us one monolithic form and
language of worship. Human beings have always worshiped God in
their cultural milieu, and God has incarnated himself and revealed
himself to worshipers in settings that are culturally familiar.

In this chapter we will take a walk through history and show
how the church, and segments within the church, have sought to
make worship culturally relevant, just as many churches in many

cultures today are attempting to make worship culturally meaningful and relevant.

The Early Church and the Middle Ages

Just as culture influened worship during the Old and New Testament
eras, it continued to do so for the next two thousand years. Church
leaders and theologians struggled over the centuries not only to make
sense of the Christian faith in a non-Christian dominant culture but to
make worship meaningful and apropos to the ordinary Christian's
everyday experience. There were times when they were successful;
other times they were scratching where there was no itch.

During the second and third centuries, the church struggled with
its relationship to the Greco-Roman culture that surrounded it. Its
general attitude could be described, in H. Richard Niebuhr's words,
as "Christ against culture."[1] Such would be expected in a period of
intermittent persecution. Frank Senn suggests that Christians'
antagonism to the culture of classical antiquity was "perhaps one of
the reasons for the tenacity of Jewish forms in Christian worship."[2]

The scanty evidence we have shows not only the retention of the
basic forms of the synagogue liturgy but a continuing crystallization
of distinctively Christian worship elements and order. The *Didache*,
a document written toward the end of the first century or the beginning of the second, presents for the first time an order for the Communion service. In the document we find set prayers to be used at
the Table. Yet there is also some latitude: the prophets are encouraged to "give thanks as much as they desire"[3]; in other words, they
should not be fettered by the prescribed prayers.

The document also provides us with information about the liturgy of the Word, baptism, fasting and prayer. Ferdinand Hahn
notes that

> even more markedly than in the Pastoral Epistles we find the juxtaposition or
> superimposition of an earlier charismatic community organization (chapters
> 11-13) and an institutional form of leadership on its way to gaining the upper
> hand (chapter 15). It is interesting that in this case the transition took place

without tension, because the charismatic talent fell into abeyance and the functions of the charismatics must have been taken over by the official leaders.[4]

Our next insight into postapostolic worship comes from a letter by Pliny, governor of Bithynia-Pontus (A.D. 111-113), to the emperor Trajan. The secrecy of Christian worship provoked the letter. Pliny informs Trajan that "the substance of their fault or error was that they were in the habit of meeting on a fixed day before daylight and reciting responsively among themselves a hymn to Christ as a god."[5] The letter also shows that the community assembled for prayer, praise and proclamation in the morning, and communion in the evening.[6] Although the text does not give a liturgical order, it does give us a window into secret worship during a period of intense persecution.

The *First Apology* of Justin Martyr gives us significant information about the content and structure of worship toward the middle of the second century. I quote from chapter 67:

> And on the day called Sunday there is a meeting in one place of those who live in cities or the country, and the memoirs of the apostles or the writings of the prophets are read as long as time permits. When the reader has finished, the president in a discourse urges and invites [us] to the imitation of these noble things. Then we all stand up together and offer prayers. And, as said before, when we have finished the prayer, bread is brought, and wine and water, and the president similarly sends up prayers and thanksgiving to the best of his ability, and the congregation assents, saying Amen: the distribution, and reception of the consecrated [elements] by each one, takes place and they are sent to the absent by the deacons.[7]

Christian worship services in the third century remained virtually the same as described in Justin Martyr's *Apology*. Believers continued meeting in the intimate setting of house churches, with the Word and Communion being central. Although there were no essential changes, Robert Webber does note that some ceremonial additions were made.[8] The chief officiator was either the bishop or the minister (large congregations had more than one minister). Deacons directed the people, read Scripture, led in prayer, guarded the entrance, kept order, presented and assisted in the distributions of the elements. Up to this time rank-and-file members were also involved, participating and assisting in the readings, dramas, responses and prayers. The evidence we have of this period leads us to conclude that even though certain parts of the worship service were fixed, there was a certain amount of freedom and flexibility.

Up until the fourth century the life of the church must be understood against the background of hostility and persecution. In such a setting one should not expect much liturgical innovation. But with the 313 Edict of Milan, which gave Christianity legal status in the Empire, and with the conversion of Emperor Constantine, the church and its liturgy began to undergo considerable change. A significant worldview shift took place in this "classical period" (fourth to sixth centuries) of the church's liturgical life. Instead of "Christ against culture," the slogan could be "Christ of culture." The church began to build bridges to surrounding non-Christian cultures. Many of the practices and festivals of the popular mystery cults, for example, began to be adopted and incorporated into the life of the church. It seems quite likely that these mystery cults strongly influenced the growing view of worship as mystery. But it is certain that festivals such as Christmas originated at this time, as new converts brought with them their old feasts of celebration and gave them a Christian "baptism."

At this time the Greek dichotomy between sacred and secular made its way into Christian spirituality as well. This shift from a wholistic view of spirituality to a dichotomized view, I reckon, has done more damage to Christians' view of worship than anything else. Because of this, worship and everyday living have been separated.

There was also a shift from intimate worship to worship as theater.[9] With the influx of new converts, the need arose for larger buildings. Senn notes that, in turn, "bigger buildings necessitated a more elaborate choreography just to move clergy and people through the great basilicas."[10] The choreography included special dress worn by church leaders. Bishops now wore the garb and insignia of the senatorial class. And, interestingly, even after this Roman style of flowing garments gave way in the larger culture to the short tunics of the Goths, clergy continued to officiate in worship in the old-fashioned clothing.

One of the important liturgical developments during this period was a move from Greek to Latin. Up to the middle of the third century, Christians in Rome worshiped in Greek. Greek language and culture had dominated not only the liturgical life of the church but to a great degree its worldview. Even its rhetoric left a lasting mark on liturgical texts.[11] But as the church grew, it adapted to local cultural situations. The church recognized that the language of worship needed to be intelligible to the worshiper, and this required use of the lingua franca of the people.

But even after the church expanded westward beyond Rome, and Latin was no longer the language of the masses, the church retained Latin as the language of worship. This worked to undergird the concept of worship as mystery. According to Webber, because the people did not understand what was happening, the aura of mystery around the clergy and the Mass was enhanced. Furthermore, he says, "the church distanced itself from the people even more as it increasingly viewed itself as a hierarchical institution rather than a body. The church dispensed salvation. The liturgy, especially the Eucharist, became the means of receiving this salvation."[12]

Although Rome became the dominant center of Christianity in the fourth century, other influential ecclesiastical centers emerged throughout and beyond the Roman Empire. These centers began to develop particular styles of worship that reflected local culture. The church in each area recognized the necessity of relating to the political, social and cultural circumstances in which it existed.[13] Not only the basic structure of worship (focus on the Word and the Table) but the style of the liturgy reflected local cultures.

Two basic styles developed: the Eastern, or Byzantine, and the Western, or Roman. The Byzantine Rite (a technical term for the way the liturgy is celebrated) reflected the Hellenistic love for the aesthetic. This liturgy made extensive use of ceremonial signs and symbols. Eastern worship was "highly ceremonial, gloriously beautiful, and deeply mystical,"[14] reflecting the ostentation of Greek culture.

The Western Rite, on the other hand, reflected the Roman "spirit of pragmatism."[15] Relative to the Byzantine Rite, it was simple and sober, lacking ostentation and not as highly ceremonial.

Though these orders of worship were the most prestigious and widespread, there were many others—witnessing to the fact that worship was being adapted to varied cultural settings. For example, variations of the Byzantine Rite developed not only in Greece but in Romania and the Slavic countries.[16] Other liturgies include the Eastern and Western Syrian rites, the Maronite Rite of Lebanon, the Coptic in Egypt, the Ethiopian and the Armenian rites.[17]

The Roman liturgy probably was most influential in Western Christianity during the first millennium of Christendom. But other Western rites existed—for example, the Gallican (in what is now southern France), the Celtic (Great Britain), Mozarabic (Spain) and Ambrosian (Milan). These, to a large degree, differed from the simple, practical and sober Roman Rite; they were generally characterized by a more dramatic, emotional, sensuous, colorful, poetic approach to worship.[18]

A new development in worship occurred or intensified during the medieval period. Some worship became more introspective, personal and pietistic. First, this is highlighted in monastic movements that protested against the growing institutionalism, worldliness and prosperity that characterized church and society,[19] and promoted a more privatized, noninstitutionalized worship. Second, the choir usurped more of the congregation's role in the service, and economic well-being allowed more private masses to be celebrated. These two developments contributed to a large degree to the disintegration of the communal institutional and traditional worship. No wonder, says Senn, that people "turned to paraliturgical devotions such as the rosary or the way of the cross, where their participation was assured, or to forms of contemplation and meditation,"[20] as offered in monasticism.

The Reformation Through the Eighteenth Century

The sixteenth century was a time of great change in the Western world, particularly in northern Europe. The rise of nation-states, the shift toward a capitalist economy and the blossoming of Renaissance humanism, and all the learning that came with these, signaled a massive worldview shift. Reformers like Martin Luther "articulated the whole new consciousness of the individual"[21] at this dawn of modernity in the West. Their call for a religious reformation was in tune with and was heeded by the peoples of Europe. Because the reformation movements were in touch with the times, the various liturgies that burgeoned among them reflected the cultural ethos of the peoples. The Reformation (and even the Catholic Counter-Reformation) was thus very contextual.

Before we survey some of the changes that affected worship between the sixteenth and eighteenth centuries, it is worthwhile to note that one of the most significant developments during this time was the growth of rationalism. This, more than anything else, moved worship into a cerebral mode.

The Age of Reason, or the Enlightenment, reached its peak in the eighteenth century and was strongest in Germany, where it affected Lutheran and Reformed liturgy more than Anglican or Catholic. But its effect seeped into all liturgy to one degree or another, so that generally "ritual action gave way to verbal pedagogy"[22] as the church endeavored to prove Christianity or reinterpret the faith in nonsupernatural ways.[23] Senn goes on to point out that

> a certain liturgical deterioration had already occurred under Pietism, where the fixed and recurring liturgical elements were often made to yield to more subjective and extemporaneous ones. But under Rationalism the historic liturgy disappeared altogether. The Age of Reason valued religion according to its ethical results. Consequently, the church became a lecture hall and the minister a moral instructor. He felt free to rearrange the service at will, even to devise updated texts of the Lord's Prayer and the words of institution and distribution at Holy Communion.[24]

One of Luther's greatest contributions was putting worship in the vernacular of the people and encouraging congregational singing through the use of popular tunes. These changes, of course, did not have their genesis in the mind of Luther. They were part of the Renaissance and humanist push to make worship intelligible.

Overall, however, Luther did not make as significant a break with his Catholic liturgical heritage as did the other Reformers. Lutherans (as well as Anglicans) retained much of the ancient form of worship. Calvin and the Reformed community went further. Martin Bucer was a main figure in the changes. Before Bucer, worship at Strasbourg included many of the Lutheran and Catholic ceremonial elements. Bucer reduced the liturgy to its simplest forms, giving precedence to preaching and the singing of metrical psalms. The lectionary disappeared; the minister picked his own text and preached for an hour. Organ and instrumental music was abolished in favor of the human voice singing biblical texts.

Ulrich Zwingli and the Anabaptists of the Radical Reformation made an even greater break with the past. Zwingli, the Swiss Reformer, emphasized that people should give ear to the Word alone. He advocating doing away with anything that would "distract from" the hearing of the Word, such as organ and other musical instruments, vestments, and pictures.

The Anabaptists went further, rejecting not only the liturgical ceremonies but formal worship itself. This is understandable in their historical situation as a people persecuted by both Protestants and Catholics. Their worship meetings generally had to be secret, unscheduled and impromptu. But "it was their conviction that the true church was an obedient and suffering people whose daily walk with God was of utmost importance. This walk climaxed in the gathering of Christians together for prayer, Bible reading, admonition, and the Lord's Supper in the informal atmosphere of the home."[25]

In the period following the sixteenth-century Reformation, much evolution took place in liturgical practices. One of the most significant developments was the free church movement. Webber discusses three trends in its worship.[26] First, there was a fresh understanding of how salvation is received. No longer is it appropriated through the sacrament, but through personal understanding and experience. Ceremonies, signs, symbols and forms that were part of sacramental worship were now viewed as idolatry. Worship was to be understood and participated in as a spiritual event.

The antiliturgical movement that originated with the Puritans in England is an example of this new conviction. The formal prayer book used in Anglican liturgy was abandoned in early Baptist, Congregationalist and Quaker worship. The free church view of worship was one of the foundations of pedagogical worship in the seventeenth and eighteenth centuries and the evangelistic approach to worship in the nineteenth century.

The second trend was a stress on Scripture. This encouraged pedagogical worship—often three- to four-hour services spent in biblical instruction. The Word and its exposition became dominant in Presbyterian worship, for example. "Presbyterianism rejected the use of all 'ceremony' in worship unless it was prescribed in the New Testament. For this reason worship remained simple and appealed to the mind alone, not to sight, smell, taste, and hearing (other than the Word of God)."[27]

The third trend was an emphasis on personal experience. Pietism, Moravianism and revivalism illustrate this trend. Pietism was a movement in Lutheranism that reacted against dead orthodoxy in both Protestantism and Catholicism. Its concern was to effect a personal faith-reform in the believer. It rejected established worship as being dependent on external form. Such externalism "prevented personal involvement motivated by an openness to the Spirit."[28] With Pietists' stress on personal conversion, worship no longer centered on the corporate act of the church; rather, the personal experience of the worshiper was central. The converted worshiper need not depend on others in the liturgical experience.

The Moravians' most lasting contribution to liturgy was in hymnody. Moravian hymns created a subjective experience because of their emphasis on personal experiential worship. These hymns were "emotional, imaginative, sensuous, with a minimum of intellectual structure."[29] John and Charles Wesley, who were strongly influenced by the Moravians, composed songs that mostly stressed the subjective personal experience and conversion.[30]

During this period the Roman Catholic Church was changing as well.[31] The Counter-Reformation was forged in the context of opposition to Protestantism. The Council of Trent in the sixteenth century reformed the Roman Rite. This Tridentine liturgy became the obligatory form of worship for Western Catholicism for the next four hundred years.[32] Its unbending rigidity was not decisively questioned until Vatican II, in the second half of the twentieth century.

The Nineteenth Century and Beyond

In Europe the nineteenth century was a period of Romanticism and a revival of folk culture and fairy tale, chivalry and Gothic architecture. People looked "for a golden age in which to take refuge from times of uncertainty."[33] In England the high-church Oxford Movement with its ritualism paralleled the Romantic movements in literature and art. In Germany the revival movement sought to restore sixteenth-century liturgy, hymnody and chant. Even in Roman Catholicism, Ultramontanists and others sought to idealize medieval church order and theology.[34]

In the United States a different trend appeared, one that eventually influenced liturgy around the world. In reality it was not one trend but a series of trends growing out of the cultural and social milieu of the period. James F. White summarizes these trends as four liturgical eras in the last 150 years. They are revivalism, respectability, the recovery of tradition and pluralism.[35]

The dominant Western culture of the nineteenth century was marked by pragmatic optimism. There was a general philosophy that one could accomplish anything if the right techniques were used. Worship was viewed in a similar manner in this era of revivalism. The techniques of preaching, prayer and music, used rightly in worship, could and did make converts. Revivalism had an accurate and pragmatic understanding of human behavior, and manipulated it (in both positive and negative ways) expertly.

This period of revivalism saw the growth and development of the

Holiness and Pentecostal movements.[36] The Holiness movement produced new denominations such as the Free Methodists and the Church of the Nazarene. These nineteenth-century groups sought an intense religious experience in worship. Their camp meetings, in particular, were characterized by spontaneous freedom. There was much shouting, weeping and wailing, and groaning aloud.

The Holiness movement strongly influenced modern Pentecostalism, which began with the Azusa Street revival of 1906 in Los Angeles. Pentecostal worship was characterized by spontaneity, freedom and individual expression. With a focus on Spirit-led worship, speaking in tongues and prophetic utterances (for strengthening and encouraging) became staple features of worship. Singing and music were also highly valued in Pentecostalism. Pentecostal churches broke with the pipe-organ tradition and introduced musical idioms and instruments from popular culture, including the guitar and drums.

The era of revivalism was followed in the second quarter of the twentieth century by the period of respectability. "Emphases during this era included sobriety over the ecstatic, refinement over the primitive, restraint over the boisterous, and intelligibility over the emotional."[37] This reflected a general American cultural trend: people were becoming more educated and sophisticated. Many old white-frame meetinghouses were replaced with neo-Gothic church buildings. Full choirs replaced the old gospel quartet. Vestments for choir and clergy replaced the everyday garb of worship leaders.

After World War II the recovery-of-tradition period began. Senn summarizes the background to this period: "The experience of the war crushed the shallow theology of the social gospel. Neo-orthodox theology emphasized the sinfulness of humanity and had a correspondingly high Christology. Wilsonian optimism gave way to the calculations of the cold war. We lived under the shadow of the bomb in the age of anxiety."[38] People sought a sense of security. The recovery of tradition met that need. Yet historic rites were appreciated more for aesthetic than for theological reasons.

The 1960s brought a paradigm shift in the culture of the United

States. Some say that the society came unglued. The culture lost any sense of consensus on hairstyles, clothing, lifestyles, morality. Racism, classism and gaps between the generations intensified. Experimentation was the order of the day. It was an age of cultural pluralism that affected worship. This period, says Don Wardlaw, "brought new and heady wine into many of our sanctuaries."[39] Liturgists began to be more inclusive and socially responsible in their liturgical planning and preaching.

Roman Catholic worship changed during this period as well. The rigidity in which the church had been locked for four hundred years was broken with Vatican II reforms. The changes included new texts for worship; new music and songs; worship in the vernacular instead of Latin; more participation by the congregation in singing, praying and responses; restoration of biblical preaching; and a greater integration of the liturgy with local cultures.[40] The church also, while still holding on to many of the traditional liturgical elements and practices, became more charismatic in a number of places, making worship relevant in an era when freedom and charismatic expression were coming into vogue.

As the church, both Protestant and Catholic, embarks upon the twenty-first century, it is faced with the same dilemma and opportunity that has faced God's people throughout the ages (from the Hebrews, the Jewish and Greco-Roman Christians, and the Europeans to a culturally diverse worldwide church): how to make worship culturally relevant yet utterly God- and Christ-centered. It is a challenge to which we must respond both corporately and individually.

Constancy
& Diversity

The Christian church is universal, or catholic. The church is also local.
The church's worship is constant as well as diverse. On the one hand,
we are attached to the concept that there is such a thing as a universal
or catholic culture. Yet on the other hand, we have a tendency toward
insularity. Much of the tension over worship practices stems from this
tension. To what extent should the needs of a local culture take precedence over what seem to be universally accepted practices? Will the
church become insular if local cultural expressions dominate the liturgy
and thus give short shrift to what is constant? A great challenge the
contemporary worldwide church faces is determining what is historically and culturally conditioned and thus changeable, and what is
essential and unchangeable in the worship experience.

The Lutheran World Federation's "Cartigny Statement on Worship and Culture" states that "the task of relating worship and cul-

ture is ultimately concerned with finding the balance between relevance and authenticity, between particularity and universality, while avoiding eclecticism and/or syncretism."[1] I argue that constancy—those common factors and universals at the core of worship—must be balanced with diversity, particular practices grounded in the local setting. What remains essential and constant in all cultural traditions must not be the mechanics of the liturgy, for these lend themselves to cultural adaptation. It must be those core elements that transcend both time and space.

To make this distinction is difficult for many traditionalists. For them, any changes in the worship service constitute an attack on the core (which for them is all the liturgical elements that have always been part of their worshiping experience). Let us not be too quick to condemn. For as Don Wardlaw has pointed out, these traditionalists fear the loss of refuge and safety:

> The sanctuary for many clergy and laity alike serves as the last bastion against shifting values and eroding absolutes. As we gather to worship we wonder about what has happened to all those fixed truths about inevitable progress, human potential, honesty in government, making the world safe for democracy, liberty and justice for all, or women's place in the home. We had those absolutes so nicely wrapped, ribboned and displayed in the windows of our nineteenth century minds. But someone threw a brick through the display window. The church is running out of hiding places in the face of the world's demands that we radically reorient our thinking if this globe is to survive at all. No wonder we resist the current move to get rid of pews. Pews symbolize one of the few things in our lives that remain solid and bolted down. And when we cannot afford pews, we opt for chairs stained and padded like pews, weighty and substantial like pews. A significant part of our emotional investment in liturgy is wrapped up in the fixity and immutability embedded in the experience. We long for one hour in the week when at least some of the ground beneath our feet is not shifting sand. "Good old" hymns, sermons in the language of Canaan, prayers that soar on the sounds of more innocent years, sung responses fixed in our bones, become ingredients so many of us depend on for a questionable sense of stability in a runaway world.[2]

Still, though we can sympathize with the comfort, security and safety these elements of worship bring to a congregant, we cannot elevate the forms to the level of absolutes.

Misrepresentation of the constants or core elements in worship is not limited to some contemporary conservative traditionalists. Theologians and denominations throughout the centuries have struggled with the question of what is core and what is not. The history of the debate over the Eucharist, or Lord's Supper, is a case in point. Is the ceremony or sacrament of the wine and cup a constant or not? If it is, it must be celebrated at each worship service. If not, the Communion service is important but not core. A universal is more than what is important. It is what cannot be dispensed with *every time* we gather for the purpose of worshiping. Any one symbolic element cannot, then, be a universal.

What *are* the constants? The biblical section of chapter one, along with the historical survey in chapter two, gave us a clue. A study of liturgy in the Scriptures and Christian history help one discover what remain as essential elements from one generation to another, in every corporate worship setting, and what changes as a result of cultural adaptation and historical circumstances.

The basic forms of Christian worship, remember, were developed from the Jewish synagogue services and other Jewish rites. These ancient rites included sabbath assemblies, festivals, prayers and exhortations. From these emerged the Christian eucharistic or love feast and weekly worship services. By the middle of the second century (at least in Rome), worship had come to consist of a fixed sequence of Scripture readings, sermon, common prayer and Communion. This pattern as the essential shape of worship has remained fairly constant.

It seems fair to deduce that the ageless, universal, common and core factors in worship are (1) an assembling or gathering of the people of God to experience the numinous (or divine presence) in encounter with their neighbors, (2) a celebration of festivals and sacraments, (3) the presentation of the Word in Scripture readings, study and sermon, and (4) prayer.[3] These four elements are in keeping with the four things the new converts devoted themselves to after the Peter's Day of Pentecost sermon: "apostles' teaching" (the Word), "fellowship" (gathering), "breaking of bread" (celebration) and "prayers" (Acts 2:42). These, I believe, must remain constant if we are not to degenerate into what has been called "particularization," resulting in a narrow religious provincialism that would cause us to lose a sense of the church's catholicity.[4]

Yet particularity used appropriately is essential to the mixture of constancy and diversity. The process of understanding the relation of particularity and diversity of cultures to worship has been alternately called contextualization, indigenization, localization and inculturation. Of course no single term adequately expresses the process, but they do help us to get a handle on the particularity of contexts and the historical development and change that occur in all contexts.[5]

Much has been written on the contextualization of theology. Contextual scholars see this as a theological imperative. Stephen Bevans in his excellent discussion notes that "contextualization is part of the very nature of theology itself."[6] Theology that is contextual recognizes that theological expressions cannot ignore culture and history, nor the varied contemporary thought forms. It is a false and irrelevant theology that is not reflective of its culture, times and current concerns, as well as those in tradition and history. Bevans therefore is correct when he says that "the time is past when we can speak of one right, unchanging theology, a *theologia perennis*. We can only speak about a theology that makes sense at a certain place and in a certain time."[7] But we must be careful not to base our theology on a "fossil" culture, one that does not exist today except in some people's "romantic fantasies."[8] Culture is not static. It is always changing, in flux and adapting.

Just as theology does not make sense unless it is contextualized, worship is not authentic if it is not accommodated to particular eras and particular cultures. "The denial of cultural elements . . . fundamentally calls into question the very human quality of the liturgy itself."[9] Liturgy must take seriously the cultural and ethnic diversities in local and worldwide Christian communities.

Diversity is also historical. We have seen that the style of worship in the second century was quite different from that of the fourth and fifth centuries, just as the nineteenth-century American worship emphasis differed from today's. Recall James F. White's four liturgical eras in American culture: revivalism, respectability, recovery of tradition, pluralism. Each of these brought a different dimension and emphasis to the worship scene. In another work White discusses how diversity has characterized Protestant worship tradition from its inception, and thus he divides Protestant worship into nine liturgical traditions that have passed on from generation to generation.[10]

The diversity and particularity that especially concerns us is that of our contemporary location. To have worship in the vernacular is to make it contextually relevant to the culture. When we speak of Martin Luther reforming the sixteenth-century liturgy and putting it in the vernacular, we are talking about more than language and dialect. While these are vital symbols of inculturation and cultural expression, they are not the only ones. The way all worship rituals are enacted and understood by worshipers is culturally conditioned.

The arts, music, dance and architecture are all informed by culture. Mark Francis states that these are as much cultural

> as the more informal but no less important expressions of cultural values such as eating with a knife and fork, looking at the person one is addressing and obeying traffic laws while driving a car. [These] are just a few of the "symbolic forms" that express the values and vision of a particular culture. All of these forms have been influenced by the history of a given people in a specific place and time. There is nothing intrinsically "better" about any of these modes of behavior—or constitutive of being human.[11]

Liturgical vestments make statements about a particular culture. The fabric and design, for example, can communicate triumphalism or simplicity, fullness or frugality, gaudiness or dignity,[12] depending on what is important in a particular culture. (For example, compare the robes the Protestant African-American preacher wears in the pulpit to the simple business suit of his or her Caucasian counterpart.) The music can be the human voice or the organ, the guitar or the piano, the maracas or the harp. These all have to do with particular taste, and taste is the product of one's culture. Liturgical contextualization thus permeates every aspect of worship—the music, the arts, the dress, the language (both dialect and content[13]), the food and other material elements of celebration, and even the mode of leadership (male or female, communal or individual). All these are cultural artifacts that are not constants.

It is worthwhile to note at this point that we are experiencing what is known as multiculturalism or cultural pluralism, particularly in North America. Cultural pluralism "represents a perspective that encompasses a wide range of convictions about respecting other cultures, nurturing diversity, and challenging the hegemony of Western culture."[14] Brenda Aghaowa speaks of "liturgical imperialism," which imposes Euro-American worship preferences on Christians of non-European descent. "It is related to the notion of cultural Christianity, which links Euro-American culture and Christianity, as if the two were one, and views Euro-American worship styles as normative and superior."[15]

Such "imperialism" and "hegemony" are on their way out. The notion of North America as a "melting pot" is now generally viewed as a myth, no longer a valid metaphor for describing the American landscape.[16] More apt metaphors are "fruit basket," "vegetable plate" and "mosaic." Cultural groups do not seek to merge in a melting pot but strive to preserve their distinct ways. This is certainly true for many worshipers within the wider Americas. Caribbean people wish to preserve Caribbean ways of worshiping; Hispanics in many instances do not care to melt into the Anglo-dominated pot.

The great experiment in North American liturgical circles is how to make worship a truly multicultural experience. How can a congregation that is diverse, that speaks out of varied cultural experiences, worship together and even have their own vision altered by the honest dialogue that takes place because of this experience? We should not fear a multicultural worship experience, for as Mark Bangert has shown, we all already draw on multicultural elements in our worship:

All of us who use the traditional Western rite are multicultural, for it is a collection of liturgical contributions from the near East, Rome, Northern Africa, and Europe. Our experience at multicultural worship is yet wider. Consider how German hymnody has found its way into most contemporary hymnals. For years we have used language formations dependent on English social structures. We are becoming more familiar with African American religious music and feel increasing comfort with clapping out the rhythms. Guatemalan styles have found their way into many Gothic spaces.[17]

Much of the discussion regarding diversity and contextualization has to do with indigenization on a more global scale. For centuries conversion to Christian faith required an African or Asian to discard indigenous ways as inferior and superstitious and adopt the "superior" Western European culture. For example, Aghaowa says, missionaries required those in Africa who became Christians

to put aside many of their own worship styles and rich cultural traditions. They did this in the mistaken belief that these were connected in some instances with the worship of tribal idols. . . . Western suits and dresses often replace the more colorful, beautifully woven traditional garb at worship. Certainly, the style of worship, while spirited anyway, is still more formal and subdued than it would be without the influence of the missionaries.[18]

A relatively new movement rejects such ethnocentric understanding and behavior. Missionaries are now attempting to restrain themselves from imposing Western customs and practices on converts who are non-Western. The Roman Catholic Church and Vatican II have led the way in this endeavor, as they moved from centuries of "rulericism and liturgical uniformity"[19] toward an openness to diversity.

One of the most important and most controversial arenas of indigenization is music. In many Christian communities, worship music is fraught with contention and emotionalism. As seen in this book's historical section, this struggle is not new. Even in the Reformation era, organs and instruments were smashed to pieces, and singing went unaccompanied for years. Now the debate involves questions such as whether the organ, the guitar or the drums are suitable for worship.[20]

Many liturgists contend that we must adapt to the particularity of each local culture. Yet the adaptation practiced by many is not to local and folk-inspired music but involves, as it were, brushing a coat of folk varnish over an Anglo-European core. This is Ricardo Ramirez's concern:

> When we speak of adapting the liturgy to Hispanic cultures, we are aiming at more than a coat of varnish that automatically gives an impression of Hispanicity. Guitars, *zarapes*, English hymns translated into Spanish, colorful stoles and vestments do not of themselves provide an answer. What is needed is a renewed Hispanic liturgy that will affirm and celebrate Christian values and traditions peculiar to Hispanic cultures.[21]

Of course the liturgical indigenization process involves many other areas of controversy, such as how the church's sacraments may properly be contextualized. In the 1970s in the Caribbean, Guayanese Christians complained that grape juice, wine and flour had to be imported for the Eucharist though locally produced sugarcane juice and rice for making rice cakes were available in abundance (at a time when the economy was at a low ebb). From another cultural perspective, Stephen Bevans asks, "How can the important symbol of baptism express cleansing and inclusion when, in the Masai culture of Africa, pouring water over a woman's head is a ritual cursing her to barrenness?"[22]

Such issues need to be addressed. But they don't apply only to Asia, Africa, Latin America and the Caribbean. Even in North America the need for inculturation and liturgical indigenization is urgent—whether it be in the barrios of Los Angeles or the heart of Harlem, New York, in rural Georgia or big-sky Montana. The need everywhere is for missionaries and leaders to incarnate[23] and immerse themselves in the local culture and particular community so that liturgical expressions will not be externally imposed but will authentically reflect the people's life.

This leads us to an important point in this discussion of diversity and contextualization: *worship must be related to and relevant to the total lived life of a particular community.* If not, worship will be "sterile regardless of how emotional or unemotional it is."[24] The language of the worship service, says Paul Brown, must be the "language of experienced life."[25] It should consist of the stuff of life—congregants' faith and struggles, blessings and injustices, failures and accomplishments, joys and conflicts. The worship experience needs to demonstrate that it is in touch with the historical conditions and immediate circumstances of the worshipers. Such worship is uniquely contextual.

One important aspect of relating worship to life involves forging a liturgy that addresses the social injustices and pain that rack the society in which God's people live. The worship service must apply H. Richard Niebuhr's fifth typology and be a transformer of culture.[26] Social commitment to the transformation of social structures and injustices needs to be proclaimed and affirmed. In the eloquent words of Thea Bowman:

> We will find shelter for the homeless. We will feed the hungry, comfort the lovely, visit the incarcerated, teach the illiterate, live our concerns for the elderly poor. We will listen to people who hurt. . . . We'll be intolerant of racism, intolerant of racism and sexism and classism and clericalism and elitism and defeatism and materialism and consumerism and all those other kinds of isms that lead us to injustice and to destruction. We will use our spiritual, moral, social, economic, political, and diplomatic power to work for justice.[27]

For worship to be truly contextual it must address those social sins that God truly hates, and let "justice roll down like waters, and righteousness like an ever-flowing stream" (Amos 5:24).

But how far do we go in the indigenization process? Where is the boundary—the periphery? How much folk religion and culture do we incorporate into the worship service to make it truly incarnational without merely capitulating to culture? Moses Oladele Taiwo argues that we have failed to relate Christianity to the world of the African. He quotes words of a popular festive Yoruba tribal song to show the need to incorporate indigenous ritual in our celebrations:

> Awa O s'oro ile wa O.
> Awa O s'oro ile wa O.
> Igbagbo o pe ka'wa ma s'oro
> Awa os' oro ile wa O.

We shall celebrate the cultic festival of our home.
We shall celebrate the cultic festival of our home.
Christianity never forbids, no, Christianity never forbids participation in
cultic festivals.
We shall celebrate the cultic festivals of our homeland.[28]

For Taiwo, quite in contrast to the missionaries alluded to earlier, the boundaries have an extended range. The missionaries made the mistake of importing a liturgy of language, music and approach that was alien to the colonized culture and rejecting out of hand the folk culture and religion of the locals. The church failed then, as in many places it still does, to be "baptized" (to use Michael Marshall's metaphor)[29] with folk religion, and thus worship became unnatural.

But am I saying that there are no boundaries? In a sense yes—or rather, that the boundaries are fuzzy. In fact worship is best carried out when we do not concentrate on the boundaries but on the center, Jesus Christ. Authentic worship in any age and culture always moves from the center toward the periphery. Contemporary liturgical theologians are following this movement when they apply Niebuhr's fifth model— of Christ as a transformer of culture—to worship. Frank Senn, following Geoffrey Wainwright, argues that "any natural symbol can be baptized for use in the Christian cult. Any cultural expression or social institution can be 'christianized,' as it were."[30] Worship therefore is Christian (with "christianized" expressions) when its center is Jesus Christ and it bears witness to the gospel of Christ.[31]

Clearly the process of contextualization, inculturation and indigenization is not cut and dried. It is often a messy enterprise. "Practices that seem right and salutary in one era or within one culture may be judged silly or quaint in another,"[32] as will be seen in the following sections on African-American, Caribbean and Hispanic worship. But the process must continue as we maintain the tension between constancy and diversity, catholicity and locality in worship.

African-American Worship

"We Had Church Today!"

T he *African-American church and African-American worship are* not monolithic. They are diverse. Underneath this variety, however, there lies a commonality that makes the worship of this American subculture unique. The root of this uniqueness is embedded in the African soil with its worldview and practices.

The African Roots

Western sociologists, historians and theologians long have accepted and perpetuated the myth that black Africans came to America bereft of a meaningful past, lacking a significant religious experience.[1] The fact is, many of the distinctive practices and experiences that inform the black church and its worship today have been passed on from generation to generation by the spiritual ancestors who brought them on the Middle Passage from Africa. Furthermore, the African religious heritage survived in its primal form, almost wholly untouched by European American Christianity, for approximately 150 years.[2]

Africa has bequeathed to American society a way of worship that is rich in expression and content—its music (spirituals, gospel, rhythmic instrumentation), its expression of the Word in preaching and praying, its communal and ecstatic responses in "call and response" antiphony, the shout, the falling out. All these, which might seem "motor behavior"[3] to the outsider, are deep expressions of an African way of life and worldview. When African-Americans capture this spirit in worship, one will hear the folksy expression as they depart from the place of worship, "We had church today!"

The black church in America preserved its liturgical heritage only through great struggle. Much of this preservation took place in the heart of rural America. Early slaves had to worship clandestinely, developing what has come to be known as the "invisible institution." In these secret places, slaves took great risks to express their faith in traditional African ways.

The secret places of the invisible institution, known also as "hush harbors," "brush harbors" or "bush," were secluded in woods, swamps, deep gullies and ravines, or in slave cabins. The worshipers' exuberance had to be muted so as to avoid the inevitable persecution that would be meted out if they were discovered by slavemasters.

Peter Randolph in his book *From Slave Cabin to Pulpit* gives a detailed description of a "hush harbor":

> Not being allowed to hold meetings on the plantation, the slaves assemble in the swamps, out of reach of the patrols. They have an understanding among themselves as to the time and place of getting together. This is often done by the first one arriving breaking boughs from the trees and bending them in the direction of the selected spot. Arrangements are then made for conducting the exercises. They first ask each other how they feel, the state of minds, etc. The male members then select a certain space, in separate groups, for their division of the meeting. Preaching in order, by the brethren; then praying and singing all around, until they generally feel quite happy. The speaker usually

commences by calling himself unworthy, and talks very slowly, until, feeling the spirit, he grows excited, and in a short time, there fall to the ground twenty or thirty men and women under its influence.[4]

The architecture and furnishings of the hush harbor were developed to maintain quiet and secrecy. In some instances quilts and blankets, saturated with water, were hung to define the worship space and keep in the sound. Former slaves also recalled the use of a large black iron pot filled with water, placed in the center of the "sanctuary." The preacher, the person praying or the group of worshipers would speak and sing into the pot to deaden the sound. Using an inverted pot produced equivalent results. Patsy Hyde, a former slave from Tennessee, reported that slaves "would tek dere ole iron cookin' pots en turn dem upside down on de groun' neah dere cabins ter keep dere white folks fum herein' w'at dey was sayin'. Dey claimed that hit showed dat Gawd waz wid dem."[5]

Although African expressions of worship were preserved most widely in the clandestine settings of the invisible institution, the praise houses (or "prays houses," "prayer houses," "pray houses" or "de place way oner go fur pray")[6] of the Sea Islands were possibly the first "visible institutions" where African-American worship traditions were developed. The Sea Islands, off the coast of South Carolina and Georgia, had an African population of approximately eleven thousand (83 percent of the islands' population) in 1861. Melva Wilson Costen notes that "for generations these people of African descent had been isolated and were, therefore, able to preserve African and newly shaping African-American practices longer than in other places."[7] For the most part, however, such preservation remained underground in the United States.

Initially no attempts were made to Christianize the African slaves. Force and violence were used to prevent the slaves from practicing their own African religious rites. These attempts failed. White preachers and missionaries ultimately convinced the slavemasters that it would be in their best interest to convert the slaves to Christianity. As part of this conversion, the slaves were required to renounce their African traditions and accept wholesale the European forms of worship.

Blacks in America, to a large extent, rejected that either-or dichotomy. They appropriated the missionaries' message but remolded it. They rejected simple imitation of European forms, opting to transform them into African-oriented liturgical practices.[8] Music (both melodies and rhythm), movement (the ring shout and ecstatic seizures) and other elements served in the process of infusing into Christianity a new African paradigm.

The question was raised then, as it is still now: Is black worship, with its African orientation, truly Christian worship? Certainly black worship, rooted as it was in African cultural traditions, differed from the religious practices of white European and American Protestantism and Catholicism. The difference was significant enough, early in the nineteenth century, that a visitor from Great Britain noted that "the negro of our southern States prefers going to a church or meeting composed of peoples of his own colour, and where no whites appear. Slaves, also, sometimes prefer places of worship where greater latitude is allowed for noisy excitement . . . than would be tolerated in the religious assemblies of white people."[9]

Nevertheless, black worship is Christian worship. It is informed by Judeo-Christian religious content, Western European and American interpretations of Judeo-Christianity, and traditional African primal worldviews. As the invisible institution became more visible, the African dimension of Christian worship became more obvious. Henry Mitchell states that "as Christian worship came to be carried on without White supervision, the African cult which had been suppressed, surfaced again as Christian cult. And the African appeared again—now as Christian—with all of his native splendor."[10] Of course, as will be seen later, it is not only the infusion of African tradition into worship that gives it this unique Christian dimension. But the conditions of slavery and the black experience in America played roles in the development of African-American worship and spirituality.

Of course African-Americans do not have one uniform style of worship. Although worship in black indigenous churches around the world (whether in Africa, the United States or the Caribbean) has distinctive elements in common,[11] "different situations and circumstances under which exposure to Christianity took place for each congregation, denomination, (history and theological orientation), geography, and social life-styles are significant determinants of worship."[12]

Vattel Daniel's study of class structure in the Chicago's black community between 1937 and 1939 highlights in broad strokes the nonmonolithic nature of African-American Christianity and worship. He proposed a scheme of four "ritual types": (1) ecstatic sects or cults, (2) semidemonstrative groups, (3) deliberative or sermon-centered services, and (4) liturgical denominations.[13]

This outline may be helpful, but even within denominations and congregations we find multiplex patterns. Besides, change comes with the passing of time. For example, James T. Campbell, in his massive work on the African Methodist Episcopal (AME) Church in the United States and South Africa, reminds us that during the nineteenth century the AME Church "was clearly the most respectable and 'orthodox' of black American independent churches. While some recognizably African elements surfaced in services, AME leaders tended to disdain if not actively to suppress those beliefs and practices that scholars today celebrate as signs of Africa's persistence in the New World."[14] Yet today who would argue that the AME denomination is one of the most Afrocentric Christian communions?

The same is true in terms of class shifts. Daniel's study confirmed what has always been obvious: that class structure determines the level of Afrocentrism in the denomination or congregation. The lower the class, the more Afrocentric the church; the higher the class, the more Eurocentric. However, one of the most significant class shifts over the past half-century has been among Pentecostals. C. Eric Lincoln and Lawrence H. Mamiya's seminal study on the black church in America estimates that more than half of Church of

God in Christ (the largest Pentecostal denomination) members are now within "the coping middle-income strata."[15] And Pentecostalism continues to exhibit the vitality of its African roots of worship, in spite of its adherents' "moving on up." The fact is that today, possibly more than ever since the days of slavery and the invisible institution, blacks across the United States and across denominational lines are forging ahead (to one degree or another) in incorporating African worldviews and practices in their liturgy.

This brings us around again to ask whether we should be focusing on our differences in worship (see part one). Many in the Caucasian community and even some in the black community see it as fragmenting the church and tearing us apart. We should talk about our similarities and downplay our differences, it is argued. "But, until there is an absolute respect for our differences," say Cyprian Rowe, "and a cherishing of variety in culture and in gifts, there can be no talk about similarities that is of genuine and true value."[16]

It was in part the demeaning of African cultural and religious values that led to the establishment of the independent black churches in America. In 1819, for example, John F. Watson chastised white Methodists for singing like the "illiterate blacks of the society."[17] Thus African-Americans were forced to focus on their differences in order to give status to their values. As Rowe points out, "There were certain areas of Afro-American life that Euro-Americans were not interested in. One of these areas was the church, another was entertainment."[18] Whites were (and in many instances still are) not interested in, or comfortable with, black worship and religious life. And so African-Americans isolate themselves.

In some instances Caucasians are the ones withdrawing. Black Pentecostalism is a case in point. Black Pentecostalism (unlike organizations of black Methodists and Baptists) did not begin as a separatist movement. It began as an interracial movement from which the dominant ethnic group subsequently withdrew.[19] It must be noted that although the separation was largely due to racism, there were other factors that precipitated it. Lincoln and Mamiya note, for example, that Pentecostalism gained momentum at the beginning of the twentieth century in reaction to liberal tendencies "expressed in Darwinism, the ecumenical emphasis, and the Social Gospel movement. The antiliberal orientation of the Pentecostal movement led also to the termination of its interracial character as separatist white denominations were organized."[20]

African-Americans consider the melting-pot metaphor a myth. They have always known that the melting was meant to produce homogeneous Americans reflecting the old WASP model,[21] so that African distinctiveness would be obliterated. Joseph Bethea reminds us that "black people have been taught that the right way to worship and do anything else in this country is the way white people do them. There used to be a saying in the black community: 'If you're white, you're right; if you're brown, stick around; if you're black, get back.' 'Black' was the term used to denote error, rejection and evil. 'White' was used to denote truth, acceptance and goodness."[22] American society would never melt in such a way as to include its blackness to any significant degree. So African-Americans changed the metaphor from melting pot to "fruit plate," "vegetable dish" or "rainbow."

Using these new metaphors, which give equality to the diverse American cultures, we can agree that patterns and traditional practices in African-American worship should not be viewed as "an interim kind of state until black church members become more educated," in Brenda Aghaowa's words. "These traditions have integrity and represent Blacks historically and psychically at deep levels." They should not be done away with. Neither should they be tolerated until black folks can come up to a higher level. "Rather they are to be celebrated, preserved, refined, and shared with the world." They must not be obliterated. They must not be erased.[23]

And indeed African elements of worship in black churches have not been obliterated or erased. Since Stokely Carmichael's galvanizing of "Black Power" and the advent of the motto "Black is beautiful," African-Americans have more pride than ever before in their worship service and their church. The secular value of pride in one's blackness has spilled into the sacred space and time of worship and church life. In surveys done among black Christians, it was found that because the church is "one of the few institutions that is completely owned and controlled by black people, the sense of possessiveness, pride, and power are unparalleled in other phases of African American life."[24] Charles Hamilton in *The Black Preacher in America* argues that African-Americans manifest a completed identification with "my pastor" and "my church" that is not found elsewhere. African-Americans seldom speak of "my Democratic Party" or "my NAACP," even though they are closely associated with these institutions. However, they often speak of "my church."[25] I'm convinced that the reason for this close identification and pride lies in an African worldview which the church has incorporated and maintained in its life and worship.

A Wholistic View of Life and Worship

I have noted elsewhere that "of all the cultures which make up the pluralistic society of the United States, the African American may capture best the wholistic view of worship."[26] Worship for blacks in America is not merely a "spiritual" exercise unrelated to the rest of life. Historically, church and its related activities were not disconnected from other aspects of African-Americans' daily life. As in Judaism, where the synagogue was the center of life in its totality,[27] the black church has "served as school, forum, political arena, social club, art gallery, and conservatory of music. It was and is the place where fellowship and interaction with fellow human beings and with God takes place."[28]

African-Americans refuse to adopt the Western dichotomous view of life. They have maintained and perpetuated the traditions of their ancestors, who saw life as a whole. African society, like most Eastern societies, envisions a universe that is not compartmentalized between the sacred and the secular. The secular and the sacred are all part of the *spiritual* world—the opposite of which is the *profane*. "So the secular and the sacred, on Saturday night and Sunday morning, come together to affirm God's holiness, the unity of life, and God's lordship over all of life,"[29] in ways that persons with a dichotomous worldview cannot comprehend.

With this wholistic worldview informing the liturgy, everything done in worship manifests connectedness and interrelatedness—a wholism that involves the worshiper's total self. Thus while rational, cognitive transmission of information is important to the congregant, worship is deeply *experiential*. Within Afrocentric worship and religious experience, the emphasis is on "the subjective and intuitive (feeling), rather than objective, abstract, or rational thinking."[30] This is not to say that such worship is merely subjective or mindless. Rather, African-Americans who worship with their whole persons do not come to church *only* to learn something but also to feel God's Spirit, participate in communal sharing and involve themselves physically in the service.

Community is paramount in worship. African culture is profoundly tribal and communal in its essence. When this tribal antecedent is combined with "the African American history of group identity as slaves and the continuing reality of racial oppression . . . one discovers a potent cultural undercurrent of *collectivism*."[31]

The communal worldview is most evident in the extended family. African cultural tradition sees every woman, for example, as mother, aunt, grandmother, sister or daughter. All are family. Africans and African-Americans view life as one-in-community. Life is a two-way relationship, not individualistic. Africans and black Americans define themselves by a sense of belonging—belonging to a community.[32] This cultural worldview of necessity is carried over into worship. Worship therefore is a community happening in which kinship and mutual interdependence are affirmed.

Worship is not a spectator sport. In the African religious tradition no one was to be separated as an onlooker or observer, stranger or spectator. All were brought into the worship experience as participants.[33] The participative and relational character of African-American worship can be illustrated by an overview of what might happen in a typical service:

> Worshipers might be instructed to ask the names of those sitting next to them, to shake hands with people around them, or to turn to their neighbors and

say, "God bless you" or "I don't know what *you* came to do, but *I* came to praise the Lord." Or they might be instructed to leave their seats for a brief period of time and go around the sanctuary to hug and greet as many people as they can. Often, for the benediction, worshipers may be asked to join hands, even across aisles, for the final doxology. All will sway together rhythmically in time to the music as they sing a gospel version of "Praise God from Whom All Blessings Flow." The clasped hands are lifted to the ceiling as the final Amen of a threefold "Amen" concludes the doxology.[34]

Although worship is a cooperative community event, not just an isolated effort of an individual, individuality is encouraged in the worship service of African-Americans. This is illustrated by Henry Mitchell's discussion of the extended family and the person in relation to music:

> White people read music and are criticized when they do not follow what is on the paper. A Black person who is trying to be middle class and wants to be like White folks says, "She don't know how to play what's on the paper. She play anything she feel like playing." Well, that is exactly what African art invites, because African art is done with the understanding that everybody is artist. Everybody fulfills himself/herself as he/she feels like being fulfilled, in whatever it is one happens to be doing. There are subtle and careful adherences to the melody and the rules of the medium, but self-fulfilling improvisation is the rule.
>
> If you hear a black gospel rendition and a person improvising on the theme, you must understand this. It is understood that everybody fashions his own offering of praise to God in his own way. That is what one is supposed to do. One is supposed to know the theme well enough to use it in the fashion that befits one's spirit. You will hear folk in the congregation say, "Sing your song, child!" And when they say it, they themselves are, in a vicarious way, fulfilled. It is understood that it is "your song" and that Beethoven, or whoever, just sort of gave you the initial theme on which you thereafter improvised.[35]

Even in such expressions of individuality there is a sense of community, "vicarious" though it maybe. Worship is not worship if it is not a community event. It is almost as if the individual is subsumed into the community. Thus C. Michael Hawn is correct in his observation that "the question so often voiced—'Were my needs met?'—would be unthinkable in the midst of African worshiping communities. Strength for the individual is found in what strengthens the community."[36] Worship for African-Americans is not an "entering into oneself."[37] It is an encounter between God, the worshiper and the worshiping community and family.

Worship as Liberation

W. E. B. Du Bois in his classic 1903 work *The Soul of Black Folk* states that "the history of the American Negro is the history of . . . strife—this longing to attain self-conscious manhood, to merge his double self into a better and truer self."[38] In order to alleviate the pain resulting from this strife, early African slaves, like their ancestors, turned to the supernatural. In a later essay in the same work, Du Bois writes:

> Endowed with a rich tropical imagination and a keen, delicate appreciation of Nature, the transplanted African lived in a world animate with gods and devils, elves and witches; full of strange influences—of Good to be implored, of Evil to be propitiated. Slavery, then, was to him the dark triumph of Evil over him. All the hateful powers of the Under-world were striving against him, and a spirit of revolt and revenge filled his heart. He called up all the resources of heathenism to aid,—exorcism, and witch-craft, the mysterious Obi worship with its barbarous rites, spells, and blood-sacrifice even, now and then, of human victims. Weird midnight orgies and mystic conjurations were invoked, the witch-woman and the voodoo-priest became the center of Negro group life, and that vein of vague superstition which characterizes the unlettered Negro even to-day was deepened and strengthened.[39]

The fact that the slaves were introduced to Christianity did not diminish the enslavement, marginalization, oppression and denial of respect perpetrated by the very ones who initiated them to the new religion. The refuge they now found was in the Christian God and his worship. This had a liberating effect. No matter what the slavemasters did, the oppressed knew that they had "a *somebodiness* that is guaranteed by God who alone is the ultimate sovereign of the universe."[40]

Their worship services became the place where liberation was enacted and most keenly felt. Particularly in the "hush harbor" of the invisible institution, the slaves found answers and ways to cope. Delores Williams suggests that the use of the overturned pots functioned symbolically as a "resistance ritual."[41] Worship among the early African-Americans brought together both as a passive community of refuge where their "somebodiness" was liberated and an active, resisting community where God's support of them in their struggles was affirmed.

The passing of slavery and gaining of political freedom did not bring full liberation to blacks in America. Life for African-Americans continues to be plagued by trouble and suffering, difficulties and disappointments, trials and tribulations, cares and woes. Life for most African-Americans is a daily physical, economic and emotional grind.[42] Weekly worship is a welcome refuge—a "bridge over troubled waters;" a place where they "take their burdens to the Lord and leave them there," finding instead joy, relief, solace, affirmation, escape and shelter. Church is "a very positive alternative," says Aghaowa, "to what is waiting at home. It is a pleasure for many African Americans intentionally to leave behind the stresses and strains of home life"[43]—stresses and strains that are intensified by their political, social and socioeconomic circumstances in America.[44]

Socioeconomic factors, to a large degree, explain the extended time black people spend at church. Aghaowa notes that "of nearly 2.5 million black families in the United States, about 31 percent (almost one-third) live below the poverty level (according to 1993 U.S. Census Bureau statistics). This compares with 12.3 percent for the general population." She goes on to suggest that "given these economic realities, there often is little money for expensive diversions. Thus the church serves as a social meeting place as well."[45] There is no rush to leave this place of refuge and fellowship.

Socioeconomic factors are not the only struggles from which blacks feel the need to be liberated in weekly worship. The vast majority of African-Americans, including those who are highly educated and have gained a certain measure of professional and financial success, still "endure a profound sense of alienation and precariousness of position in a mostly white society."[46] African-Americans feel excluded, humiliated and oppressed by the majority society. They feel that they have not arrived at a place of full acceptance and equality. Disenchantment, marginalization, dehumanization and second-class citizenship mark their experience of life in the broader culture; worship, on the other hand, provides the full acceptance and equality they long for. As J. Wendell Mapson Jr. writes:

> It provided a place for the free display of talent and potential that could not be utilized and appreciated in America's marketplace. Those who were powerless had access to power within the black church. Those who had neither title nor position elsewhere could hold office in the black church. Those who could not release their feelings in the everyday world could be heard on Sunday morning. The black church was and is both a place of temporary withdrawal as well as a place to refuel for the journey.[47]

That period at the end of the week is a time when "self-confidence is bolstered." Hope is "spawned and incubated." Sense is made of the "inexplicable set of circumstances"[48] that blacks face the other six days of the week.

Now we can understand another reason African-Americans are in no rush to get out of worship. "When people have faced the experience of dehumanizing oppression all the week and in every other setting, they are not so anxious to get away from the one setting that gives them personhood and assures them that they are somebody."[49] So authentic, liberating worship among African-Americans cannot be limited to a specific schedule, rigid rules or precise planning. Freedom reigns.

A word must be said about the worship service as an activist forum for political and social liberation. Lincoln and Mamiya discuss this a number of times in their volume. African-Americans have tended to be liberal in their political views. Even black evangelicals who are theologically conservative are often politically liberal.[50] The results of several surveys over a twenty-year period demonstrate that there is a consensus and broad support for a social, political, prophetic role for the black church. Overall, African-Americans support a more activist political role for their church than Euro-American Christians do. Significantly, "as far as it is known, black churches have not suffered the kinds of loss in membership and financial support that some more liberal white denominations have experienced because of their involvement in social and political issues."[51]

Because black worship is wholistic, its ritual and preaching must reflect the problems African-Americans face, "affirm their worth in the sight of God, and inspire them to militantly seek solutions to their problems."[52] Therefore the pulpit serves not only as a platform for bringing hope and liberation amid daily struggles but as a forum for active political involvement to demand change in the here and now.

"Worship is a catharsis for the oppressed."[53] It is therapeutic.[54] "Worship in the black idiom functions to heal individuals, to celebrate and support black identity, to offer blacks a sense of place and significance in the continuity and flow of a troublesome life."[55] In worship, pent-up emotions and frustrations are released in a flood of emotion.

William B. McClain is correct in noting that, contrary to popular opinion, black worship is different from white fundamentalist emotionalism. The mode of worship and faith articulation is derived from the experience of the worshipers. "The White experience in its critical essence is not the Black experience."[56] What African-Americans bring to worship, how they act in worship and what they take from worship can be significantly different from the experience of other Americans. An observation by Albert Pero is apropos:

> Whereas the [mainline, white] churches struggle to make worship "relevant" to the rest of the week's work and play, the black experience is to make the week's work and play and struggle the stuff of worship. Put more simply: Where white Christians try to take something away with them from worship (such as "inspiration," or sermon ideas, or warm memories of moving experiences), black ... Christians should be able to render that need unnecessary by what they *bring* to worship.[57]

Worship as Celebration

Authentic African-American worship is celebrative. It is not a polite observance at the end of the week. Rather, it is the high point of celebration when God's love and redeeming acts amidst the troubles and trials of the week are affirmed.

God, having brought them safe thus far, is reason for rejoicing. Therefore the authentic black worship service is never boring but highly enjoyable. The joyous elements in the liturgy, filled with spontaneity, come together to form a service that often elicits the folksy response "We had a good time in the Lord!'

There is no rushing away from such an experience. Worshipers don't ask, "How long will the service be today?" Time constraints are not an issue. Church members almost never complain that the service should be scaled back to an hour. A typical African-American worship service is a celebration lasting two to three hours. It is unhurried. Every element is celebrated to its fullest, whether it be the music praise by the congregation, professional vocalists and instrumentalists; the offertory; the announcements; the preaching; the prayer or the call to discipleship. "No element or moment in the service is considered dull, a waste of time, unimportant, or uninspiring," says Aghaowa.[58]

Liberation is experienced in worship, and the fruit is joy and ecstasy. Worshipers cannot keep silent. Throughout the service exclamations break out: "Thank you, Jesus!" "Praise the Lord!" "Hallelujah!" "Amen!" These are charismatic proclamations of the goodness of God and the gladness worshipers feel in their souls.

It is difficult for the uninitiated observer to understand what is taking place in such a service. Many see it simply as entertainment filled with physical excitement. But the foremost late-twentieth-century black theologian, James Cone, points out that "black worship is essentially a spiritual experience of the truth of black life. The experience [is] of the Holy Spirit in their midst." He goes on to say that "it is the presence of the divine Spirit who accounts for the intensity in which black people engage in worship." A detached observer cannot understand. Rather, "one must come as a participant in black reality, willing to be transformed by one's encounter with the Spirit."[59]

Worship in the African-American community is unique because it was conceived within a peculiar experience. It is an experience with roots in the African continent with its primal worldview, but also an experience growing out of "a long and bitter night of slavery, segregation, discrimination, oppression, deprivation, exclusion, alienation, and rejection in this country."[60] These experiences have helped black believers realize that African culture has integrity, and within them is embedded the matter that gives them the strength to cope. This cultural perspective, added to the good news of Jesus, gives reason for an ecstatic, joyous celebration. In worship African-Americans find answers to the question of what it means to be black in the United States—what it means to be a pilgrim, socially and spiritually. Through music, the spoken word and their response, African-Americans celebrate their culture and the God who brought them through. When the celebration is carried out to its fullest, they always say, "We had church today!"

African-American Music

It is impossible to "have church" without good music. In the African-American community, music is to worship as breathing is to life. So important is music (particularly vocal music) to the worship service that it has been said it is possible to "have church" without an outstanding sermon, but not without good singing. Some say that "a good sermon ain't nothing but a song."[1]

Music is possibly the most permanent characteristic of the heritage blacks brought from Africa. Thus a study of their music "is in essence a study of how black people 'Africanized' Christianity in America."[2] Black music is also perhaps the most vivid conveyor of the social and spiritual struggles of a people in a strange and hostile land.

Music permeates the entire of African-American life and thus continually ministers to the whole person. Music in black thought, reflecting the African worldview, cannot be easily compartmental-ized into sacred and secular categories. Such dichotomized labels fail to recognize the wholism that is essential to black life and thought. In a discussion of the characteristics of music in black wor-ship, J. Wendell Mapson argues that music "must hold in tension the emphasis on this world and the expectations of the new age. It must be 'this worldly' without being materialistic and earthbound. It must be 'other worldly' without being disconnected from the con-cerns of social justice."[3]

If music is to worship what breathing is to life, then it is possibly the most essential ingredient in the liturgy. Mapson says that it is more than a mere ingredient; it is the "yeast" that gives "shape, sub-stance, and content"[4] to the service. It is not an extra, a sort of icing on the cake or a refreshing interlude in the action. It is not a periph-eral addition or an afterthought. It is central. "It is not a moment of pleasure tucked in between the serious parts. It is not even a means of entertainment for a bored congregation."[5] Of course it is enter-taining in the sense that it makes the worshiper feel good in the Lord and in the company of fellow worshipers. But it is not enter-taining for entertainment's sake. Entertainment is only part of the wholistic ministry that music serves in worship.

Vocal Music

An old African adage states that "the Spirit will not descend without a song."[6] In the African-American experience, worship without the Spirit is nonworship. Vocal music plays a vital role in the evocation of the Spirit. It not only prepares the worshipers for the Spirit but "intensifies the power of the Spirit's presence with the people."[7] We must make it clear that the Spirit can't be made to come through manipulation. But by means of song "the people know whether they have the proper disposition for the coming of the Spirit."[8]

Vocal music is more than a melody set with lyrics, with the latter the more important. Singing involves lyrics, melody, rhythm and improvisation. In many instances the latter three are emphasized over the lyrics—unlike in White culture. Don Cusic's discussion of early African-American music expands on this point:

> While the early white settlers placed a heavy emphasis on the words with the music being incidental—a handful of tunes were used, often interchangeable with different sets of lyrics—the black American felt a need to emphasize music over the words. But it was more than just a different melody—it was a whole new rhythm, an entirely new "feel" to the songs which became defined as black gospel. So, even though the Blacks and whites often sang the same words, learned from the same sources, the results were two entirely different songs, with the black gospel songs rhythmical in a way the white songs never were. These rhythms, often complex, are attributed to the African influence.[9]

It was, and still is, typical for a black composer to take a song written by a white composer, reshape it and improvise it in a folk-like manner, or "blackenize"[10] it, giving it new life. This is the genius of worship in the African-American experience.[11] African-Americans made each song uniquely their own.

To the outside observer during the days of slavery, the sound of black singing often seemed wild and weird.[12] But it was typically African. African singing is characterized by "high intensity and use of such special effects as falsetto, shouting, and guttural tones."[13] It is rhythmic and includes a call-response structure. African-Americans have expanded on these basic characteristics. Their singing utilizes extensive melodic ornamentations, such as slides, slurs, bends, moans, shouts, wails and grunts, as well as complex rhythmic structures—all of these rooted in the principle of improvisation.[14]

The call-response pattern is important in the worship music of blacks because of the communal worldview of African-Americans. In Africa, music-making is participatory; music is not a spectator sport.[15] More often than not, there is little distinction between the congregation and the choir, small ensemble or soloist. The audience participates as a community, whether through singing along, antiphonal response to selected phrases, humming, clapping or swaying. The presentation may be punctuated throughout with affirmations such as "Amen!" "Well!" "Yes!" "Thank you, Jesus!"

"Sing your song, chil'!" In this way the song is shaped by the total community and is the property of every worshiper. It is more than an entertaining performance. "It is a communal happening"[16] in which everyone improvises.

Yet as was noted in the previous chapter, although community is basic, individuality is encouraged. Each person is encouraged to fashion his or her music and response in praise to God in his or her own way. "Sing your song, chil'!" affirms the soloist's or group's uninhibited improvisation.

The freedom to improvise is important for blacks. In African-American worship a song changes each time it is sung. Each performance is a unique experience for both performer and audience. "The inventiveness on the part of black singers renders it nearly impossible to transcribe this music in sheet form," says Cusic. "Although it is put on sheet music it is rarely sung by blacks exactly as it is written because the song essentially remains in the oral tradition. The sheet music serves as a source of lyrics for the singers and a guide for basic chords for piano players."[17] A white choir, he notes, will purchase individual sheets of music from which each member will sing. The black choir, however, generally learns a song by ear, and only the director and piano player will have sheet music. "For that reason, the sheet music for blacks will usually only include the lead melody line and piano accompaniment while sheet music for Whites will have all the parts—soprano, alto, bass, tenor—written out."[18] Sheet music cannot capture the feel, freedom and spontaneity that are essential to singing in black worship.

In the days of slavery various missionaries, European visitors and white American observers described the worship songs of the slave as "wild hymns," "barbaric songs," "nonsensical chants" whose strains were weird and strange and combined with disjointed and meaningless texts, not sung but "yelled," "hooted" and "screamed."[19] Portia K. Maultsby argues that "these inaccurate and biased descriptions demonstrate the need for extreme caution when imposing western European musical forms and aesthetics upon musical traditions having a non-European cultural base." She continues:

Black spirituals are grounded in a West African aesthetic which defies characterization and qualitative assessment from a purely European frame of reference. The use and performance style of Black spirituals, therefore, can be described accurately and only from an African-American cultural and musical perspective. The musical norms and aesthetics that govern the singing of Black Americans are representative of a cultural value that places emphasis on free expression and group participation. In view of this perspective, Black spirituals were almost always accompanied by gestures, dance, and verbal interjections, and represented an intrinsic part of the religious service.[20]

The assault on the unique singing and music of African-Americans is not limited to Americans of European origin. A number of black Americans have themselves expressed disgust. Most famous among them was Daniel Alexander Payne, sixth bishop of the African Methodist Episcopal Church and founder of Wilberforce University. He was unrelenting in his denunciation of spirituals, which he called "cornfield ditties." He said they might produce "the wildest excitement amongst the thoughtless masses"[21] but have no place in the repertoire of Christians who are enlightened. He also attacked the "self-made fugue tunes" as "transcripts of low thoughts, ignorance, and superstition."[22] One of his priorities as minister and bishop was to replace such music with a fare that would engage both the spirit and the understanding.

In his history of the A.M.E. Church, James T. Campbell says this assault "struck directly at one of the most distinctive and vital features of early African American Christianity." He notes that many of the songs in the first African-American hymnal (*A Collection of Hymns and Spiritual Songs from Various Authors* by Richard Allen) came from evangelical revivals and camp meetings. "Often spontaneously created and passed down by word of mouth, these 'spiritual songs' were ideally suited to the lowly and illiterate. The images were vivid, the sentiments straightforward. . . . Most of the songs circulated without music, . . . enabling congregations to adapt them to different tunes and to mix and match choruses and verses." Black revivalists sang these songs in the "husking-frolic method" of

Southern slaves, according to one white observer. Another was appalled to hear a hymn sung to the popular tune "Fol de Rol."[23]

Through his derisive attacks Bishop Payne and others like him attempted to denigrate the folk essence of African-American music and song. Had they succeeded, a significant cultural aspect of American life would have met its death.

Instrumental Music

For Africans the main musical instrument, apart from the human voice, was the drum. As far as the missionaries and slavemasters were concerned, the drum was a symbol of heathenism. Their negative attitude toward this musical instrument contributed significantly to the "drum being deferred in the diaspora."[24] But it was not the drum that was the cause of the so-called paganism, says Jon Michael Spencer. It was rhythm. Rhythm was largely responsible for the percussiveness that produced the power that helped Africans to dance and moved them into a state of Spirit possession. "Had missionaries, slave traders, and slave masters calculated this, they would have attempted to remove rhythms from the blood and bones of the African."[25] This of course was an impossibility.

The culture of the diaspora largely succeeded in "dedrumming" African-American religion and worship. But it failed to "derhythmize" black expressions of worship and praise. "With the drum banned, rhythm, which was both its progenitor and its progeny, became the essential African remnant of black religion in North America."[26] In the Caribbean and South America, use of the drum continued despite restriction.

The drum was not totally eliminated, even though stringent laws prohibited its public use. It simply went underground until the twentieth century, which saw its resurgence in the worship setting. Up to that time the basic instrument of African-American accompaniment was the human body—handclapping and footstomping. With the coming of the twentieth century and particularly the rise of the musical idiom called gospel, more rhythmic instruments were added. Tambourines, piano, trumpet, saxophone and guitar became staples in the worship setting. The Hammond organ, however, became the most vital instrument of accompaniment in the black service.

Today, in addition to the Hammond organ, most large African-American churches will have a pipe organ and ensembles featuring strings, brasses, synthesizers, and other electronic and percussive instruments. The sound in worship is enhanced, but the rhythm remains the same as it has been for millennia.

Metered Hymns

Although the invisible institution had to remain in "hush harbors," many Christian slaves attended church with their masters—sitting in segregated sections, of course. It was likely here that they learned the English hymns popular in American churches.[27] As African-American congregations and denominations proliferated and their members became more literate, a great deal of hymn borrowing was done.[28]

The hymns of Isaac Watts and Charles Wesley were the most popular at that time, with those of Watts favored. Although Wesley wrote more than seven thousand hymns and songs and set the musical tone of English and American Protestantism, fewer than one hundred are used in African-American churches today.[29] James Cone suggests that the major reason for the lack of favor of Wesleyan hymnody among blacks is that it, like European hymnody in general, seldom focuses on liberation. "Freedom has always been an intimate concern of the Black church, and in its pilgrimage toward that goal, the much used songs of Charles Wesley seemed increasingly inexpressive of the urgencies felt by Black people."[30] Watts's hymns may have been preferred because the text and music were more straightforward[31] or the imagery was more in tune with the African-American experience.[32]

"Dr. Watts" became the popular term for the style of singing known as metered hymn and "lining out." All hymns, but especially those of Watts, were adapted and reshaped to the dictates of the congregation. The original meter was thrown out, and each was remade into a "unique expression of faith."[33]

The "lining out" tradition traces its roots to the old Scottish custom of the responsorial psalm, in which a line was sung by the precentor and repeated by the congregation.[34] But it also resonates with the African tradition of polyphony, work-song antiphonal singing, and call-response modes. There was unmistaken "Africanity"[35] in the "Dr. Watts" songs. The process of "lining out" consisted of the preacher, deacon, precentor or song leader chanting or "tuning" one or two lines of the lyrics in a singsong manner and ending on a definite pitch. The congregation would then pick up the same line (often before the "liner" had completed his or her recitation) and elaborate on the tune. This would be followed by the moaning or humming of the verse.[36] This lined tradition, although most popular in the antebellum and postbellum eras, continues to be a distinctive aspect of African-American religious culture.

Spirituals

African-American slave forefathers and mothers not only borrowed and transformed existing hymns but created new songs and invented new tunes.[37] Though some would argue that the earliest black spirituals have their genesis in the white culture, having arisen from the British and European folk tradition,[38] most African-Americans will argue that the black experience is at the heart of the creation of the Negro spiritual.

The date of origin of the spiritual as a musical genre cannot be determined with precision. It apparently emerged on Southern plantations during the antebellum slave period and evolved as a musical form in the "praise houses" of the South and independent black churches of the North. The spiritual developed as "the signature of serious black involvement in American Christianity"[39] and has been identified as "the first authentic American folk song form."[40] Of all the musical forms, the spiritual is indigenously American—not born in Africa but emerging out of the experience of a people in serfdom in the United States.

The African influence in the spiritual, however, is revealed in its functional character. "In Africa and America, Black music was not an artistic creation for its own sake; it was directly related to daily life, work and play," says Cone. "Song was an expression of the community's view of the world and its existence in it." Thus "in the spirituals, black slaves combined the memory of their fathers with the Christian gospel and created a style of existence that participated in their liberation from earthly bondage."[41]

The spiritual expressed the full range of emotion and life experience of the slave—negative and positive.[42] In the first place, they were "Sorrow Songs," as W. E. B. Du Bois called them.[43] They were "the music of an unhappy people, of the children of disappointment."[44] They spoke of pain, fear, futility, despair, struggle, sorrow, suffering, servitude and death. They were stories and commentaries of a depressed and disfranchised people. Again, Cone is on target when he argues that "no theological interpretation of the black spirituals can be valid that ignores the cultural environment that created them." The experience of the African-American is "a history of servitude and resistance, of survival in the land of death. It is the story of black life in chains and of what that meant for the souls and bodies of black people."[45] It is such an experience that gave birth to such Spirituals as "Sometimes I Feel like a Motherless Child" and "Nobody Knows the Trouble I've Seen." These lyrics express the sorrow of an unhappy people undergoing hardship—a people struggling to survive. "Survival," states Gayraud S. Wilmore, "became the regulative, moment-to-moment principle of the slave community, particularly among field hands."[46]

A classic example of a spiritual filled with the struggle motif is "We Are Climbing Jacob's Ladder." Wilmore, following John Lovell, suggests that the story in Genesis 28 is only the point of departure. The slaves, in song, painted a picture of themselves climbing round by round out of their misery and degradation. "The Jacob experience has been chosen," says Lovell, "because it is the most available, the most dramatic, the most impressive and acceptable simile" to express the sufferer's determination to ascend the ladder of material, spiritual [and I would say social] success.[47]

In the second place, these were songs of hope. Du Bois states that "through all the sorrow of the Sorrow Songs there breathes a hope—

a faith in the ultimate justice of things. The minor cadences of despair change often to triumph and calm confidence." The hope is always there that "sometime, somewhere, men will judge men by their souls and not by their skins."[48] These songs expressed a joy that amidst the harsh struggles they could affirm "I ain't tired yet."

At the heart of this vibrant affirmation is the theme of God's active involvement in the people's liberation. Biblical texts, narratives and images served to express the assurance of God's intervention in their lives. Consider the words of these spirituals:

Didn't my Lord deliver Daniel
And why not every man?
He delivered Daniel from the lion's den,
Jonah from the belly of the whale
And the Hebrew children from the fiery furnace,
Any why not every man?

Go down Moses
Way down in Egypt land
Tell old Pharaoh
To let my people go.

God's salvation was portrayed in images such as train, ship, chariot and heaven: "Freedom Train A-Coming," "Swing Low, Sweet Chariot," "Walking in Jerusalem Just like John." But worshipers were beginning to experience that liberation even amidst the hardship and struggle. They sang:

Sometimes I'm tossed and driven
Sometimes I don't know where to roam
I've heard of a city called heaven
I've started to make it my home.

Through many dangers, toils and snares
I have already come
'Twas grace has brought me safe thus far
And grace will lead me home.

Spirituals served a dual purpose for slaves. These songs were transcendent and otherworldly. They were pervaded with hope for a final eschatological deliverance. But the slaves sought imminent liberation and social change. So they used spirituals as songs of protest and political communicative devices, which would, for example, provide signals for the time and place of the next Underground Railroad "train."

"Heaven" referred to a celestial place but also designated earthly places of freedom such as the Northern states, Canada and Africa. Slaves sang, for example,

Swing low, sweet chariot,
Coming for to carry me home.
Swing low, sweet chariot,
Coming for to carry me home.

I looked over Jordan and what did I see[49]
Coming for to carry me home
A band of angels coming after me
Coming for to carry me home.

"Home," like heaven, was the free states or Canada; "Jordan" was the Ohio River. And the "band of angels" was Harriet Tubman (who went to the South nineteen times and brought over three hundred persons to freedom) or another conductor.

Spirituals were used to mask a call to escape:

Steal away, steal away to Jesus
Steal away, steal away home

I ain't got long to stay here
My Lord calls me, he calls me by thunder

The trumpet sounds within my soul
I ain't got long to stay here.

Here Jesus' name is used to mask the invitation to sneak into the woods either for a secret slave meeting or to escape to freedom.

Other spirituals with dual meaning emphasize revolution and protest:

Joshua fit the battle of Jericho
Jericho, Jericho!
Joshua fit the battle of Jericho
And the walls came tumblin' down.

While the Jericho spiritual evoked battle and destruction, the following was a warning to the slavemaster:

When Israel was in Egypt's land,
Let my people go.
Oppressed so hard they could not stand,
Let my people go.

Go down, Moses, way down in Egypt's land,
Tell old Pharaoh, let my people go.[50]

Following emancipation, the spiritual fell into a period of decline. However, it was revived following its popularization by the Fisk Jubilee choir and other tour choirs from black colleges and universities. These anthemized arrangements made the spiritual genre more acceptable to the general white American public as well as the more sophisticated and elite black churches.

The creators of the original spirituals were formally illiterate and untrained. But the arrangers of these songs as concert anthems were, in general, among the finest musicians in the nation, having been educated at the nation's and the world's most prestigious universities and conservatories of music.

Composers Europeanized spirituals into the anthem style by taking the text and the tune and arranging them "into a homophonic (occasionally contrapuntal) setting for choir, with or without a featured soloist and piano accompaniment."[51] C. Eric Lincoln and Lawrence H. Mamiya suggest that "this modernization process did not necessarily improve the spiritual, but it did solve the problem of assimilating it into the sophisticated worship services of the elite black churches."[52] They go on to argue that

on the one hand, the African American religious tradition is maintained through the modernization of spirituals; while, on the other, the arranged spiritual ceases to be authentic and actually becomes an anthem. It ceases to be the congregational folk song that the worshipers sing, or to which they can clap, sway, and respond verbally. It becomes a concert piece to be appreciated artistically. Anthemization, then, has replaced one of the remaining African remnants of religious antistructure with even more structure. It has taken much of the spirit out of the spiritual and has replaced the cathartic with the aesthetic. Critics complain that it has made the Black Church more like the white church and less like itself.[53]

During the twentieth century the use of Spirituals continued to decline as part of the folk repertoire of the black churches. However, with the rise of the civil rights movement of the 1950s and 1960s, a renewed interest in spirituals focused on liberation and freedom. Songs of racial pride became prominent— such as the black national anthem, "Lift Every Voice and Sing" by J. Rosamond Johnson and his brother James Weldon Johnson. Other songs like "We Shall Overcome" joined the old spirituals in a renewed call for liberation in a land that had failed to deliver on its promise one hundred years after emancipation.

Gospel

Black gospel[54] music is the Northern counterpart of the Negro spiritual of the South. Like metered hymns and spirituals, gospel arose in a social context. It emerged at the turn of the twentieth century in the midst of the great black exodus from the South. As African-Americans arrived in Chicago, Detroit and New York, too often they found themselves living in rat-infested ghettos and falling on hard times—a life not much different in essence from what their slave forefathers and mothers had to endure. Like these ancestors, they created a new musical form that would deal with the sorrows that afflicted them as individuals and as a people—but these were songs of hope.

More than spirituals, gospel music emphasized the immediate. It was also more optimistic (with its modern jazz, blues and ragtime rhythms) than the spiritual or white gospel.[55] The gospel music of Ira D. Sankey and Dwight L. Moody suppressed emotional outburst and tended toward introspection, but black gospel developed a character that was joyous, upbeat and reflective of the "good news" of the gospel.[56]

Black Gospel expresses a theology—but not a theology of the academy, seminary or university. It is not a formalistic theology, writes William B. McClain; it is a *theology of experience:*

> the theology of a God who sends the sunshine and the rain, the theology of a God who is very much alive and active and who has not forsaken those who are poor and oppressed and unemployed. It is a theology of imagination—it grew out of fire shut up in the bones, of words painted on the canvas of the mind. Fear is turned to hope in the sanctuaries and storefronts and burst forth in songs of celebration. It is a theology of grace that allows the faithful to see the sunshine of His face—even through their tears. Even the words of an ex-slave trader become a song of liberation and an expression of God's amazing grace. It is a theology of survival that allows a people to celebrate the ability to continue the journey in spite of the insidious tentacles of racism and oppression and to sing, "It's another day's journey, and I'm glad about it!"[57]

The first black gospel composition appeared at the turn of the century. Charles Albert Tindley, a Methodist preacher from Maryland, gained fame with such classics as "I'll Overcome" (later reshaped to become "We Shall Overcome") and "Stand by Me."

But it was Thomas A. Dorsey, a young talented blues and jazz musician influenced by Tindley, who gave the new form the name *gospel.* His influence on the development and spread of this musical idiom earned him the title "the Father of Gospel." As a composer, publisher, performer, teacher, organizer, choir director and minister of music at the Pilgrim Baptist Church in Chicago, he defined gospel and gave it its distinctive identifiable sounds.

Dorsey's biggest hits were "Peace in the Valley" and the number-one gospel song of all time, "Precious Lord, Take My Hand." Other songs by Dorsey included "I Surely Know There's Been a Change in Me," "It's My Desire," "When I've Done the Best I Can," "How Many Times," "I'm Gonna Live the Life I Sang About in My Song," "Singing in My Soul," "Life Can Be Beautiful" and "The Lord Will Make a Way."[58]

Thomas Dorsey, along with composers and arrangers such as Kenneth Morris, J. Herbert Brewester, Roberta Martin, Sallie Martin, Theodore Frye, Lucie Campbell and James Cleveland, made the period between 1930 and 1969 the "golden age of gospel."[59] From 1932 to 1944 Dorsey toured the United States with singers such as Mahalia Jackson promoting this new idiom.

Gospel's distinctive sound and feel are due mostly to the blues and jazz idioms Dorsey added to the lyrics. The keyboard accompaniments were "most often quite rhythmic, 'bluesy,' highly syncopated, and intricately necessary as a *vehicle* of support for properly communicating the message of the text"[60] in the context of black urban America. Significantly, like their African foreparents, American blacks showed little concern for maintaining a sharp distinction between the sacred and the secular. Thus the blues and the spiritual could naturally share stylistic elements.[61]

The vocal characteristics of black gospel are just as distinctive as the instrumental idioms. Melva Wilson Costen describes the genre's distinct flavor as involving

> vocal agility, tone color, and an extensive vocal range. Vocal timbres of the best Gospel singers range from well modulated "straight tones" to strained, full throated growls and shrills, with lots of controllable vibrato. Melodies are "best" executed if the leader can improvise with spontaneous interpolations, ornamentations, bends, and portamentos (scoops and slides). The use of the falsetto voice has enhanced Gospel music since the 1960s adding a new dimension to other features that have popularized this genre.[62]

Costen notes that the tempo of gospel is often left to the discretion of the leader. "Slower tempos are subject to elaborate vocal embellishments. Faster tempos lend themselves to rhythms that are more syncopated." In addition to all this, "the repetition of words and phrases, in combination with other musical devices, helps to create an emotional impact on both the singers (leader and choir) and the congregation."[63]

The contemporary period of gospel began around 1970, when a new generation of gospel artists expanded the venue from worship in the sanctuary to worship in concert halls with strings, brasses, synthesizers and electronic instruments. This era is dominated by artists who are for the most part Pentecostals, such as Walter Hawkins, Edwin Hawkins, Tremaine Hawkins, Andrae Crouch, Sandra Crouch, Elbernita Clark (of the Clark Sisters) and such clergy as James Cleveland, Al Green and evangelist Shirley Caesar.

The link between Pentecostalism and gospel needs to be mentioned, because as has been noted elsewhere, "gospel music has played a critical role in the development of Pentecostalism, and reciprocally, Pentecostalism has performed an indispensable service in the development and acceptance of contemporary gospel."[64] This may be one of the reasons there tends to be a denominational and congregational bias in some quarters against gospel.[65] But as the contemporary charismatic movement expands in both Protestantism and Catholicism, the use of gospel and Pentecostal "praise songs" will increase.

The praise song, as used by black Pentecostals, has many of the characteristics of African-derived music. There is much improvisation and a simple structure. Each time a song is offered it is sung differently. There is also the call and response:

> *Leader:* I'm a soldier
> *Congregation:* In the army of the Lord
> *Leader:* I'm a soldier
> *Congregation:* In the army.
> *Leader:* If I die, let me die
> *Congregation:* In the army of the Lord
> *Leader:* If I die, let me die
> *Congregation:* In the army.[66]

Michael G. Hayes also notes that "Black Pentecostals sing their praise songs in a way similar to the way jazz musicians play their instruments. Just as jazz musicians have an inventory of jazz riffs and chord progressions to call upon, so have the Pentecostal praise leaders an inventory of familiar calls at their disposal for leading the singing of praise songs."[67]

It may be that with the rapid growth of the Pentecostal and charismatic movements and their influence on American Christianity, gospel music will continue to have a significant impact on worship services across North America.

Gospel music is evolving, however. Christian hip-hop is its newest form. It began about 1989 in the concert hall (like contemporary gospel) rather than in the liturgical setting. However, it is finding its way into the black churches as youth are finding worship more meaningful when it draws on sounds and idioms that speak to them. Among the hip-hop artists popular with today's youth are DC Talk, PID (Preachers in Disguise), ETW (End Time Warriors), SFC (Soldiers for Christ), Witness, D-Boy Rodriguez, Helen Baylor, Michael Peace and Fresh Fish.[68]

I have noted elsewhere[69] that black gospel has been criticized by whites and blacks alike. A number of factors contribute to this unsympathetic view. First of all, many see gospel as mere entertainment being utilized by opportunists. But this can be said regarding any musical form. Another argument is that it has its roots in African-American secular musical idiom and forms. In response it must be noted again and again that the African worldview refuses to make a dichotomy between the sacred and the secular. Besides, *both* white gospel and black gospel grew out of a people's history and culture. If we uplift one while denigrating the other, we must stand condemned of crass ethnocentrism!

In conclusion, music for African-Americans (to paraphrase Grayson Brown's words)[70] is a vehicle that permits them to move from the frustration of inarticulate emotion to the point of adequate, satisfying expression. Music allows them to express their worship wholistically, from deep inside, comfortably and freely. Music moves them one more step away from inadequacy.

The Spoken Word

I*s there a word from the Lord?"* For many African-Americans, that is the most important question asked each week as they assemble to worship. For them the word spoken by the preacher must be a word from the Lord.

Preaching is central in the black church. Survey results consistently demonstrate the importance and centrality of the event.[1] In the black tradition, however, preaching is more than "the sermon." It is an event in which the congregation and musicians are caught up with the preacher in a highly emotional and cognitive drama directed by the Spirit.

The Preacher

Not only in the sermonic event but in the life and history of African-Americans, the preacher plays a pivotal role. In 1903 W. E. B. Du

Bois wrote that three things characterized the religion of the slaves: "the Preacher, the Music, and the Frenzy."[2] He summarizes the first:

> The Preacher is the most unique personality developed by the Negro on American soil. A leader, a politician, an orator, a "boss," an intriguer, an ideal-ist—all these he is, and ever, too, the centre of a group of men, now twenty, now a thousand in number. The combination of a certain adroitness with deep-seated earnestness, of tact with consummate ability, gave him his pre-eminence, and helps him maintain it.[3]

The roots of the African-American preacher go back to the motherland. The parallels between the African-American preacher and the African priest/medicine man are striking. In Africa he (for it was basically a male institution) presided over the crises of the community: "birth, death, sickness, puberty, trouble, domestic discord, marriage, etc."[4] He was "leader, diviner, seer, and medium."[5]

Not only were the earliest preachers former African priests and religious specialists,[6] but the preacher on the American soil retained these roles and added more, adapting to the needs of his fellow oppressed community. Not only was he accepted not only in the role of priest and spiritual leader, but the influence of Judeo-Christianity propelled him into the charismatic authority of prophet and politician. He achieved a position of dominance and became the voice of God to the people.[7]

In the pulpit the preacher was and is expected to be at his or her peak. There preachers display the African priestly heritage as "doctors of soulology"[8] and the Judeo-Christian charismata in being the mouthpiece for God. In Harold Dean Trulear's words,

> The preacher is "God's man," and increasingly "God's woman," set forth to "break the bread of life." As such, much of the sacred aura and awesomeness that is part of the nature of God, God's "holiness," comes to be seen to reside in the pastor. During the sermon event, this becomes most pronounced, for in this context the preacher is expected to speak for God. The preacher must establish in the early parts of the sermon, or even before he/she begins to

preach, that what is to be said is "what thus saith the Lord." The preacher then becomes a symbol of God, in the context of the sermon event.[9]

Much of the staging of the preaching event and the preacher's appearance (the robes, capes, attendant nurse with orange juice and fresh handkerchiefs) is important to the ritual drama that make the statement "This is God's spokesperson, with God's message, to God's children, in this sacred place." The "God-aura"[10] and high expectation surrounding the preacher in the context of worship set him or her apart in the black community to a level that is unmatched in Euro-American society.

Cerebral Versus Emotive

As mentioned earlier, black worship does not emphasize only the objective but highly encourages the subjective; it embraces not only the abstract and rational but also the intuitive and feeling. The preaching event is not merely an intellectual cerebral exercise but an emotional experience in the Spirit. Preaching has to be both a "cere-bration" and a "celebration."[11] The former is affective and emotive; the latter is reflective and intellectual. The black preacher holds these together in a wholistic tension:

> One doesn't simply abstract the rational part and try to operate with that alone. . . . This is a radical difference between the two [African American and Euro-American] cultures. So it is that a sermon in African tradition is an *experience* and not merely an idea. It is an experience of truth, to be sure, but the authentic Black preacher *don't know how* to give one of those stone-cold, dry and exclusively cerebral lectures. Any time I "gets up" to speak, I'm going to do something that involves my whole person, body and soul, and this again is something that I can't help. That's just the way I be.[12]

The African-American preacher who attempts to make the preaching event an exercise in dry, abstract intellectual discourse will find that no matter how brilliant the content, it will not go over well with the worshiping congregation. The preacher will know it. Members will let it be known, sometimes in kind, subtle ways (as with the "compliment," "Good talk" or "Good lecture," and not the ultimate, "You preached today!"), sometimes in not so subtle ways (uncomplimentary remarks or stone silence).

Great preachers like Martin Luther King Jr. and Jesse Jackson "consistently package sophisticated theological and political concerns in a charismatic, colorful fashion so that their audiences not only *learn* something important intellectually that relates to their faith but also *feel* God's Spirit active in their midst."[13] Although the great African-American preachers can present significant philosophical and theological arguments and cite the likes of Brunner, Barth, Bultmann and Bonhoeffer, black churchgoers prefer the word to be less discursive and more human. They want it to relate to life. They desire it to inspire and move them emotively. The preacher must be able to "tell the story"; that is, he or she must communicate "in language, symbols, and symbolic mannerisms that speak directly to the needs of worshipers"[14] in a wholistic way.

Frank A. Thomas, in his excellent book *They Like to Never Quit Praisin' God: The Role of Celebration in Preaching,* discusses at length this issue of the cerebral versus the emotive. Preaching, he says, is analogous to music in this regard:

> Music does not ignore the cognitive to secure emotive movement, but includes it as part of the process because it is not possible to move anyone without musical cognitive logic, i.e. measures, beats, scales, harmonies, etc. The very best in the field of music clearly do not stop at the level of the cognitive, or the emotive, but intend to move the listener as part of the emotional process to register meaning in the intuitive.[15]

In the same way the preacher does not ignore the cerebral aspect of sermonizing in order to secure the emotive[16] but "includes it as part of the process, because it is not possible to move anyone without the cognitive logic of the sermon, i.e. exegetics, theology, words, and rules of communication that inform rational discourse."[17]

Thomas points out, however, that most African-American preachers use what is called *homiletical exegesis.* There are two steps in this process: first, the traditional exegetical method of attempting to discern what the text means; second, an experiential hermeneutic that relates the meaning to the existential condition of suffering, tragedy and evil in the world. Beyond intellectualizing and philosophizing, this approach grounds the Word in the day-to-day experience of the worshipers.[18]

For this method to be effective, the member in the pew must hear, see, taste, touch and feel the sermon. The senses must be involved in the emotive process. When churchgoers complain that a sermon is boring and lifeless, in part they mean that it failed to appeal to most of their senses. "Without our senses being stirred, we do not have a means of identification, and if there is no identification, there is no release of emotion that sustains interest."[19] And if there is no emotive release, the worship event falters and fails.

Gifted black preachers particularly appeal to the sense of hearing. "Black preaching is aimed primarily at the ear as the route to the heart," says Wyatt Tee Walker, "as over against being aimed at the eye as the route to the mind. Black preaching is far more oratorical than it is literary. You will enjoy it much more if you hear it than if you read it."[20] The poetic recitation and dramatization move the listener. The preacher's creative use of metaphors and "greater number of nouns, adjectives and adjectival clauses rather than verbs and verb forms"[21] lend to a grandeur and picturesqueness of language that move the hearer to say, "The preacher said the right thing rightly!"

Spontaneity is a key element in black preaching. Although the thoughtful African-American preacher will always be prepared to preach from well-researched notes or manuscripts, he or she may feel the Spirit moving in an entirely different direction. It is common for a preacher to say something like this to the congregation: "Church, I was planning to preach from Isaiah 6:8 today, but the Lord is directing me to deal with 2 Peter 3:10 instead. So just bear with me." The congregation will invariably respond heartily with "Help yourself, Rev!" "Well that's all right!" "Amen!" "Fix it up real good now!" "Take your time!"[22] With this the preacher has the freedom from the Spirit and the congregants to expound the given Word in ways that will appeal to the intellect and the emotions.

Prophetic Elements

Although the black preacher functions as a priest in the African and Judeo-Christian traditions, in the pulpit he or she is primarily a prophet proclaiming the truth of God's Word. The sermon is a prophetic oration that "tells it like it is." It therefore falls more in the Old Testament prophetic genre than in the New Testament pastoral mold. McClain illustrates:

> I pointed out in an article that I wrote for *Christianity and Crisis* in 1970 that the Sunday morning on which the four Black children were bombed to death at Sixteenth Street Baptist Church in Birmingham, a survey of the sermons preached in that city on that sad Sunday morning revealed that almost without exception, the Black preachers preached from the Old Testament. The white preachers *without exception* preached from the New Testament. This was not a coincidence. Black preaching tends to announce the judgement on the nation, and to call into question the institutions in society in a prophetic fashion, whereas white preaching tends to be of a pastoral nature.[23]

In this light it is not surprising that African-American preaching is declarative more than suggestive. The preacher is not tentative or timid. There is no hesitancy in proclaiming, "Thus saith the Lord."

The Bible is the basis and grounding of all black preaching. James Cone notes that the slave preachers, like their contemporaries, were inerrantist. Yet in contrast to their white counterparts, African-American preachers were not enslaved to the words of the Bible. Rather, the biblical texts served as starting points for an interpretation relevant to the lives of the people. James Weldon Johnson speaks of an occasion when a preacher "who after reading a rather cryptic passage took off his spectacles, closed the Bible with a bang and by way of preface said, 'Brothers and sisters, this morning—I intend to explain the unexplainable—find out the undefinable—ponder over the imponderable—and unscrew the unscrutable.'"[24]

McClain notes that "while the white middle class Protestant church suffers through small homilies on small subjects, lectures, and advice on 'how to use your leisure time' and other such mundane subjects in search of relevancy, the Black Church finds poignancy, relevance and a continually guiding Word in the Old Book."[25] Black preachers weave the Word into the existential situations of the worshiping congregation. The Word must relate to their lives and needs and feelings. It must address the predicaments that constantly plague the black person and the larger African-American society—the hazards of life, the age-old scourges, the economic, social and political adversities.

> Preaching cannot be based upon a white Jesus with silky locks and blue eyes. The Jesus that Black preaching must proclaim has to be able to walk the dark ghetto streets of the North and the hot dusty fields of a sharecropper's farm in the South. The Jesus that Black preaching proclaims must be the Christ of faith who is relevant to the needs, feelings and aspirations of Black folk. That Jesus is the One whose face and image we can see in the rat-bitten, mutilated faces of children, and his suffering we see in the agony and pain and scars of dull and dirty needles in the body of a dope addict nodding in a stinking, dirty alley. That is the Jesus who is not only the Liberator and Emancipator, but He is the Bishop of the souls of Black folk. It was this Jesus that our forefathers knew and sang about: "O fix me, Jesus, fix me." It was this Jesus that I heard Aunt Jane ask in her prayers for Him to be a "bridge over troubled waters" long before Simon and Garfunkel ever knew that there are rivers that seem uncrossable and waters that you cannot go through.[26]

Biblical preaching by African-Americans provides a sense of hope in hopeless situations. In "telling the story" it allows people to experience the assurance of grace[27] and helps them to keep holding on.

"Telling the story" in African-American prophetic preaching can mean entering what Westerners would call the political arena. There is broad consensus in the black community for a sociopolitical prophetic role for black churches and preachers.[28] From the time of slavery, the church was the one "free" institution where pastors had the freedom to address and respond to social and political issues without fear. The black church is thus more politically active than are white churches. When the question is asked,

"Can the Rev tell the story?" the expectation is that he or she should act on and speak out on any issue that impinges on the daily struggle of black people.

Drama and Musicality

Unlike cultures that make a dichotomy between content and style (as in the sacred-secular distinction), black culture holds together *what* is proclaimed with *how* it is proclaimed. Black preaching is drama—musical drama. Wyatt Tee Walker says the African-American folk-preacher is the "Shakespearean actor of our culture." No one, he says, can tell the story and make you see it like the black folk-preacher. He illustrates with an anecdote about the great African-American preacher Dr. Gardner Taylor. One Thursday morning he was preaching. "As he was bringing the Prodigal son home, he did so with such vividness and power that I found myself, along with others, looking back over my shoulder to see if he was coming down the aisle of Coburn Chapel."[29] Walker says, "There is a genius in drawing a word-picture so powerful that the hearers are on the verge of expecting something to materialize."[30] E. Franklin Frazier notes:

> Preaching [in the times of slavery] meant dramatizing the stories of the Bible and the way of God to man. These slave preachers were noted for the imagery of their sermons. One slave preacher, John Jasper, achieved distinction, according to his biographer, because of his lofty dignity which was combined with his fiery and thrilling oratory despite his "tempestuous and ungrammatical eloquence."[31]

Black preaching is a "kratophany." As *theophany* is a manifestation of the deity in concrete objects, *kratophany* is the manifestation of power in preaching through the spoken word replete with drama and musicality. Kratophany is expected to move people and cause a reaction. Worshipers will respond percussively by clapping, stomping or shouting. Or they'll nod the head, shed a tear, sing, hum or say amen.

The sermon is characterized by a slow and deliberate buildup, interspersed with dramatic pauses that force the congregation to reflect on what is said and anticipate what is to follow. McClain describes the pattern as the four Rs: "rhetoric, repetition, rhythm, [and] rest."[32] Many times the path taken is winding, with a number of detours; but the preacher is heading someplace very deliberately. Every now and then someone in the congregation will call out, "Take your time, preacher!" as the pulpiteer symphonically orchestrates the sermon. "One can wait in anticipation of an adagio movement, which could gradually build up to a scherzo celebration, or a sonata allegro form with numerous recapitulations and a lengthy coda."[33] An old preacher in Alabama gave McClain some good advice in a dictum:

Start low; go slow,
Go high, strike five.
Sit down.[34]

Another way to describe the dramatic mold of African-American preaching is to compare it to jazz soloing: "characterized by improvisatory vocal inflection, such as the bending and lowing of pitches, sliding from tone to tone, grace notes, and tremolo." And "just as an enthusiastic applause from an audience can impel a jazz artist to return to the stage for an encore, so do exuberant responses from a congregation inspire a minister to stand back up and 'whoop' just a little longer." Jon Spencer notes that some preachers are known for improvising two or three encores, each crescendoing to a higher climax,[35] moving the congregation to greater ecstasy.

To a large extent the power of sermons lies in the preacher's ability to "sing" the sermon, because preaching is musical. (This was a qualification that the slave preachers had to possess.)[36] Surveys show that "the preacher who is particularly skilled at this kind of musical eloquence is usually highly regarded as adept in his profession, and his church is almost certain to be blessed with a large and faithful membership."[37]

Of particular importance to the black churchgoer is whether the preacher can "whoop." Whooping involves intonation, chanting, "tuning," a moaning or singsong style; some will ask, "Does he (or she) got a nice hum?" The principal melodic mode of whooping is the pentatonic scale.[38] This five-note scale has its roots in Africa. Black preachers' African ancestors

> chanted their oral history and folk stories, and Africa's North American prog-
> eny moaned bluesy hollers and vendors whooped street cries. Additionally,
> just as Africans chanted tribal laws, stories, and proverbs, so have black
> preachers intoned biblical laws and stories. Moreover, as Africans have pre-
> served their history and theology in song, so have black preachers perpetu-
> ated African-American experience and religious beliefs in their "spirituals"
> [i.e., their musicality in preaching].[39]

There are those who disdain intonation and whooping, consider-
ing it a vestige of folk religion that is inappropriate for the preaching
of the gospel.[40] However, William Turner has shown that whooping
is not restricted to those of limited educational attainment, nor is it
the domain of particular denominations. "It continues to span the
gamut from the preaching of Father Andrew Bryand and Andrew
Marshall at the beginning of the nineteenth century to Martin
Luther King, Jr. and Charles Adams in the twentieth century, from
the 'cornfield preacher' to the 'Harvard Whooper,' from the 'No D'
to the Ph.D., and 'every D in between.' "[41] He also points out that
this style is found among some white Pentecostals (such as Jimmy
Swaggart)—and it is not surprising that such white churches and
movements attract a substantial black audience.[42]

Three other aspects of the musicality of African-American
preaching are worth highlighting. First, there is the rhythm. Rhythm
lies at the base of black preaching. "Ministers often drum upon the
podium to stress important words in key sentences, so that percussive rhythmic variations evolve syntactically."[43] In many churches
an actual drum serves this purpose.

Second, intonation and whooping are especially effective when
accompanied by a homophonic (harmonic) instrument, usually the
organ. Spencer suggests that "some preachers do their best 'tuning'
when an organist is intricately engaged in the 'song.' "[44]

Third, preaching moves through key modulations. Just as the

spiritual "We Are Climbing Jacob's Ladder" modulates by semi-tones verse after verse, some preachers are able to modulate their chanting "in order to facilitate the most potent kratophany."[45] In moments like these, the congregation is transported to exalted moments of celebration.

Dialogical Style

The interaction between the "preacher in the pulpit" and the "preacher in the pew" is possibly the most folksy part of the African-American worship service. Black worship is dialogical. Black preaching is not a monologue. Walter Pearson is correct when he states that it is actually a "trialogue" that involves "the Lord, who reveals; the speaker, who declares; and the congregants, who affirm."[46] The event of preaching is not hierarchical; it is a communal experience in which antiphony predominates. This is unlike most Eurocentric worship experiences which are spectator oriented, where the congregation sits and listens. In Afrocentric worship the worshipers participate in the preaching.

The root of this dialogue is in the "call and response" of the African tradition. In preaching it produces a colorful interaction between pulpit and pew while the sermon is taking place, not after its completion. "Sometimes a mediocre and unpoetical preacher can be brought to new life, brilliance and lyrical power when there is the cooperation of the pew, the help and expectancy and the encouragement and enthusiasm of the congregation."[47] For this to happen, however, all participants in the service must listen ardently to each other—the preacher, the congregants and even the organist or pianist, who can enter the dialogue with appropriate rhythms and other musical responses.

Congregational responses to the preacher include phrases and exclamations like "Preach it!" "Tell it like it is, Rev!" "Help yourself!" "Go ahead, brother preacher!" "Well!" "Amen!" "Hallelujah!" "Praise the Lord!" "Bring it on home!" or nonarticulate responses such as moaning, humming, nodding the head, shedding a tear, clapping, waving the hand, swaying or making unidentifiable sounds. I believe Cone is right on track when he states that

> if the people do not say "Amen" or some other passionate response, this usually means that the Spirit has chosen not to speak through the preacher at that time. The absence of the Spirit could mean that the preacher was dependent too much on his own capacity to speak or that the congregation was too involved in its own personal quarrels. Whatever the case, the absence of a "hallelujah" and "praise the Lord" when the preacher speaks God's Word is uncharacteristic of a black worship service. For these responses let the preacher know that he is on the right track, and that what he says rings true to the Spirit's presence in their midst.[48]

The Prayer

Prayer and preaching developed in parallel fashion within the black church; both, like music, are a continuation of the African religious heritage. "If preaching is indeed the Heart of Black Worship," states Walker, "then Praying has been its Strength."[49] From the days of slavery, "exhausted from their daily labors, worshipers . . . often found physical and mental relief in prayer."[50] That "little talk with Jesus" did make it right—all right.

Praying time in black worship is an event all by itself, yet it has all the characteristics of preaching. Those who pray "tune" or intone their prayer like the preachers and use vocal inflections and ornamentations "with bends, twists, and quavers, providing a musical flow."[51] The prayer event can be just as dialogical as the preaching event:

> Rather than passively listening to a prayer, the gathered community becomes involved with the prayer (prayer leader), using a variety of responses. There might be verbal "witnessing" to what is being prayed, such as "Amen!"; "Thank You, Jesus!"; or "Yes, Lord!" There might be direct urging or nudging of the leader to "pray your prayer!" or "tell it to the Lord!" There are often injections of admonitions to God to "Come by here"; "Oh, help him, Jesus"; "Hear us . . ."; or "Help us now, Lord!" Some participants moaned or hummed in perfect cadence with the prayer leader. Some rocked, swayed, cried softly, or merely nodded their heads in assent. The "prayer event" often

reached full intensity as the leader and congregation filled with the Spirit, demonstrated that everyone's heart was spiritually "in tune."[52]

In this setting, prayers need to be heard and not read. Read prayers, whether printed in the bulletin or read aloud, interfere with the spontaneity that is expected in the prayer event. To many worshipers, reading diminishes the power of the Spirit and the communication between the divine and human. The word of prayer must not be shackled in any way in the African-American worship service.

The Response

U*sually when the phrase "We had church today!" is uttered at* the close of a worship service, it is not only because the music was inspiring and the preaching powerful, but because the worshiping congregation responded with their whole being. Although African-Americans respond to and in the worship event in a variety of ways—formally and informally, personally and communally, with spontaneity and in a regularized manner[1]—"the genius of Black worship is its openness to the creative power of God that frees and enables people . . . to 'turn themselves loose' and celebrate God's act in Jesus Christ," says Melva Costen.[2] The creativity that is inspired by this freedom allows the black worshiper to express him or herself physically, vocally and communally rather than meditatively and individualistically.

Although African-Americans respond as individuals, their

response is in the context of being one community of faith. Worship is a community event. Kinship is affirmed. Interdependence is highlighted. Spiritual and social hospitality is evident. Even when statements such as "I'm so glad I'm here in Jesus' name" are used, the first-person singular pronoun is meant to represent first-person plural as it is understood in the African worldview.[3]

This relational character of worship gives a feeling of togetherness in the worship setting and allows more physical contact—like shaking hands, hugging, joining hands and other touching—than would be acceptable in a Eurocentric culture. "The point is that spiritual togetherness is reaffirmed and heightened by a ritual form of physical togetherness."[4] In this way the worshiping community's response is not only at the metaphysical level but at the physical level as well.

In most Afro-American churches the physical response is initiated by the supernatural working of the Spirit. George Ofori-atta-Thomas speaks about persons in the black church who register a certain quality of spirituality in the worship service. These are the "Aunt Janes" who are the thermometer or the thermostat, "not so much as intending to measure or cut off the spirituality of worship as to be a conduit through whom the Holy Spirit would be manifested."[5] These devout women are the " 'movers and shakers' in the worship service and they are the guardians of the spirituality in the experience of 'having church.' "[6] The physical demonstration of the Spirit's working by these persons is captured by the rest of the congregation and is expressed in diverse forms, particularly as the service is drawing to an energetic close.

The Dance

One of the African traditions that survived the Middle Passage and continues as a worship response is the dance. Dance in traditional religions was not separate from music.[7] Dance was a response of the physical person to the rhythms of music by the moving of the Spirit. In Africa, worship is not solely a cognitive experience. One worships with one's whole body. Henry Mitchell tells of when he and his students in West Africa worshiped with a community: "the women of the group did something which in this country would probably be called 'the Funky Chicken!'"[8] But it was their worship response with their muscles, bones and nerves.

Like the drum, dancing, which was essential to black worship, was disapproved of by slavemasters and missionaries. Yet it persisted underground and in the invisible institution. It is claimed that one of the purposes of the overturned pots at the entrance of the worship place was to keep in the noise that the dancing worshipers generated.[9] As a matter of fact, this African worship practice began to influence white worship practice to the point that John F. Watson expressed outrage that this "most exceptional error" was seeping into the white Methodist liturgy. In his book *Methodist Error: Or, Friendly Christian Advice to Those Methodists Who Indulge in Extravagant Religious Emotions and Bodily Exercises*, Watson not only condemns the practice but gives us a description (though biased) of the black worship dance:

> In the black's quarter, the coloured people get together, and sing for hours together, short scraps of disjointed affirmations, pledges, or prayers. . . . These are all sung in the merry chorus-manner of the southern harvest field, or husking-frolic method of the slave blacks; and also very like the Indian dances. With every word so sung, they have a sinking of one or other leg of the body alternately, producing an audible sound of the feet at every step, and as manifest as the steps of actual dancing in Virginia.[10]

Although the prohibition against dancing was respected by even the African-American churches (particularly those with white affiliations), dance in one form or the other endured in the United States' black community. It is significant that in those parts of the New-World African community where dancing was prohibited and nearly eliminated (e.g., Venezuela and Colombia), that African religious tradition disappeared.[11] In North America, however, rhythm and dance endured in worship, and thus the African cultural ethos survived.

The Shout
W. E. B. Du Bois identified the "Frenzy" shout or ring shout as the

third important characteristic of black religion with roots in the motherland:

> The Frenzy of "Shouting," when the Spirit of the Lord passed by, and, seizing the devotee, made him mad with supernatural joy, was the last essential of Negro religion and the one more devoutly believed in than all the rest. It varied in expression from the silent rapt countenance or the low murmur and moan to the mad abandon of physical fervor,—the stamping, shrieking, and shouting, the rushing to and fro and wild waving of arms, the weeping and laughing, the vision and the trance. All this is nothing new in the world, but old as religion, as Delphi and Endor. And so firm a hold did it have on the Negro, that many generations firmly believed that without this visible manifestation of the God there could be no true communion with the Invisible.[12]

While Du Bois's assessment of the shout was quite positive, for opponents and outsiders it was at best mere frolic, and at worst grotesque, barbaric, a remnant of heathenish idol worship. Even James Weldon Johnson came to the conclusion that shouts were "neither true spirituals nor truly religious." Rather they were "semi-barbaric remnants of primitive African dances," only "quasi-religious."[13]

The most vigorous African-American opponent of the shout was A.M.E. Bishop Payne, who, in his *Recollections of Seventy Years*, described a ring shout observed during a 1878 visit to the South:

> About this time I attended a "bush meeting," where I went to please the pastor whose circuit I was visiting. After the sermon they formed a ring, and with coats off sung, clapped their hands and stamped their feet in the most ridiculous and heathenish way. I requested the pastor to go and stop their dancing. At his request they stopped their dancing and clapping of hands, but remained singing and rocking their bodies to and fro. . . . I then went, and taking the leader by the arm requested him to desist and to sit down and sing in a rational manner. I told him also that it was a heathenish way to worship and disgraceful to themselves, the race, and the Christian name.[14]

Although Bishop Payne's efforts succeeded to a large degree in driving responses like dancing and Spirit possession to the margin of African Methodism, the ring shout has stubbornly remained a significant element of worship in many African-American churches across the country. Interestingly, black Christians rejected the suggestions that the shout was akin to secular dancing. They pointed out that in the latter, one's feet had to be raised and crossed, while in the ring shout the worshiper refrained from lifting the feet or crossing one foot over the other. Instead the shoulders were pressed close together and there was a slow shuffle, while the bodies of the "dancers" swayed in the circle that was formed.

The choreography of the dance varied according to era and geographic location.[15] The following, however, is a basic description of the shout as a worship response:

> After the regular religious services were over, or on special "praise nights," the benches in the early black churches or "praise houses" would be pushed back against the wall so that the dancing could begin. The dancers or "shouters," as they were called, would form a circle and to the cadence of a favorite shout song or "running spiritual" would begin a slow, syncopated shuffling, jerking movement "bumped" by the handclapping or body slapping of those waiting on the sidelines. The tempo gradually quickened, and during the course of the dance (which might last for seven or eight hours), shouters who became possessed, or who dropped from sheer exhaustion, were immediately replaced by others waiting to take their places.[16]

Joseph Murphy notes that the movements of the shout in many instances mimicked the actions of biblical characters. For example, "as the participants sang repeatedly, 'We're traveling to Immanuel's land,' they would move through the gestures of Joshua's army surrounding Jericho or the children of Israel leaving Egypt."[17] The shout was thus part of the liberative experience of African-American worship.

The shout, or "getting happy" (as it is also called), is not only liberative (in contrast to the oppressed status of blacks in a white society),[18] it yields an emotional catharsis (because the dancer willingly yields to the power of God)[19] and is psychotherapeutic. Brenda Aghaowa refers to a study on the black church as a therapeutic community. The study takes a look at "acting-out" in black worship and suggests "that because of the emotional release many experience in black worship, rates of mental illness and hospitalization in mental institutions are lower for African Americans than for whites."[20]

The ecstatic, cathartic experience of the shout persists even today in many charismatic churches, crossing denominational lines. Rhythmic gospel music frequently prompts the shout or holy dance. It must be noted, however, that there is a method for determining whether a worshiper is dancing "in the Spirit" or "in the "flesh": "By suddenly halting the gospel shout music, one is able to check for authenticity. If the dancing continues without the music, it is assumed that it is genuine and induced by the Holy Spirit. But if it ceases, apparently it was not so holy after all and was merely rhythmically induced."[21] The revival of Spirit-filled physical expression and response in black liturgy in the African-American community has brought an explosion of the shout as another major response to the experience of communal worship.

The Testimony

As a response to the Spirit's presence within the total worship experience, black Americans often testify during the service. This may have grown out of the mechanism of sharing in the slave brush harbor, called storytelling, in which they shared what God had done in their lives.[22] An often-repeated phrase is "I believe I will testify for what the Lord has done for me." It is a time of praise in which the worshiper can articulate his or her conviction that "God is good, all the time."

But the testimony time is also used to articulate the trials and tribulations worshipers are undergoing. A typical example of testimony of an individual's specific trouble would run like this: "I thank God today, because the other night, I was at school, so keep praying for me 'cause I am trying to make it at school. The devil is so busy trying to get me into the same things those other kids are into, but I'm going to keep holding on."[23]

In many instances tears of sorrow as well as joy are a response of the listening congregation to the testimony. Harold Dean Trulear notes that tears are a common expression of trouble and sorrow in the black church. It's part of the phenomenon of testimony. "Through tears, the worshiper brings her/his sorrow into the church for processing."[24] It is expected that trouble and sorrow can and must be expressed in the context of worship. In worship African-Americans can take their "burden to the Lord and leave it there."

Other Responses

There is not space to discuss all the responses that take place in an African-American worship service, because they are many and varied. The freedom of expression that is allowed as the Spirit moves brings a diversity of creative as well as traditional responses.

One response that is less significant to black congregations than to Euro-American churches is the Lord's Supper. One reason may be that though Communion was celebrated in interracial worship services during the slavery era, there is no evidence for its practice in the invisible institutions and praise houses.[25] It seems to have taken a backseat to other sacraments in the black church such as anointing, sprinkling and the touching of holy articles.[26]

The altar call, on the other hand, is indispensable in the black church. It is rare that a service ends without the worship leader saying, "The doors of the church are open," and then inviting people to come forward and make a public declaration of their faith. The call is at times extended to all in the congregation to recommit themselves to Christ in response to what he has done for them.

Another response of great importance is the tithe and offering collection. Hans A. Baer and Merrill Singer note that the collection is one of the most elaborate ritual events during the morning service in African-American churches. They illustrate with the Eternal Hope Missionary Baptist Church in St. Louis:

> At EHMB "tithers" first drop their envelopes with money in a special box in the front of the sanctuary. Afterwards, the ushers bring their contributions to the collection tables and systematically guide the congregants, one block of

pew at a time, to bring their contributions to the tables. "After the money has been collected, there follows another period of multi-focused activities— announcements, reports of lay persons who have attended conferences, introduction of visitors, appeals for further money to supplement a 'special collection,' and short homilies by the pastor. During this period functionaries at the collecting tables count the receipts for the day" (Simpson 1970:107). After the money is counted, the pastor or an ordained assistant may say the benediction; the choir may sing it, or the congregation may repeat it, phrase by phrase, as the pastor leads them.[27]

Thus a liturgical point that in other churches is often considered mundane is transformed into an elaborate sacred event in which worshipers respond overwhelmingly.

Verbal and nonverbal, formal and nonformal responses in African-American worship are as natural as breathing. James Cone summarizes it well:

When a song is sung right and the sermon is delivered in response to the Spirit, the people experience the eschatological presence of God in their midst. Liberation is no longer a future event, but a present happening in the worship itself. That is why it is hard to sit still in a black worship service. For the people claim that "if you don't put anything into the service, you sure won't get anything out of it." Black worship demands involvement. Sometimes a sister does not plan to participate too passionately, but before she knows what is happening "a little fire starts to burning and a little prayer-wheel starts to turning in her heart." In response to the Spirit and its liberating presence, she begins to move to the Spirit's power.[28]

When worshipers like these are set on fire, the response is overwhelming, contagious and uncontrollable. They'll dance, run, clap, wave their hands, shout, sing, chant, hum and moan. They'll say "Amen," "Hallelujah," "Praise the Lord." The response is ecstatic and climactic because it is an expression of liberation in Jesus Christ. They call out with gusto, "*Yes*, Lord!" as William A. Jones Jr. said in his sermon "From the Bottom Up":

He's my Rock, my Sword, my Shield,
He's my Wheel in the Middle of a Wheel.
He's my Lily of the Valley, He's the Bright and Morning Star.

—Friend of the friendless
—Hope for the hopeless
—Health for the sick
—Food for the hungry
—Water for the thirsty
—Prophet without a peer
—Priest without an equal
—King of Kings, Lord of Lords
—Chief Rabbi, Sovereign Ruler
—Potentate of the Universe
YEEES—YEEEES-YEEES
—Dyingbed Maker
—Host at the coronation
YEEEES, LORD.[29]

Part 3

Caribbean Worship

An Adventure
of the Spirit

C aribbean, *for our purposes, refers to the English-speaking* regions in the Caribbean sea.[1] The term (and its synonym *West Indies*) encompasses also the islands of the Bahamas, Belize in Central America and Guyana in South America. All these territories have in common the fact that they have been (and in a few cases still are) colonies of Great Britain.

Although a large percentage (in the case of Jamaica, nearly 90 percent) of the population have a dominant African heritage (except Trinidad and Guyana, where perhaps 40-50 percent in each case are East Indian), Caribbean peoples are biologically and culturally mixed. For the most part, not only are the nationals creole but the culture is creole. The mixture of European, African and even Asian genes and mores have produced a culture that retains elements from these varied dominant cultures.[2]

The Caribbean has been a class-conscious society—more so prior to the 1970s than now, yet classism remains an unfortunate reality in this geographic region. This fragmentation generally follows four interrelated orientations: (1) a Euro-centered ("white skin") elite, (2) a Euro-oriented creole ("brown skin") upper class, (3) a creole and black intellectual elite, and (4) the African-Caribbean ("black skin") bulk of the population.[3] The ratio varies from territory to territory; but the basic structure, I believe, is constant. We may note that these distinctions are not quite as noticeable in the large centers of the Caribbean diaspora in the United States and Canada. However, when intense discussions over issues of social taste and worship forms arise, the immigrants (consciously or unconsciously) argue out of a class cultural background.

The peoples of the Caribbean are extremely religious. In Jamaica, church membership is high, and nearly everyone is baptized. The Anglican Church claims the largest membership, but Baptists, Roman Catholics, Pentecostals, Seventh-day Adventists, Presbyterians, Wesleyans, Moravians, Congregationalists and a number of other bodies make up significant percentages of the Christian population. In Trinidad, on the other hand, Roman Catholicism is the Christian denomination of preference. But Anglicans, Presbyterians, Methodists, Baptists, Seventh-day Adventists and Pentecostals boast high memberships as well.[4]

Census numbers do not give a complete picture of the religious life of the Caribbean people. On the one hand, many will claim membership in a denomination, a church that they may attend once or twice per year. On the other hand, many don't attend organized churches but are found in faithful attendance at street-corner meetings and cottage meetings held in a yard off the main road. In many instances, attendance at these meetings is higher than attendance at the traditional churches.

Census numbers also do not accurately reflect the marginally Christian and African-based religious communities throughout the Caribbean. Such religious groups as Orisha (Shango) in Trinidad and Grenada, and Pocomania in Jamaica claim to have as many adherents as some of the traditional churches. Many people attend both African-based semi-Christian ceremonies and European-based traditional services. This crossover is important in the evolution of all churches in the Caribbean. For while the traditional churches continue to remain Euro-American in essence, they are being influenced by the Afrocentric nontraditional groups.

The revival and reemergence of things African has opened up a new world to Christians in the Caribbean, bringing about a creolization of religion and Christianity—a new synthesis in which Afrocentrism and Eurocultural elements appear hand in hand. Contemporary Caribbean worship therefore can be an "adventure of the spirit."[5] Yet the historical journey to this place has been arduous.

A Historical Survey

The modern period of the Caribbean territories began with the arrival of Columbus in the 1490s. The centuries since then have witnessed the extermination of the indigenous population of Caribs, Arawaks and other Amerindian inhabitants of the region. Approximately one million Africans were brought through the Middle Passage to replace the indigenous people and to work as slaves on the plantations of European colonizers. Thus there came to be two cultures (three if we count the native Indians) with different worldviews operating side by side.

For nearly five hundred years, however, cultural communication went only one way: from the "civilized" peoples of the North to the "backward and primitive" inhabitants, people of color, of the West Indies.

> The mores of the Arawak and Carib Indian, and even more those of the African slaves, were denigrated and European things were promoted and idolized. The former were considered pagan, the latter were to be emulated. Thus the slaves and natives learned to dress, eat, speak, and worship like their masters. They desired to have children whose complexions were as light as possible. There was a cultural miscegenation. African and Indian traditions were subsumed.[6]

Chief among the traditions that were subsumed was religion. As a matter of fact, the view of Richard Ligon (an early settler in Barbados) in 1647, that the Africans did not know any religion,[7] most likely was widely held by the European inhabitants. In their opinion, the system of belief adhered to by the slaves could not be described as religion. It was nothing more than "heathenish superstition."[8] Many believed that the slaves were incapable of religious sentiment because they seemed "void of genius and . . . almost incapable of making any progress in civility or science."[9]

Dale Bisnauth in his *History of the Religions in the Caribbean*[10] makes it abundantly clear that not only were the slaves religious but in fact religion pervaded their lives. Their religion and belief system came from Africa. Some slaves had had contact with Islam. For example, the Mandingoes in Jamaica were literate in Arabic and felt that the Europeans were "a race of formidable but ignorant heathens."[11] Islam did not survive the rigors of plantation life or the policy of prohibiting the assembling of slaves for cultic purposes.

Many indigenous African religious ideas and practices (particularly the Yoruba traditions) survived the difficulties of estate life. The Yoruba people attempted to hold tenaciously to their ritual, as it provided a "source of consolation in a foreign environment."[12] Yet even though such religious ideas and practices remained recognizably African, they have undergone significant changes throughout the centuries. Bisnauth suggests that two factors are mainly responsible for these changes. First, the religious ideas of the Africans were capable of modification in response to new circumstances such as the realities of plantation life. Second, because African religious practices were frowned on by the plantocracy, slaves were forced to worship irregularly and clandestinely. Thus some of the elements of African religious practice necessarily disappeared.[13]

Despite the efforts of the estate masters through legislation and encouragement, the worship of African divinities and the accompanying rituals survived, as is evidenced in Trinidadian Orisha, Cuban Santería and Haitian Vodu. But as will be shown in a bit more detail later, some significant changes took place that made these Caribbean cults different from their counterparts back in Africa. For example, the role of the priest shifted. In West Africa his role was a social one: he mediated between the tribe and the gods. Thus worship services were public affairs. One of his functions was to challenge the work of the evil *obayifo* (from whose name *obeah-man* is derived), who used his supernatural powers to injure or kill people. But throughout the centuries of slavery the distinction between the priest and obeah-man became blurred, and people went to the same person for healing and to seek revenge on enemies.[14]

Into this African religious life the European missionaries came. Caribbean Christianity from the beginning was thus influenced by the religious ideas and practices of Africans. True, many of the churches founded by the missionaries, particularly in the eighteenth century, turned out completely orthodox (that is, more or less following the practices and belief of the parent churches in the United States and Great Britain). Some, however, either broke away and developed independent traditions or incorporated African religious ideas and practices into their Christianity.[15] The Revivalist traditions in Jamaica and the Spiritual Baptists in Trinidad are examples of this development.

The introduction of Christianity to the slave population in the Caribbean did not happen without a struggle. Letters and reports witness to the persistent and widespread objection of the estate authorities to missionaries' attempts to Christianize their slaves. Arthur Dayfoot relates one missionary's experience in 1705 in Montserrat and St. Kitts:

> The negroes, of whom there were 2,000 in his [Dr. Francis Le Jau's] three parishes, were "sensible and well disposed to learn" but were made stubborn by "the barbarity of their masters." ... If a minister proposed the negroes should be "instructed in the Christian faith, have necessarys" &c, the planters became angry and answered "it would consume their profit." They also objected "that baptism makes negroes free"; but Dr. Le Jau believed the true ground of their objection was that they would be "obliged to look upon them

as Christian brethren and use 'em with humanity."[16]

In Dayfoot's account this attitude is evident as late as 1808. Colin Donaldson, a clergyman in Jamaica, wrote a tract commending Bishop Porteous for his religious instruction of the slaves. Donaldson mentions that the bishop was told he "had no business interfering with the rights of private property."[17]

By the nineteenth century this scenario possibly was the exception rather than the rule. The missionaries had succeeded in converting a large segment of the slaves to Christianity. But African religious traditions continued to be practiced, albeit condemned and prohibited as "black magic."[18] Prohibition took the form of legal ordinances like the one passed by the Common Council on June 15, 1807, in Kingston, Jamaica:

> Whereas, it is not only incumbent upon, but the first and most serious duty of all magistrates and bodies political, to uphold and encourage the due, proper and solemn exercise of religion and worshiping of God. And whereas nothing can tend more to bring true devotion and the practice of religion into disrepute, than the pretended preaching, teaching, and expounding the word of God as contained in the Holy Scriptures, by uneducated, illiterate and ignorant persons and false enthusiasts. And whereas the practice of such pretended preaching, teaching and expounding of Holy Scriptures, by such descriptions of persons as aforesaid to large numbers of persons of colour, and negroes of free condition and slaves assembled together in houses, Negro-houses, huts and yards thereunto appertaining . . . and during such pretended preaching, teaching and expounding and pretended worshipping of God, divers indecent and unseemly noises, gesticulations and behaviour often are used and take place to the great annoyance of the neighbours and to the disrepute of the religion itself.
>
> No person not duly authorized [shall] . . . under the pretence of being a teacher, or expounder of the gospel, or other parts offer up public prayer or sing psalms in any meeting or assembly of negroes, or persons of colour . . . [Violators] shall suffer such punishment by fine not exceeding one hundred pounds or by imprisonment in the common goal for any space, not exceeding three months, or both. . . . And be it further enacted and ordained by the

authority that no person or persons whatever . . . shall use public worship . . . earlier than the hour of six o'clock in the morning, or later than sunset in the evening, under the penalty (as described above). . . . And be it further enacted and ordained that . . . in case any owner, possessor, or occupier of any house, out-house yard, or other place whatsoever, shall permit any meeting, or any description or persons for the purposes of hearing or joining in any such pretended teaching, preaching, praying or singing of psalms . . . such owner if a person of colour or black, of free condition . . . shall suffer same punishment.[19]

Such ordinances of prohibition were outgrowths of the negative attitudes held by European and traditional churches toward African-oriented ceremonies and rituals. They were seen as wild, senseless and mad.[20] An anonymous nineteenth-century writer's description of a funeral ceremony betrays the typical negative attitude toward Afrocentric ritual:

During the whole of the ceremony, many fantastic motions and wild gesticulations are practiced, accompanied with a suitable beat of their drums, and other rude instruments, while a melancholy dirge is sung by a female. . . . This species of barbarous music is indeed more enchanting to their ears than all the most exquisite notes of a Purcell or Pleyel, and however delighted they might appear to be with the finest melody of our bands, let them but hear at a distance the uncouth sounds of their own native instruments, and they would instantly fly from the one to enjoy the other.[21]

A development beginning in the middle of the nineteenth century has had an enormous, long-lasting effect on Caribbean religious life, particularly in Jamaica: the Great Revival. This religious movement seemed to have commenced among the Moravians and gradually spread to all parts of the island. Multitudes gathered "as often as twice a day to sing, fast, pray, and reach the conviction of sin and personal salvation in the blood of Christ."[22]

The mood was right for such a movement. The country was in an economic depression, there were shortages due to the Civil War in the United States, and people were frustrated in their hopes for social change. An apocalyptic mood was in the air. A newspaper article written by a "Son of Africa" in the 1860s saw Jamaica as "engulfed in the ultimate confrontation with the biblical forces of imperial evil, Gog and Magog." That very year, says the article, "eastern Jamaica would erupt in a bloody rebellion which is remembered today as a critical defeat for Jamaica's 'sons and daughters of Africa.' "[23] With all these forces swirling around, the millenarian message of the revival took on a sense of urgency.

According to William Garner, who witnessed the revival, "the hearts of thoughtful and good men were gladdened by what they witnessed in the changed lives and characters of people for whom they long seemed to have laboured in vain." Yet in too many districts, Garner says, the movement also brought "much of wild extravagance and almost blasphemous fanaticism." He claims that this was the case in places where the native Baptists had considerable influence.[24] As will be seen later, the native Baptists effectively combined African ritual with Christianity.

The intensity of the revival died down; but the expression of Christian spirituality in African ritual forms became a permanent feature of the worship of masses of Jamaicans.[25] Revival and Revivalism became the name of an ongoing movement dedicated to the Afrocentric expressions of the 1860s revival.

The Moravian work in Jamaica and the rest of the Caribbean had begun long before the 1860s. As early as 1754 we hear of them establishing a small mission to the slaves. Other missionary denominations followed suit in the 1820s. But these missions were never staffed in significant numbers.[26] The African Methodist Episcopal Church from the United States was also active in the Caribbean. But its numerical success was minimal—possibly because when they came they found a number of predominantly white denominations well established, or because their financial resources were not abundant. Dayfoot also implies another reason: "The Negro churches in the United States arose out of tensions within American churches between white and black members. There blacks are in the minority both in society and in the major denominations. But in the West Indies it is the whites that are in the minority."[27] Whatever the reasons, the black American church never took significant root among the black population of the Caribbean. Yet Christianity and para-Christian bodies independent of European and white American leadership continued to flourish as the nineteenth century came to a close.

Where the A.M.E. Church had failed to be effective, the Pentecostals succeeded in the early twentieth century. As the Native Baptist movement weakened at the turn of the century, Pentecostalism took up the reins and began a significant movement along the lines of the revivalist tradition.[28]

Still, not until the 1960s did a social and political paradigm shift arouse the church and make it wake up, listen and attempt change. The advent of independence, beginning in Jamaica in 1962, made the nations of the Caribbean more sensitive to their African heritage. Many before had attempted to arouse the people. Marcus Garvey, the Jamaican national hero, had chided black ministers decades earlier for not teaching their people to appreciate their African heritage. Now, as I have noted elsewhere, "many Caribbean people have begun to ask questions of identity, while moving away from the attitude that whatever is foreign is superior to that which is indigenous. The colonial umbilical cords are being cut."[29]

Besides the independence movement, the black power movement of the 1970s awakened a great awareness of cultural identity. This forced innovators in the Roman Catholic Church in Trinidad, explains Joanne Stephens, to take a serious look at their culture. One result was indigenization conferences,[30] which assisted the church in recognizing that the European culture is not necessarily superior to that of the African.

Stephens is quick to point out that the black power movement should not be given all the

> credit for pushing the church to address issues of decolonization. There were other forces. Besides the independence movements and the struggle towards selfhood, there was the inclusion of courses at the University of the West Indies in Caribbean history and sociology. These forced West Indians to take

cognizance of their roots and social progress. "All this helped bring about a greater awareness and consciousness which dispelled many old notions about the inferiority of non-white races and cultures."[31]

In addition, the theology of liberation that was sweeping across Latin America in the 1960s and 1970s made an impact in some Caribbean circles, with the effect of making worship services more Caribbean and thus "adventures of the spirit."

Afrocentric Worship Communities

Today many mainstream denominations and some up-and-coming churches are attempting to make their worship more Caribbean and relevant, following what a number of Afrocentric communities have been doing for years, decades and possibly centuries. These religious communities have been able to reach the Caribbean people of African descent where European and white North American religions have failed.[32] Traditional Christian churches are intentionally or unintentionally borrowing from these bodies elements of worship that will allow their theology to remain orthodox but make the liturgy relevant and meaningful to their congregations.

A brief survey of some of these communities will allow us to see what aspects of their worldview and worship have impacted the wider society. It must be noted at the outset that these religions are not easily categorized. Stephen D. Glazier mentions that George Eaton Simpson had tried to divide them into five categories: "remodeled African religions, ancestral cults, revivalist cults, spiritist cults, and religio-political cults." But there is considerable overlap between these categories. Thus I believe Glazier is correct in concluding that a typology of Caribbean religions is not very useful at this time. "Caribbean religions are in a constant state of flux; the dynamics of Caribbean religion should command most of our attention."[33]

Although the majority of these religious bodies have many worship elements in common, the supreme religious experience of almost all is possession by a spirit or the Spirit (as is true in many

African-American churches). Of course Simpson is correct in pointing out that the religions of the Caribbean and black America do not have a monopoly on the phenomenon of possession. It is found in Asia, Africa, Europe and among the nonblack population of North America.[34] Because these Caribbean religions have developed a culture that contains elements from Africa, the United States and Europe, one has to ask, from where did they derive the phenomenon? Simpson addresses this issue:

> We have to discard immediately one type of European possession, the private trance of experience of European mystics, because the commonest and most important kind of spirit-possession in these countries occurs publicly. The other type of possession, found in Great Britain and Ireland and like that of the camp meetings in the United States, differs in two important ways from spirit-possession in the Afro-American cults. In the first place, those possessed were almost always possessed by the "spirit," presumably the Holy Ghost; only a few were possessed by the Devil, the only other spirit we have seen mentioned in accounts of revivals such as the Scotch-Irish revival in Ulster in 1858. . . . In Trinidad, and in other New World countries where Afro-American cults are found, devotees are possessed by a variety of gods.[35]

Nevertheless, not all the religions we will look at involve devil-possession or other god-possession. The more Christian the religion, the more possession is solely by the Holy Spirit. But I believe the manifestation and emphasis on possession come from both Western Christian and African roots—though I will contend that the African influence is stronger.

These Caribbean religious communities all (to one degree or another) give priority to their African roots and thus have been associated with "black pride." This factor not only has precipitated growth in these religions but has contributed to a freedom of Afro-centric expression in their liturgies and ceremonies, allowing adherents to worship more wholistically than their counterparts in religious bodies that are non-Afrocentric. Following is a brief survey of a number of these nonconventional religions.

Orisha. In most of the literature and to most people on the street, this religion is known as Shango. But adherents, like Rawle Gibbons of the University of the West Indies, are quick to point out that Shango is only one (albeit possibly the most powerful) of the Orisha deities.[36] These deities have their roots in the Yoruba religion of West Africa.

A lack of historical records makes it difficult to reconstruct the inception and development of this religion in the Caribbean.[37] It seems, however, that indentured laborers who arrived in Trinidad and Grenada[38] were responsible for the introduction of Yoruba beliefs in the Orishas. Although there has been much migratory movement between Trinidad and Grenada, apparently Yoruba religion was introduced into each island by separate groups of immigrants, since there are major differences between the practices on the two islands.

The Orisha religion in Trinidad particularly combines elements of Yoruba traditional beliefs and practices with Roman Catholic beliefs and practices and, to a lesser extent, those of Anglicans and Baptists. Thus in its theology and ritual it has striking similarities with Afrocentric religions in other parts of the Americas that are predominantly Catholic: Santería in Cuba, Vodu in Haiti and Xango in Brazil.[39] All these religions, states Simpson, "retain the names of prominent African divinities, include animal sacrifices, feature drumming, dancing, and spirit possession, and utilize thunder stones and swords as ritual objects. Each of these groups believes in a total magico-religious complex which includes cosmological, theological, ceremonial, magical, and medical aspects.[40]

In an interview Gibbons emphasized that Orisha is not Christian per se but uses Christianity, particularly Roman Catholic saints, who are equated with the Orisha divinities. Gibbons said:

Orisha people . . . don't have a problem with Christianity because we know that all religions come from African traditional religion, from Egypt and spread throughout the world. So we know that there is no problem with that. But we don't limit ourselves, or we don't define ourselves as Christians, but we accept the Christian saints, we accept Jesus Christ. . . . So there is an element of Christianity in terms of the prayers, in terms of the identification of the saints, and in terms of some of the icons that you will see when you go to shrines."[41]

Gibbons explains that religious services center on the use of the drum, which issues a call to the Orisha and to worshipers to enter and participate. For every Orisha there is a specific drum and a specific chant. Total participation in the service is of vital importance. The Orishas will not come without the full participation of all present. "If people stand and they don't participate, and they don't sing, they don't clap, they don't keep the rhythm in one way or another, the Orishas won't come, and if they don't come they will be displeased."[42] Thus it is very important that attenders not remain passive observers. In worship, everyone sings and dances and moves around in a circle. Everyone gives of their total self. It is when their total selves are given and surrendered that they come in contact with the spirit and the manifestation of possession takes place.

Molly Ahye, one of the few female Orisha priests in Trinidad, points out that Christian prayers and psalms often form part of the service. But prayer in the ritual is not simply meditative or verbal "but involves drumming, singing and dancing under the experienced eyes of priests and priestesses who help to mediate between ritual behaviour and the spirits which such ritual can evoke."[43] Like drumming, dancing is a dominant feature in Orisha worship. "Dancing can link you with the cosmic vibration of the earth, it can connect you with the sky," says Ahye.[44]

It is impossible to determine the number of Orisha adherents in Trinidad and Grenada. Many followers have preferred to remain "in the closet" because of the perception that has stigmatized them for decades.[45] For many Trinidadians "Shango," or worship of the Orishas, was heathen and diabolical. This perception drove it underground and caused people to deny their affiliation with it. More recently, as Afrocentrism has come into vogue, it has become more acceptable to acknowledge one's affiliation with the religion.

Increasingly there is traffic between the Orisha community and Christian (and semi-Christian) groups, particularly the Spiritual Baptists. Gibbons pointed out that often you will find an Orisha shrine and a Baptist chapel next to each other; and people who are Baptist can be seen in the Orisha compound. These crossover Baptists participate in the Orisha prayer meetings, drum songs, dance and healing ceremonies; however, they will not participate in the sacrifices. Orisha devotees also attend Roman Catholic, Anglican, Methodist, Presbyterian and Pentecostal churches with a degree of regularity.[46]

Such mixing has had the singular effect of aiding Christian denominations to be sensitive to their African roots and in so doing has made their worship more Spirit-filled. But Simpson alerts us to a broader influence of this religion on the total culture system of Trinidad: "its utilization of African, as well as European, cultural elements, thus contributing to the perpetuation of the multi-cultural heritage of the island"[47] and, I would add, of the entire Caribbean region.

Revival. The revivalist tradition seems to have its roots in the Great Revival that swept Jamaica in the 1860s. Revivalism appears to constitute a combination of the fervor of the Native Baptist movement and myalism, an African belief system. But scholars like George Eaton Simpson and Joseph Murphy point out that its roots actually go back to Afro-Christian traditions that were being developed in the late eighteenth century.[48] The African slaves in these traditions, as they explored the world of the Christian Bible, found common ground with their African experience.

On another front in the late eighteenth century were several hundred United Empire Loyalists who migrated to Jamaica from the United States. Many of these brought slaves who had been converted to Christianity, and these became missionaries to the Jamaican slave population. They seemed to have been the founders of the Native Baptist movement. This movement reinterpreted Christianity in Afrocentric ways. By the 1830s they were fully integrated into the black Jamaican culture, and their teaching constituted serious competition for the Christianity of the European missionaries. As a matter of fact, even though the official missionary movement gained significant numbers of members between the 1820s and 1840s, by 1865 it had lost between a quarter and a half of them to the Native Baptists. By the 1860s Great Revival, the Native Baptists appeared to be stronger than European orthodoxy.[49]

Revivalism in Jamaica comes in diverse strains and forms today. For this reason scholars are divided as to whether the movement is closer to the Orisha tradition or the Spiritual Baptists tradition in Trinidad. Bisnauth argues that it is like Orisha, except that the latter is the Africanization of Catholicism while Revivalism is the Africanization of Protestantism.[50] Simpson, on the other hand, equates Revivalism with the Spiritual Baptists, who are more Christian than Orisha followers. In a sense both are correct, depending on which of the traditions within Revivalism one has in mind. If it is Myalism, Cumina or Pocomani (Pukkumina), the similarities to Orisha are striking. But if it is Revival Zion, the Spiritual Baptists are closer.

Cumina, the most culturally African of the Revivalist religions, is similar to the Trinidadian Orisha tradition in recognizing the Yoruba god Shango as a most powerful deity. Also as in the Trinidadian community, drumming, dancing and spirit possession are important ingredients of Cumina worship ceremonies. Walter Pitts Jr. tells us that along with Shango, "earth, sky and ancestral powers called zombis possess members who, like the revivalists, form a ring to bring on possession trance through singing and drumming."[51]

Because the majority of adherents to Revivalism come from the lower class, the middle-class perception of Revivalism is mostly negative. It is seen as primitive religious expression and ridiculed as "a little madness" and "over-enthusiastic" Christianity.[52] The word used to refer to these revivalists is *Poco* (a shortened form of *Pocomania* or *Pukkumina*). So strong is the negative connotation of Poco that Murphy writes the following in a footnote of his study:

> An index of the stigma of the label of *pocomania* is that in recent censuses of Jamaican denominationalism only a tiny fraction (0.01) of [the] Jamaican population publicly identifies itself with *pocomania*. Yet every researcher indicates

that among the working and unemployed classes of Jamaican society, who make up the majority of the Jamaican population, *pukkumina* and other revival traditions can claim more adherents than all the mainstream traditions combined. It is likely that most members of revival churches identify themselves as Baptists.[53]

Members of Revival Zion churches attempt to distinguish themselves from Pocomania, pointing to the biblical foundation for all their activities. However, Revival Zionists are also perceived as unorthodox and polytheistic by the traditional denominations, because of their appeal to spirits. Although Revival Zion is categorized as "a fundamentalist Protestant cult with African overtones,"[54] the similarities with the Pocomania tradition are strong. The differences, according to Pitts, "center on the nature of possession and of the possessing spirits."[55] The structure of their rituals and ceremonies is quite similar.

The four common elements found in Cumina, Pocomania and Revival Zion worship services are drumming, singing, dancing and offering of sacrifices. The Revival Zion groups observed by Simpson in West Kingston[56] begin their services with a half-hour of vigorous drumming on the snare or "rattling" drum and a bass drum. The drumming is accompanied by hand-clapping and shaking of tambourines and rattles. Edward Seaga also reports that Zionist rituals usually begin with "speeches, Bible-reading, praying and the singing of choruses . . . accompanied by drumming."[57]

The songs most popularly sung in Revival Zion churches come from the Sankey and Moody hymnal: "How Sweet the Name of Jesus Sounds," "I Heard the Voice of Jesus Say," "Just As I Am Without One Plea," "I was a Wandering Sheep." It is quite common for these songs to be sung over and over again for a period of ten minutes or longer. The songs are initially sung without syncopation, and the rhythm remains unaltered. But as the service progresses with singing and prayers, the congregation moves into what is called *trumping*.

"Trumping" or "laboring" is a dance or posturing peculiar to the

Revival tradition. Simpson describes it:

> It is done counterclockwise around the altar, or the center of a ring, and has the appearance of a forward moving two-step stomp. With the step forward, the body is bent forward from the waist so sharply as to seem propelled by force. At the same time the breath is exhaled, or inhaled, with great effort and sound. The forcefulness of the action gives justification for the use of the word "laboring." The word "groaning" is used in connection with the heavy expulsion and sucking in of the breath. In . . . Pocomania the breath is exhaled when the body bends down and inhaled on the upswing; in Revival Zion, the process is reversed.[58]

As the trumping increases, the drumming stops and the pounding of feet takes over and supplies the rhythm and percussion.

One of the purposes for this spiritual dance is to facilitate possession by the Holy Spirit or other saints. The possessed may run, crawl, shout, quiver, moan, spin around, fall and roll on the ground. During a violent possession, a person could remain on the ground for days or even weeks.

Possession is desired by all Revivalists because through it the Holy Spirit or other saints and spirits use the person's body and teach him or her spiritual truths. The initial possession is felt to have a cleansing effect, while subsequent possessions assist in one's growth and development toward maturity.[59] It is believed too that the Holy Spirit and the prophets, disciples and ancestors desire to return to the world by using the worshiper for their enjoyment and edification.[60]

Revivalists believe that the high God, the Creator and ruler of the universe, does not leave his throne in the high heaven to attend service, nor does he ever possess a worshiper. Jesus Christ is in attendance at the service, though he never trumps. On the other hand, God the Holy Spirit is the chief spirit in the revival, and he not only attends but trumps as well.[61]

Pocomania and Cumina theology differs from Revival Zion in this respect. Being more African in their worldview, these sects perceive a closer relation between the spiritual and natural worlds and a close affinity between human beings and nature. Because God is an integral part of nature, he does not move away or stay away from humankind. But it is the duty of the worshiper to attract God into the circle.[62] In these ceremonies, therefore, nature becomes central as the link is formed between heaven and earth.

Spiritual Baptists. As was noted earlier, the Spiritual Baptists (or "Shouters") of Trinidad most resemble the Revivalist traditions of Jamaica because of their strong Protestant orientation. However, they did not have their roots in a strong revivalist movement as did their Jamaican counterparts.

It appears the religion came to Trinidad from the island of St. Vincent around 1900, but it may have been initially introduced into St. Vincent by American missionaries from the Southern states.[63] There is some debate as to whether many of the elements in Spiritual Baptist worships should be attributed to the influence of the Orisha tradition or the black church in the United States. Because their roots go back to these overseas communities, one is tempted to think that the linkage is stronger with fundamentalist black churches. Yet we cannot rule out the influence of the Orisha religion on the Spiritual Baptists. Although to a lesser degree, Spiritual Baptists will have lithographs of Catholic saints and will be "possessed" by them, along with possession by the Holy Spirit and African "powers" as well.

Some of the elements of Spiritual Baptist worship that point to a strong linkage with the United States churches are shouting, chanting, hand-clapping, trances, dancing, "rejoicing" and extemporaneous forms of prayer. There are a number of differences, however. In the first place, drums were not used widely in U.S. churches until recently. Singing in the North American church was normally accompanied by hand-clapping and tambourines. In the second place, trances, possession by the Spirit and "speaking in tongues" are less African-oriented in the United States than in Trinidad. In earlier camp meetings and today's Pentecostal-style ceremonies, possession by the Holy Spirit is provoked by powerful sermons and emotional rhythmic singing. In Trinidad Baptist churches, says Angelina Pollak-Eltz, "the faithful are possessed by 'powers' of spirits, who speak through them or use their bodies to perform cleansing rituals or other ceremonies, as it is customary in Africa and African American religions, but seldom in Protestant sects."[64] It appears, then, that the Spiritual Baptists were strongly influenced by both the Orisha movement with its strong African roots and the fundamentalist Protestant churches of the United States with their more modified Africanisms.

Like the Revivalists in Jamaica, the Spiritual Baptists of Trinidad appeal to the poor and black lower class, who are aware, or becoming more aware, of their African heritage. Early in the twentieth century they were perceived as a major threat to the established European-oriented denominations, which were rapidly losing members and money. It is purported that these groups were behind the government's decision to outlaw the movement as a public disturbance. The Spiritual Baptists were accused of shouting too loudly, and thus in legal documents they were branded as "Shouter Baptists"—a designation they detest and reject.[65] The Shouter Prohibition was passed in 1917 and remained in effect until 1951.[66]

The persecution during this period seemed to have had the effect of strengthening the Afrocentric dimension of the religion. In the 1930s through the 1950s, Spiritual Baptists developed and espoused widely the concept of the Black Divinity. This belief holds that Jesus Christ was a black African and that Africa and Africans occupy a very central place in history and antiquity.[67] In an interview Mother Monica Randoo, a leader of Spiritual Baptist churches in Cocorite, Trinidad, stressed that Africa is the center of civilization. "So we keep that African part of us. We are here, we have come from a land that is far away, but the land rests within our spirit. We believe that Africa is the cradle of civilization. We believe that all things came out of Africa."[68]

Although they are Afrocentric, Spiritual Baptists hold to much of the traditional theology espoused by conservative fundamentalist groups, especially in the United States. Among the beliefs held are the inerrancy of the Bible, the virgin birth of Jesus, the substitutionary atonement, the physical literal resurrection of Jesus, and the authenticity of the miracles recorded in Scripture.[69] But the Spiritual Baptists, unlike their counterparts in the United States, do not use these tenets as political lightning rods against their opponents in the liberal and scientific communities.

Worship and ceremonies are vital in the life of Spiritual Baptists. The *Constitution and Government of the West Indian United Spiritual Baptist Order* requires three services each Sunday: Divine Service commencing at 4:00 a.m., Communion Service commencing at 9:00 a.m. and Evening Service starting at 7:00 p.m. and terminating not later than 10:00 p.m., "except [as] the occasion necessitates."[70] Most of the religious ceremonies last from three to six hours and include rites of purification (intended to cast out evil spirits from the place of worship), bell ringing, singing, preaching, dancing, shouting or trumping, and possession.

Singing and drumming are central to the ritual of Spiritual Baptists. Music is used, reports Glazier, "to dispel unwanted spirits, to demonstrate power and authority within the church, to 'guide' candidates for baptism, for mourning, to offer prayer and supplication, and to invoke the presence of the Holy Ghost."[71] As among the Jamaican Revivalists, the use of Sankey hymns is prevalent. These hymns are usually begun with the leader lining the verses for the congregation to sing. But after a couple of verses, the rhythm changes to produce a trance, and the percussive singing commences. Hand-clapping, bongo drums and rattles are introduced; the tempo becomes faster, and the hymns take on a swing idiom that moves the worshipers into a state of spiritual ecstasy.[72]

During such periods, worshipers are possessed by the Holy Ghost—jumping up and down, gesticulating intensely and in many instances going into a trance. Trances sometimes take the form of short jerks and tremors which cause the possessed to swirl around as the Spirit descends. During the trance, speaking in tongues is common. At the end the person usually collapses on the floor. The Spirit may also manifest itself through "shouting," which may take the form of a grunt, a whisper or a sigh.

We should note that this frame of the worship resembles the ring shout of early African-American worship. In the case of the Spiritual Baptists, however, there are more emotional prayers during this period and an incessant ringing of bells, intended to produce a trance and bring about possession by the Holy Spirit.

Manifestations of the Spirit are usually followed by periods of illumination and contemplation during which Scripture is read and short homilies are given by worshipers. Interestingly, many of the homilies contradict each other. But as each successive speaker points out the error of the previous person, all pray for greater enlightenment. Before the main speaker gives the final interpretation, there is a ritual of sharing and touching. The intended purpose of this is to diffuse the power of the Holy Spirit which was previously concentrated in the speaker. Prior to this it is believed that the speaker is in "a most dangerous and supercharged state."[73] If the speaker's power is not shared, he would be destroyed by it. After the main sermon, there is a brief period of speaking in tongues, shouting and bell ringing, followed by a benediction.

The Spiritual Baptists continue to have an increasing influence on Trinidadian society, particularly the lower and working classes. As was noted in the case of the Orisha adherents, there is much crossing over. Because of this, many traditional churches are incorporating elements of spiritual Baptist worship into their service. Mother Monica is convinced that they are fearful of losing their members. "Fear, fear have them mooping," she says with a sigh.[74]

Other semi-Christian groups. There are a number of other Caribbean movements that have similar characteristics to the ones discussed above. Walter Pitts Jr. describes two. The first is Shakerism on the Island of St. Vincent. The Shakers are fundamentally Christians, but their religious practices are similar to the ring shout in the United States and practices of revivalism in Jamaica. As in other such groups in the Caribbean, the majority of Shakers are socially, economically and racially stigmatized, being poor and black. Citing Simpson, Pitts states that they are an amalgam of European Christianity and African religious traditions, blending a Methodist base with some Anglicanism, Catholicism and African ritual.[75]

A typical Shaker service begins with the singing of hymns, recitation of prayers and consecration of the four corners of the meeting place. The Apostles' Creed is repeated, and worshipers kneel and repeat the General Confession and the Lord's Prayer followed by another prayer and the singing of the Gloria Patri. Trance, which evidences itself in a form of trembling (hence the name of the group), rarely occurs during this traditional segment of the service. However, following the sermon the preacher begins to sing and worshipers enter into a shaking trance, similar to that of Afrocentric religious movements described earlier.

A second but contrasting movement also based in St. Vincent is called Streams of Power. Its ritual begins with fast, loud singing accompanied by various instruments. There is also hand-clapping and stomping of feet. Worshipers then enter into a trance while speaking in tongues. This is followed by the sermon, benediction, and the singing of European-derived hymns.

A third movement is totally different from any of the movements discussed because it is possibly the Caribbean's only totally indigenous religion. Rastafarianism claims no roots in European Christianity or African Yoruba traditions. It arose out of the Back to Africa movement during the first half of the twentieth century in Jamaica.

Although Rastas use the Judeo-Christian Bible extensively, they claim to know the truth intuitively. "This, they make out, is possible since, as the ancient Israelites reincarnated, they have been with God from the beginning of creation."[76] This ideology has encouraged Rastafarians to express enormous creativity in the visual and plastic arts, handicrafts and music. The most famous of the musical idioms invented by this movement is reggae, Bob Marley being its most internationally famous artist. Rastafarianism continues to greatly influence society and church in the Caribbean. And reggae music is fast becoming an acceptable form in worship services, paralleling its growing popularity throughout the world.

Pentecostalism. In one sense Pentecostalism should not be included in a discussion of religious traditions that are Afrocentric, for it makes no such claims. Besides, unlike most of the traditions surveyed above, Pentecostals are thoroughly orthodox Christians who reject all aspects of the African spirit world. Yet of all mainstream Christian movements or denominations in the Western world, Pentecostalism displays most characteristics of the wholism in worship that African-rooted religions possess. We might continue to wonder how much influence the African worldview has had on this movement both in North America and in the Caribbean (and, as we will see later, in Latin America).

Pentecostalism was reportedly the fastest-growing religious body in the Caribbean in the twentieth century. Data from Jamaica and Trinidad and Tobago bear this out. In Trinidad and Tobago it grew from 0.46 percent of the population in 1960 to 3.45 percent in 1980. Only the Seventh-day Adventist Church has demonstrated similarly rapid growth—from 1.5 percent in 1960 to 2.5 percent in 1980.[77] In Jamaica, Pentecostalism grew from 6 percent in 1960 to 25 percent in 1982.[78] Given such growth, one can hardly question the influence this body of Christians is having on Caribbean society and Christian worship in the region.

Studies and general observation show that Pentecostals come from the lower economic strata of society. However, increasing numbers of middle- and upper-middle-class persons are joining the movement.[79] Interestingly, based on data from the 1950s, in countries with less socioeconomic stability, like Jamaica and Trinidad and Tobago, Pentecostal growth is more rapid than in islands like Montserrat where economic changes have been more stable.[80] With the changing demographics of Pentecostalism, however, perhaps that tendency will not hold as we enter the twenty-first century.

There is disagreement even within Pentecostalism as to the influence of African elements on Pentecostal worship services and behavior. John Hopkin, in his study of Jamaican Pentecostalism, has noted its Native Baptist roots. When North American Pentecostal missionaries brought their religion to Jamaica at the beginning of the twentieth century, it was "grafted to the tree of the local Native Baptist tradition."[81] Thus like the Native Baptist movement, Pentecostalism became an important part of the Revivalist tradition on the island. In reality Jamaican Pentecostalism, though having roots in the North American tradition as well as in an indigenous Jamaican movement, has become a movement in its own right.

Hopkin has demonstrated some fundamental differences between white North American and Caribbean Pentecostalism that are enlightening for our study. In the first place, the styles of religious expression are different. Both emphasize the immediacy of religious experience as worshipers seek to be filled with the Spirit. However, the Jamaican music, rhythm and movement in the service take on what Hopkin says is "a religiously potent quality in themselves." He explains:

> Where white Pentecostals bring on the experience of the Holy Spirit by concentration and prayer, the Jamaican church members bring it on by cultivating religious fervour and excitement through these sense-oriented forms of self-expression, and through losing themselves in their active participation in the communal events of the church service. Where for the Americans singing a hymn is an act of praise, for the Jamaicans the song and all the dancing and rhythm that accompany it are a religious experience in themselves.[82]

In the second place, Pentecostal worship, like African-based religious services, is a communal affair. In part this may have grown out of the theological belief that Christians ought to keep themselves separate from the world. This otherworldly orientation has brought on a strong sense of community in and outside the service, where members are still addressed as "brother" and "sister."[83]

Increasingly these two characteristics, which have their genesis in the Jamaican African heritage, are becoming more and more widespread and acceptable even in traditional churches. A burgeoning number of denominational traditions—and local churches—are giving their members free rein to express that intense, immediate and tangible religious experience, as well as emphasizing the communal aspects of worship.

A quite different study has been done by Christopher Walker of the Pentecostal community on the island of Tobago, particularly the

Scarborough Peoples' Church. Pentecostals here go to great lengths to deny their African heritage in their worship experience. This may be due in part to a reaction against association with Spiritual Baptists. For Pentecostals these Baptists are "counterfeit" devil worshipers. Even though the movements are parallel in such elements as fundamentalism, belief in water baptism, Holy Spirit possession, glossolalia, healing and exorcism, Pentecostals reject Spiritual Baptists as being of Satan. Pentecostals, says Walker, at a purely doctrinal level reject anything that is non-Christian, and thus reject anything from Africa.[84]

Walker further discovered that the Pentecostal church in Tobago had more affinity (in terms of preference) with the white American than the African-American church. In his field work he was told that Trinidad and Tobago churches prefer to have white North American guest speakers, for they find the black preaching style incomprehensible. And conversely, West Indian preachers more often than not speak in Caucasian churches when they travel north.[85] Walker suggests that the discomfort local Pentecostals have with their black North American counterparts may lie in the similarity in style with Spiritual Baptists.[86] Elements of black worship are therefore discounted or denied because of their association with a movement that is perceived as demonic.

Many Pentecostals throughout the Caribbean will not admit the suggestion that in part the growth of West Indian Pentecostalism has to do with the indigenous nature of the movement's worship.[87] In a survey in Trinidad, the most popular explanations given for why people joined the Pentecostal faith were that there they received the teaching of the Word and spiritual food, or they found spiritual growth and fulfillment, or they wanted to learn more about God and have a relationship with him.[88] Just about all the responses were "spiritual"; none included a sociopolitical dimension. Nevertheless, it seems to me undeniable that the underlying indigenous nature of Pentecostalism will continue to make it attractive to Caribbean peoples seeking a wholistic worship experience.[89]

An Indigenous Worship

As the nations of the Caribbean cut the colonial umbilical cord, the church, consciously or unconsciously, is recognizing the importance of decolonizing its theology. And decolonization includes an effort to make the liturgy more indigenous. Gaining independence has awakened the peoples of the region to their distinctive historical experience. These experiences for the most part had not been fully represented in the "divine hour" worship service. Apart from the religious traditions surveyed above, very few churches sensed the need to be truly Caribbean.

The majority of churches that fall under the umbrella of the Caribbean Council of Churches (e.g., Lutheran Church of Guyana, the Methodist Church in the Caribbean and Jamaica, the Presbyterian Church of Trinidad, the Roman Catholic Church of the Caribbean, the United Church of Jamaica and Grand Cayman, the Baptist church in Trinidad, the Jamaica Baptist Union, the Anglican Church, the Moravian Church in both Jamaica and the eastern Caribbean) have in the past been essentially European and North American in doctrine and worship. Not only have they given "divine sanction"[90] to the concept of the superiority of the Northern/Western culture, but they have denied their African heritage.

In the 1970s several Caribbean theologians such as Idris Hamid, William Watty and Ashley Smith challenged the church, particularly the mainline church, to "take seriously and responsibly the cultural milieu and environment in which it finds itself thereby recognizing the cultural and social experiences of that milieu."[91] This was and still is a mammoth undertaking; survey after survey demonstrates that there remains a "sincerity gap between the rites and ceremonies and real life."[92] Yet more and more worshipers are asking questions about their cultural identity and are desiring that it not be separate from their worship experience.

Anglican, Roman Catholic and other mainline churches have been making steady progress in the indigenizing of their liturgy as they incorporate gestures, bodily movements and broader participation—all vital components of the everyday life of the people. African customs such as drumming, rhythmic movement and reception of the Spirit are being incorporated into the traditional Euro-based liturgy. Some have gone even further by experimenting with native elements in the Communion service, such as cassava or rice bread and sugarcane juice or rum, and incorporating indigenous styles of music such as calypso and reggae.[93]

The indigenization process is not limited to forms and mechanics in the service such as song and dance. Indigenization of the liturgy is taking account of the broad realities of Caribbean society: "hunger, disease, ignorance, illiteracy, unemployment, frustration, and the struggles of people for liberation, justice and peace."[94] Worship increasingly is becoming not only a place where resistance against *all* oppression is affirmed, but a place where triumphs over daily hardships and systems of exploitation are celebrated to the glory of God as evidence of the power of the gospel of Jesus Christ.

As the Caribbean emigrants spread across Canada and the United States, they too are asking questions about their identity in a foreign land. While incorporating aspects of the Canadian and U.S. cultures into everyday life, many have been insistent on retaining their Caribbean cultural heritage. In fact I have come upon churches in Toronto, Los Angeles and New York that are more indigenously Caribbean than many "back home." Worshipers are creating and celebrating liturgies in which the design, style, language and worldview reflect Caribbean vernacular and culture. Their praise, prayer and preaching, like the new liturgical breeze blowing in the Caribbean itself, are certainly an adventure of the spirit.

Caribbean
Music

W*hat is Caribbean worship music? Since the 1970s church* musicologists and theologians have struggled with this question. At a seminar that dealt with this issue, the following elements of indigenous folk music were identified:

☐ the influence of both European and African culture in its rhythm and melody

☐ syncopation and complex rhythms

☐ antiphonal style

☐ repetition

☐ dialect used with melodic rhythm that is closely related to the words

☐ harmony that, when present, is simple[1]

These elements serve to define secular indigenous music; Caribbean worship music, however, remains ill-defined.[2] Certainly part of the problem lies in the nonmonolithic character of Caribbean society and its varied cultural makeup from island to island, or nation to nation. Yet I reckon that at the heart of the problem is how European *or* African true Caribbean worship music should be.

The struggle between European musical idioms and style versus African idioms and style probably dates back to the first African slaves' arrival in the Americas. These slaves brought with them their rhythm, dance and musical instrumentation such as drums, rhythm sticks, bongos and musical bows.[3] But European missionaries and colonizers saw no value in African-oriented music and went on the offensive against it. As was mentioned earlier, an anonymous writer described the music of the slaves as a "species of barbarous music,"[4] for, he said, the slaves would rather conduct their ceremonies with "many fantastic motions and wild gesticulations . . . accompanied with a suitable beat of their drums, and other rude instruments . . . [than listen to] all the most exquisite notes of a Purcell or a Pleyel . . . however delighted they might appear to be with the finest melody of our bands."[5] Sister Donatine Prince reports similar remarks by Sir Hans Sloane:

> The Negroes have no manner of religion by what I could observe of them. It is true that they have several ceremonies as dances, playing, etc., but these for the most part are so far from being acts of adoration of a God that they are for the most part mixed with a great deal of bawdy and lewdness.[6]

This attitude toward the music and worship of the slaves has remained dominant in churches that have strong European and North American roots. Not until the 1970s was there an intentional effort to revive and give respect to music with African elements as a valid part of the liturgy in traditional churches of the Caribbean.

Caribbean church musicologists and liturgists have argued, to some degree successfully, that just as earlier Europeans took popular folk music and "baptized" it into acceptable worship hymns and songs, so the Caribbean church should appropriate the music that is meaningful in the everyday life of its people. Thus more and more reggae and calypso, mento and revival rhythms are seeping into worship services.

It is wrong to identify these musical idioms as "secular." What is true is that the nonreligious world and pop culture have adopted these idioms. Reggae, for example, arose out of the religious Rastafarian movement. Rasta's emphasis on drumming and rhythm is itself an outgrowth of an African religious emphasis.[7] Calypso (associated with Jamaican-born Harry Belafonte and Trinidadian the Mighty Sparrow) also is not new "secular" music. Although it "retains vestiges of Spanish contribution,"[8] it originated in Trinidad and Tobago among some of the first Yoruba and Mandango slaves from West Africa. It is likely that calypso is a derivative of these slaves' native music, *kaiso*—a Yoruban word meaning "to bring the world together." Russ Smith notes, "For enslaved Africans, *kaiso* was a means of communication and a way of preserving hope along with African customs and culture."[9] The more modern idiom *soca* (abbreviation of "soul of calypso"), which emerged in the 1970s, attempts also to revive the tradition of *kaiso* as it voices the passion of Afro-Caribbean people.

Many Caribbean worshipers struggle with the use of reggae and calypso in the liturgy because of their strong associations with what is termed "the world." European music, by contrast, is associated with things religious. Yet it is the African-based musical idioms that express the daily social and deep spiritual concerns and feelings of the people.[10]

The church cannot and must not deny its European heritage. Many Caribbean traditional worshipers are, however, attempting to address an imbalance by reviving their African musical heritage and making it part and parcel of the worship service. Caribbean Pentecostals have been accomplishing this fairly successfully—and thus other churches that make such attempts are quickly dubbed "Pentecostal"! The truth is, such churches are not attempting to be Pentecostal clones but are seeking to recapture the African wholistic worship spirit both in instrumentation and in song.

Instrumental Distinctives
As in Europe and North America, the organ has been the instrument

of preference for most Caribbean churches that can afford it—whether it be the pedal, electronic or pipe organ. Worshipers' response to this instrument, says Althea Spencer, tends to be quiet reverence, for the organ is not a Caribbean or African instrument but a European one, suited to the smooth ploddings of hymns from that part of the world. This, Spencer argues, is unnatural for a people "whose bodies are rhythmic."[11] Caribbean music generally calls for instrumentation that evokes a more rhythmic response. Thus instruments such as drums (especially the conga), tambourines, shakers, mouth organ, guitar, flute, violin, bongo, rumbo box and maracas are growing in popularity in Caribbean churches.

As mentioned in the discussion of African-American worship, rhythm is vital to wholistic worship for people with African roots. Yet many Caribbean people, particularly of the older generation, have looked down on indigenous rhythmic music as "sacrilegious, sensual, ungodly, and carnal."[12] Like African-Americans, Caribbean people tend to be naturally rhythmic. Not only do rhythmic expressions give freedom to sensuality, but Iris Hamid sees them as a key phenomenon in communication—even in worship.[13] As we have seen, indigenous groups such as Spiritual Baptists and Revivalists, as well as Pentecostals, have made rhythm an integral aspect of worship, even to the point of transforming European hymn tunes to an African rhythmic form.

It is because drums accentuated rhythm in worship that it was particularly targeted and criminalized[14] by the colonial masters. But even though the African diaspora was to a large degree "de-drummed," it was not "derhythmized"; for as Funso Aiye Jinai from Nigeria says, "Drum language does not necessarily have to come via the drum. It can come via the voice of the people, via the movement of the body. . . . So that when you go into the traditional African-American church, what you are really hearing [in] the 'gimme' and 'amens,' 'say it man,' etc., . . . is the . . . drum language."[15]

The drum and other rhythmic instruments were not totally suppressed in the Caribbean as they were in the United States, thanks to movements such as Revival, Spiritual Baptists and Pentecostalism. Today the taboo on drums in many traditional churches is disappearing, and rhythm in worship is being revived to the glory of God.

Another instrument that for decades found little place in the worship setting is the steel pan. It has been said that this is the only new major instrument to be developed in the twentieth century. Indigenous to Trinidad and Tobago, it has become a cultural artifact throughout the Caribbean. Prior to the 1960s it was looked upon with scorn by members of the upper class, in part because of its local origins: anything not European had to be inferior! Thus any attempts to introduce it into the church setting met with great resistance. As the church made strides toward making its liturgies reflect the Caribbean culture, however, the introduction of the steel band was a natural step.[16] Today, though there are still pockets of resistance to this "worldly" instrument within and without the Caribbean, many churches and worshipers find the steel pan to be a significant aid in worship, one that glorifies God in their cultural setting.

Although Pentecostal churches have taken the lead in the use of diverse rhythmic instruments in worship, many non-Pentecostal churches within and without the Caribbean are finding it appropriate to diversify, and thus the character of their worship is coming to resemble that of the Pentecostals. The description of Pentecostal music by John Hopkin[17] therefore applies to a musical trend in many Caribbean churches.

Hopkin notes that the types of instruments used to accompany singing and dance vary from one congregation to another. The most popular instruments are the guitar, tambourine, rattles, piano, drums (snare, sometimes tomtom, bass and cymbal), and electric organ. Depending on the size of the church, instrumental accompaniment may range from a single guitarist to an entire ensemble of five or six instrumentalists. The rhythmic tambourine is everpresent. Hopkin writes:

> In most congregations a number of individuals bring tambourines to church along with their Bibles and hymn books. During the faster songs, there may

be as many as five or six people scattered throughout the congregation playing tambourines. The tambourines' sound is loud and trebly enough to be heard clearly through the clapping and singing. No special people play them; they are often passed around during the singing, from young brethren to old women to little children. The simplest tambourine pattern—not uncommon, especially when the tambourines get into the hands of old people—consists of an alternation between hitting the tambourine and withdrawing it with a shake, producing the sequence.[18]

Besides the fact that there are not many trained church musicians in the Caribbean, most churches cannot afford to hire professional instrumentalists. So instrumentalists are recruited from among the members and usually play instruments owned by the church. They usually have a strong ear, especially for basic chords. This is an important asset, since these musicians are often called upon to accompany impromptu singing. They also help to reinforce the rhythmic pulse of the singing and dance.

Instrumentation is not limited to drums, rattles, tambourines and organ. The human body itself is used as a percussive instrument. Often the regular instruments stop while clapping, pounding and stomping continue as accompaniment to the singing and dance. This is especially true in Revival-type churches where there is "trumping and laboring."[19] But it is handclapping that has become the norm in many Caribbean churches today. Again, Hopkin writes:

> The congregations usually accompany the faster, more high-spirited songs with hand clapping, in patterns that may be fairly simple or quite complex. Although the patterns vary a great deal, worshippers can apply them to any song in a duple meter, and they clap more or less the same pattern for all songs that call for clapping. But within the song the clapping rhythms may vary a great deal, [and] may even be in constant state of flux. Everyone in the church does not clap in the same rhythmic pattern; instead, different groups of people clap a varying number of patterns at any given time, and the several patterns blend to form a complex whole.[20]

Every worshiper participates in clapping or stomping, revealing the full participatory nature of indigenous Caribbean worship. "Instrumental" accompaniment is not limited to some professional who is paid to "perform." The entire congregation sings; all worshipers are instrumentalists.

Song

As in the case of instrumental music, European and North American hymns and tunes still to a large degree dominate the Caribbean liturgical scene. Spencer addresses this issue:

> Caribbean Church songs have not yet become common currency in the local congregation. The denigration of indigenous material, stemming from and encouraging the idolization of foreign material, is perhaps the chief reason. The association of the mento and the revival rhythms with activity considered to be primitive, unsophisticated, and uneducated (in other words, African) leads to scorn from the attenders of the institutional church. Dialect is not spoken publicly by respectable persons and so cannot contribute to a dignified worship service. There are reasons grounded in history and the acculturation of the Caribbean people. This bias is common to the Caribbean society. Only a long process of education, conscientization and practice will eradicate this scourge.[21]

Yet the transformation Spencer calls for is taking place as the indigenization movement progresses. The changes brings music in two categories, according to the famous Jamaican musicologist Pamela O'Gorman: (1) indigenous folk music, including songs transplanted from indigenous churches such as Revival and Pocomania, and (2) music composed in the local idiom. In the case of Jamaica, O'Gorman notes that the latter "is usually identifiable by the frequent use of syncopation or by an inherent idiomatic rhythmic background (e.g., Mento or Rastafarian) or, along with either or both of these, the use of melodic motifs commonly found in Jamaican folk song."[22]

Much of what is called indigenous folk liturgical singing is in reality a transformation of European and North American hymns and songs into local rhythmic patterns. It is common to take straightforward metrical hymns and transpose them into the rhythms of the Caribbean. Marjorie Whylie of the Jamaica School of Music argued long ago that European songs should be set to Caribbean arrangements, since traditional hymns do lend themselves to rhythm. For example, "normal Jamaican common rhythmic patterns are all double and quadruple for the most part. . . . Therefore those hymns that are written in simple double can be arranged so as to bring in certain rhythmic components."[23] When these hymns of European and North American origin are transformed into neo-African and Caribbean form, with their "harsh vocal timbre, percussive accompaniment, rhythmic body movement, improvisation and spontaneous harmonization,"[24] they are considered to belong to Caribbean heritage folk music. Revival and Pocomania movements in Jamaica, and Spiritual Baptists in Trinidad and Tobago have transformed many hymns of Ira D. Sankey (the musician who worked closely with Dwight L. Moody) into the rhythms of the Caribbean as well as into local dialects.[25]

Many churches are following in the footsteps of these movements and are transforming a number of traditional hymns. But it is also in vogue to utilize music from Caribbean Pentecostalism in worship services. Some of these are taken from hymnals published by revivalists in the United States. But many are choruses of local composition and are passed on orally. Some short songs are actually single stanzas taken from older, longer hymns. "All of the choruses and hymns," says Hopkin, "are simple and repetitious, and have a solid, square and predictable quality in both the melody and rhythm, as well as in the chordings that the church instrumentalists give them."[26]

Singing in Pentecostal services, as well as contemporary services in many traditional churches, occupies a significant length of time—in many instances more than half the service. A typical service is described by Hopkin:

> They sing at the start of the service, before announcements, during the collection, in between testimonies, in the middle of the many brief messages, after the main sermon, and any other time a hymn may fit in. Frequently most of the

congregation stays after the service is over in order to sing still more. Occasionally the choir prepares a hymn in advance and sings it alone during the service, but for the most part the entire congregation does the singing, with the choir scarcely differentiated from the rest of the people. Sometimes the preacher calls for a song, giving a hymn-book number if the hymn is not well known, and begins singing it himself or turns to the choir to begin it. At other times some member of the choir or congregation begins singing some familiar hymn and the rest of the congregation soon picks it up. Songs frequently seem to arise almost spontaneously from the congregation, so quickly do the worshipers join in.[27]

In most Caribbean churches four-part harmony has been the norm for congregational singing, with or without instrumentation. Pentecostals, however, utilize only a two- or three-part harmony: a melody line, a line harmonizing the melody, and possibly a bass line. Again Hopkin is helpful in describing harmonization in Pentecostal worship:

The harmony parts are not always carried through; they are often broken, coming in wherever they happen to fit conveniently. No one arranges these harmonies, nor do the people read them from a book, since very few can read music. Neither do the singers memorize their parts in advance. Yet the musical tradition and its harmonic style are sufficiently engrained and well enough understood that there is general agreement among the people as to what the counter-melodies should be, and conflicts between the parts are minor and rare. The singers are capable of improvising parts in an unfamiliar song. Frequently one person, in singing two or more verses of the same song, may retain the fundamentals of a certain harmony part, but fail to duplicate it a second time around. Individuals in the congregation do not consistently sing one part, especially if there are three or four to choose from—they often skip from one to another in the course of a single hymn.[28]

Attempts to set old or foreign hymns to Caribbean tunes or rhythms have generally been applauded. However, for many this does not go far enough. Music and song need to reflect the mood, spirit, temperament and theology of the Caribbean person.[29] Caribbean churches are thus searching for songs and hymns that truly reflect their culture and experiences. Barry Chevannes has been a pioneer in this enterprise. In the 1970s, while attending a Catholic seminary in the United States, he became involved in the folk movement and was also greatly influenced by the black consciousness movement. On his return to Jamaica he began to write folk masses that reflected the theology and cultural experiences of his own people.[30]

Since Chevannes, more and more songs have been composed that express the meaning of existence of Caribbean peoples. New hymnody has blossomed that focuses on the poverty, oppression, injustice and pain borne by the masses, such as Victor H. Job's "Lord God of All the Nations"[31] (which I have had my congregation sing to the tune of "Lead on, O King Eternal").

Other recent hymns clearly reject the colonial ethos and use illustrations and metaphors to which the Caribbean person can relate. Of course, lyrics that speak of snow-capped mountains and changing seasons are foreign to everyday Caribbean experience.[32] But hymns like Hugh B. Sherlock's "God of the Earth and Sky" resonate in the soul of the Caribbean worshiper.

Caribbean liturgists are composing hymns that reflect the daily experiences and cultural and linguistic norms of the people. Although much of the contextualizing of theology, tunes, rhythms, lyrics and performances has been done by Catholics, these new songs have had some widespread appeal.[33] Father Richard Ho Lung, from inner-city Kingston, Jamaica, has been at the forefront of this enterprise. He argues that "spiritual truths must be conveyed through Jamaican local images. For example, struggle for labor, survival." Jamaican music, he says, is a "struggle religious music."[34]

Pamela O'Gorman, in her fine piece "The Introduction of Jamaican Music into the Established Churches," reports that when songs like these, with their dialect and Afro-Caribbean rhythms, were first introduced into the "higher-class" churches, clergy and the parishioners reacted with considerable consternation. Even today, she says, many worshipers react to such worship music with "stunned silence, if not outright resistance."[35] Yet these songs have become the lingua franca of many churches, vindicating of the bold moves of liturgists like Chevannes and Ho Lung. Thus the liturgical needs of Caribbean people are being more fully met by music and song that are indigenous to their daily experience.

The Caribbean church as a whole has not gone indigenous. Even many lower-class churchgoers still see the introduction of such folksy and rhythmic music into the church as an unfortunate encroachment of secularism inspired by Satan. For many, only the traditional way will do. One young Jamaican worshiper objected, "We can never do without the old traditional music because it was specially made for church."[36] But the fact is that the old taboos against Afro-Caribbeancentric worship are disintegrating. Chevannes himself expresses surprise:

> Some of the most favorite Revival Zion and Pukumina choruses are occasionally sung in church, and, much to my own amazement, I have seen congregations wave arms above their heads in imitation of the gesture of greeting the spirits. These innovations in certain quarters seem inspired by the felt need to attract and hold the youth, but overall they remain impulses, rather than part of a coherent programme of liturgical reforms. Nevertheless, they betoken a recognition that certain forms of worship indigenous to the people need no longer be condemned as expressions of the devil himself, and may be appropriated.[37]

In conclusion, let me make it clear that I am not arguing that Caribbean worship should discard the Western traditions of worship. These liturgical traditions are also part and parcel of the Caribbean culture. My desire is to highlight the incorporation of the fullness of the Caribbean experience in worship.

Too often the Euro-American ethos entirely dominates the worship service; in many such cases worship scratches where people are not itching. Too often we are wedded to the rusty old organ that has no appeal to the soul of the islander. How much more alive would the worship experience be if the steel pan and the reggae rhythms in themselves were not seen as sensual, sacrilegious and carnal but as elements that can awaken the spiritual chords of the soul.

Yes, we must be careful not to make the liturgy a musical performance or a nightclub entertainment.[38] But churches and communities that have successfully incorporated music with African elements are the ones that have made Christ central in all their musical expressions.

The Word &
the Response

A *widely held opinion throughout the Caribbean is that the three* most important persons in a town or village are the preacher, the police officer and the physician. The "parson" or pastor is held in high esteem, and many congregations expect this leader to be different from ordinary persons.[1] In a sense he or she is a superperson, because "a part of the egos of all the individuals in the congregation are collected in the leader, for he [or she] is the centre of, and [spokesperson] for, the communal religious experience."[2]

The Word

Above and beyond all else, the congregation looks to the minister to present the Word. In the Caribbean this is still the major event in the worship service. It is the psychological moment when a cross-section of Caribbean society is "most predisposed to truth and most responsive to challenge and to change."[3] William W. Watty, former president of the University Theological College of the West Indies, explains:

> No other institution enjoys such an opportunity. The nearest event compara-
> ble is the political meeting prior to elections which, in many countries of the
> Caribbean, has over the years been patterned after a Sunday night service.
> But at such meetings the people who are gathered do not wish or expect to
> hear the truth. They come partly to give moral support and partly for fun.
> They warm to promises, not challenges. They want reaffirmation, not conver-
> sion.[4]

The effective Caribbean pastor is charismatic, emanating confidence and power. The preacher (particularly the male minister) possesses positive overwhelming presence in the pulpit which the congregation feels intensely. Hopkin notes that "students of psychology might point out the sexual nature of this near-deification of the leader, describing him as some sort of father-lover figure."[5] (Some surmise this is the reason most congregations have more women than men.) The pastor is ultimately perceived as God's divinely inspired representative on earth, one who speaks for God and speaks to God on behalf of the worshiping community. In another sense he represents the congregation as he speaks and acts. For example, when he says, "I feel good today" or "I'm so happy," the congregation will always respond in the affirmative: "Amen," or "Yes, we feel good today."[6]

The most poignant moment in the service is the point when the "breaking of the Word" begins. In many churches, but especially charismatic churches, the sermon begins around noon and goes for approximately an hour. Depending on the preacher's theological training (or lack thereof), the delivery is either well structured or extemporaneous.

The Caribbean preacher may draw on a variety of styles. Quite popular are lectures in which numerous scriptural quotations are given in order to bring home the message. The European/Western influence is clearly seen in this mode, in which the overarching goal is a cerebral ascertainment of truth. But there is also the storytelling style. Consciously or unconsciously, the storytelling preacher is following an Eastern or African model. These sermons consist of a series of parables or stories around a particular theme. Christopher Walker reports on a storytelling pastor in Tobago who uses inflection, beginning with a whisper to engage the listener and then booming out with authority to drive home the point:

> Yesterday I was speaking to a young man and he said, "Brother Pressley," he said, "I heard Brother Lee the other day at Sangre Grande. And Brother Pressley," he said, "I was amzaed at Brother Lee."
>
> I said, "Why?"
>
> He said, "When I knew him years ago, he had a voice like a woman. When he start to preach, his voice would go up, up, up, up, up." [this spoken softly in an ascending scale]
>
> But he said, "Brother Pressley, I listened to Brother Lee and I was amazed." He said, "That voice doesn't go high up like a woman's anymore, but now he commands himself and preaches with such AUTHORITY!"
>
> AT AGE SEVENTY!
>
> IMPROVE YOURSELF!
>
> AMEN! [this delivered in basso profundo at full amplitude][7]

A delivery style that is gaining wide acceptance throughout the Caribbean is almost identical to black preaching in the United States, as described earlier. In John Hopkin's field study in Kingston, he found this style prevalent. The preacher usually begins with an inspirational tone that is otherwise reserved for prayer and testimony. The message is delivered "in mellifluous phrases and religiously weighted words."[8] The sermon is improvised, alternating between Spirit-inspired words and words focusing on a biblical passage or a Christian theme.

The congregation reinforces the speaker's words with "Yes man!" and "Amen!" The preacher encourages this reinforcement with "Praise the Lord!" The congregation responds, "Praise him!" This call and response aids the preacher as he or she becomes more worked up and the energy level intensifies. The worshiper's response becomes increasingly emphatic. Volume and voice timbre change by degrees, becoming increasingly raspy and covering a wide range of pitches. Gestures become more animated, and sweat pours profusely. Speech and body movements become more rhythmic.

As the rhythmic drive intensifies, the congregation is drawn in. "They become a metric punctuation, as the pauses that they fill grow more frequent and consistent."[9] As the sermon climaxes the gestures of the speaker become more animated: "he swings his arms, stalks the stage, turns away from the microphone between phrases and whirls back to deliver his next words with all his force, nearly mouthing the microphone as he shouts."[10] He pounds the podium after each phrase in rhythmic punctuation. The rhythm drives the exposition.

Often sermon consists of many such peaks and climaxes, in which preacher and congregation are driven into what one might call a state of frenzy. Then the preacher breaks the rhythm, comes down and slowly begins rebuilding to an intense climax. Each time, says Hopkin, "he creates climaxes more intense and more sustained until he reaches a degree of tension that seems to be as far as preacher and congregation can go."[11] The sermon usually concludes on a quieter tone as the appeal is made.

Musicality in preaching is also becoming widespread in Caribbean churches. During the sermon the preacher's vocal intonation ranges from "singsong" to "chantlike," though it rarely has definite pitches. This musicality induces the congregants to respond. For many the effectiveness of a sermon lies in the rhythms and pitches and the responses to them.[12]

The Response
Wholistic worship in the Caribbean involves a response to the working of the Spirit through music and the Word. Styles and levels of response vary from congregation to congregation. It has been noted that some sermons include the call-and-response element common in the African-American church. Quite often one might hear cries of "Thank you, Jesus!" Praise God!" "Praise Jesus!" "Amen!" "Hallelu-

jah!" "Preach it!" "That's right!" At times when the emotional temperature in the worship is down, the preacher might say, "Come on! Hello? Are you with me?" Such calls engage the congregation to remain in active participation in the service, even during the sermon.

One of the more popular responses is the altar call. Following the climactic end of the sermon, the preacher calls for a quieter song, during which he or she beings to speak to the congregation in lyrical tones. The altar call is more personal than communal (as was the sermon). The preacher makes a plea: "Is there anyone here today . . . is there one soul today who will come forward and lay his or her soul on the altar?" One by one, congregants move to the front while they continue to sing and the preacher calls and prays. Thus the altar call provides another opportunity for movement and bodily activity within the service.

The most intense response is in the reception of the Spirit. As noted in an earlier chapter, possibly the most important aspect of the worship or ceremonies of Afro-Caribbean religion (such as Orisha, Spiritual Baptists, Pocomania and Revival) is possession by spirits or the Spirit. For a number of churches, particularly Pentecostals, possession by the Holy Spirit is paramount—not because it is African but because they see it as a New Testament mandate.

In Pentecostal churches possession by the Holy Spirit may begin to take place during the sermon. Call-and-response exclamations may be followed by an individual's jumping and twisting and speaking in tongues. At times the person is "slain in the Spirit"—a seizure that may last three to four hours.

Of course, as Hopkin points out, manifestations of possession vary from one individual to another because the Spirit works differently through different people:

> Sometimes the seizure comes on very gradually, beginning with rocking back and forth or swinging the arms, accompanied by intermittent jerks or cries, then slowly moves to glossolalia, dancing and other manifestations. At other times some individual will jump up with shocking abruptness, screaming,

sweating and struggling in the aisle as neighbours rush to restrain her, pull from harm's way a nearby child, or guide her away from obstacles. The external manifestations of seizure always include sweating, heavy breathing, and increased heart-beat, and a facial expression revealing intense feeling. Worshippers may throw back their heads or buckle over forward, hop or stamp or just walk, flail their arms about or wrap them tightly around their body. Usually the muscles become tense and movements are, as a result, abrupt and rigid. The possessed person usually cries out or speaks in tongues and may shed tears. Afterwards they report that during the seizure they are totally or very nearly unaware of all this; that they are conscious primarily of the feeling of the spirit moving in them—a very tangible physical feeling regardless of the nature of, or absence of, accompanying emotional or cerebral experience. When a large number of people are seized by the spirit, with all the attendant cries and motion, the atmosphere of the church becomes so electric with the emotional and religious energy of the assembled throng that no one can fail to feel its excitement.[13]

Another response that is increasingly finding its niche in the worship service is dance. This grows out of the recognition by Afro-Caribbean peoples that they are whole persons, body and soul, and thus cannot worship in a dichotomized manner in which bodily movement is suppressed. Pentecostal congregations and people in other African-rooted movements worship with body, mind and spirit. More and more people from the middle classes are recognizing the need for such wholistic worship; while retaining membership in Euro-American cultural denominations, they also attend services where there is dancing and other forms of movement.

The established churches' negative attitude to dancing goes back to colonial days. In 1852 Charles W. Day, a resident of Trinidad, expressed his annoyance with the black slaves' drumming and dancing:

The drumming on the abominably monotonous tum-tum, the singing in chorus, accompanied by the simultaneous clapping of the hands, are all very well for once; but novelty over, they become extremely disagreeable.

Every night there was a dance amongst the negroes on the estate, to the banishment of all peace and quiet. The horrible drumming began about seven in the evening, and with the chorus, was kept up until daybreak the next morning.[14]

Another observer in 1862 records the emotional and physical behaviour in the church that he addressed:

The chapel was full of people awaiting our arrival. Though we were very dirty, we immediately commenced the service: I addressed them from Luke XV, 10. Towards its close, some symptoms of excitement betrayed the emotional character of the people, and I rather hastily concluded. One woman swayed her body from side to side, and was scarcely held on her seat by her neighbors.[15]

These accounts demonstrate that dance is not a modern Pentecostal phenomenon. It is natural for people of African descent to dance and move their bodies rhythmically. In a conversation, a visiting professor from Nigeria, Funso Aiye Jinai, commented on African-American and Afro-Caribbean people's intrinsic rhythm:

When you look at aspects of black life, look at black people, their mannerisms are completely different from the Caucasian mannerisms. Watch a Michael Jordan move on the court; what you are watching there is, perhaps, the rhythm now transferred into the realm of sports. We watch them greet each other, the way they greet each other after a successful basket, or a crucial basket is different from the way the [Caucasians do]. Even the Caucasian players are trying to do the same thing.[16]

Rhythm is part and parcel of the essential being of the Caribbean person. As Idris Hamid states, "It quickens the being of the Caribbean man . . . . His soul or spirit responds more to the rhythmic than any other thing."[17] It is a pity that dance has been long limited to nonliturgical events and left out of praise and worship. Haitian Frank Fouche expresses in a poem how dance is deep in the soul of the Caribbean, describing theirs as "a land of dance and song."[18]

Song and dance, music and bodily movement go together in the Caribbean psyche. If music and song are an integral part of worship, dance should be as well.

Some are concerned about sexual overtones in dance movements. In Hopkin's field study of Pentecostals in Jamaica he observed that the religious dance had motions resembling standard Jamaican dance movements. However, a careful observation demonstrated that none of the motions could be construed as erotic in nature.[19]

The same question has been raised about Cumina ceremonies in which dance is prominent. But clearly

> there is no question that the dances are religious in character. Sex offenses are not observed at ceremonials; to perform a sexual act during a Cumina is to show disrespect towards the ancestral zombies and one's own family. What appear to an outsider as movements suggestive of sexual acts are performed by old men and women, young people, and even children without any of the implications the North American would ascribe to them. Because the cultural attitude of these people towards sex is not furtive, therefore, their bodily motions, regardless of their specific character, are meant to be regarded without underlying implications and are accepted as part of the variety of dance movement.[20]

When dance is incorporated in the Caribbean worship service it is not for the purpose of giving vent to one's erotic feelings nor to bring the dance hall into the house of God. On the contrary, it is for the purpose of "recovering their authentic selves"[21] in praise to God and in a wholistic celebration of what he has done.

Part 4

Hispanic
Worship

In the Spirit
of a Fiesta

P *robably the most difficult question to answer in this section is,* Who are Hispanics? Before we can describe their worship, it is essential to define this group. The task becomes complex when we realize that *Hispanic* is only one among several competing terms to categorize this segment of peoples in the New World. Other identifying nomenclatures, such as *Latino, Latina, Chicano, Chicana, Spanish American* and *Spanish-speaking*, are all commonly used as synonyms for *Hispanic* or subunits of what some perceive as a race of people.

Almost all serious studies on Hispanics point to the inadequacy of any one umbrella term to cover so diverse a group of people.[1] It is a serious error of judgment to make sweeping generalizations regarding a people who should not be seen as monolithic and undifferentiated, as if they shared the same origins, history, culture and customs. Any generalizations need to be made with caution. Discussions that evoke an image of uniformity and ignore geographical, ethnic, cultural, ideological and social differences will inevitably fail to do justice to these complex people we call Hispanics.

Rather than offering a simple definition or characterization, it may be more productive to give an overview of the history and demographics of this segment of American society that mostly speaks Spanish and has roots in such lands as Mexico, Puerto Rico and Cuba. This will be followed by a discussion of two distinctive features of their religious life: popular religiosity and the fiesta spirit.

History and Demographics

The Hispanic is a mixture (in varying degrees) of European Spaniards, American Indians and African blacks. Each of these groups— the Spanish conquistadors and farmers, the Aztecs, Incas and Taínos, and the African slaves—has contributed to the creation of a new people and a new civilization with new cultural presuppositions.

Although this civilization is a mere five hundred years old, its historical and cultural roots are deeper in Europe, the Pacific Islands, Asia and Africa. Francis Buckley explains how cultural traits of these ancient civilizations were grafted into the modern Hispanic:

> Spanish culture from the Iberian peninsula was melded from the traditions of the Celts, the Romans, the Goths, and the Moors. So, too, the many Hispanic cultures of Latin America are themselves amalgams of values brought by those who migrated into the Western Hemisphere during the last 50,000 years. The Polynesians brought a sense of inner calm, strength, and dignity, together with a tradition of service. The Asians brought a deep devotion to family, a feel for unity within nature, a delicate sensitivity to the feeling of others (reflected in indirect communication and an unwillingness to say "No"). Africans reinforced an already existing love of ritual and plastic arts.[2]

There is not one monolithic Hispanic people, culture or story. The peoples are as varied as their backgrounds. Throughout Latin America, Hispanics with strong European backgrounds differ significantly from those with deep Amerindian roots, just as those whose forebears were mostly African slaves differ from those whose family history goes back for centuries in what is now the southwestern United States. These differences go even deeper and wider. David Abalos illustrates this when he notes that Hispanics from the urban centers of Chile are quite different from those who come from the rural areas of Guatemala. Hispanics who were born in the United States are different in attitude and outlook from those who arrived only recently. Mexicans who live on the U.S. border see themselves as distinct from those who reside on the Guatemalan border. Hispanics differ in class origins, degrees of racial mixture, facial features and complexions.[3] Each of these differences is accompanied by unique and particular histories, stories, characteristics and cultural expressions.

These histories, stories and cultural expressions can be recognized (sometimes easily, sometimes with more difficulty) in the Hispanic population throughout the United States. It is, however, more manageable to divide Hispanics into historical and geographical divisions. One common grouping is fivefold: (1) Mexicans, (2) Central Americans, (3) the Caribbean peoples (Cubans, Puerto Ricans, Dominicans), (4) the Andean peoples, and (5) the borderlands peoples of the American Southwest and California.[4] Time and space will not allow a focus on all these groupings here. Instead I will highlight those I perceive to have had the greatest impact on the North American scene: Mexicans and those from the islands of the Caribbean or Antilles.

Mexican-Americans. Although Hispanics of Mexican descent can be found throughout the United States, the largest concentration is in the Southwest (especially southern California, Arizona, New Mexico and Texas). It is common to assume the reason is that most Mexicans in the United States crossed the border illegally and settled in the nearest city. The fact is, however, that many are indigenous to the Southwest. They were here for generations antedating the annexation by the United States in 1848.[5] In Yolanda Tarango's insightful words, "the border crossed us, we did not cross the border."[6] The proximity of the American Southwest to Mexico and the continual flow of immigrants have brought about the maintenance of the Mexican language and culture in the United States even numerous decades after annexation.

Persons of Mexican background constitute the largest Hispanic group in the United States, and this group is growing faster then any other. Allan Figueroa Deck figures that the Hispanic population in California constitutes 31 percent of the entire U.S. Hispanic population and 41 percent of the entire Hispanic population of Mexican origin. Furthermore, 20 percent of California's entire population has Mexican roots.[7]

Not surprisingly, the bulk of Mexican-Americans are Catholic. In a 1970 survey done by Leo Grebler, Joan Moore and Ralph Guzman, only 5 percent of those professing a religion in Los Angeles and San Antonio were Protestants.[8] Mexican-American Protestants were not only quantitatively insignificant in Protestantism but also rather isolated from the majority of Mexican-Americans who are Catholic, as well as from the majority of Protestants who are non-Hispanic.[9] This isolation and relative insignificance have changed in recent decades with the mainstreaming of Protestantism within the Hispanic world, particularly due to the enormous growth of Pentecostalism (a phenomenon that will be discussed more fully later).

Caribbean peoples. The same is true for Puerto Ricans, who constitute the second largest Hispanic group in the United States. Most are concentrated in the Northeast, particularly New York and New Jersey, But there is a significant presence in the Midwestern industrial states, especially the Chicago area.

Puerto Ricans are particularly racially diverse. A large group are white, descendants of the Spanish colonizers. There is also a significant percent of the population that exhibits a mixture of Indian and Spanish. In certain regions the African element is more pronounced. During the latter part of the eighteenth century and the beginning of the nineteenth, the slave population grew markedly due to the importation of Yorubas from West Africa.[10] This group was influential in the Africanization of popular religion on the island.

The third largest Hispanic community in the United States is the Cubans. As the twenty-first century begins, the majority of Cubans are still first-generation immigrants[11] who reside mostly in south Florida, particularly Miami. Large concentrations, however, can be found in the New York and New Jersey areas.

This large number of Cuban immigrants is a consequence of four waves of migration from Cuba following the 1959 revolution led by Fidel Castro. The first wave brought the so-called golden exiles,[12] members of the Cuban upper clear who brought with them professional skills and investment capital. They were well educated, older and overwhelmingly white.

In 1966 and 1973 two more waves of Cubans brought fewer resources. In 1980 the final wave arrived in a fleet of small boats. These people were known as the *marielitos* or "Mariel Cubans" (Mariel being the point from which they left). They were quite different from the earlier immigrants: younger, poorer and mostly black. Among them were mental patients and prisoners. Though they were settled in various parts of the United States, most seem to have returned to Florida.[13]

The first wave of Cubans assimilated into mainstream American society much more than the later immigrants. Their rate of intermarriage with non-Hispanics is very high, and they have transformed south Florida, especially Miami, into a thriving business mecca.

Other Hispanic groups. Other Hispanics in the United States come mostly from the Dominican Republic, Central America and South America. The Dominicans (many of whom are undocumented immigrants) have come mostly from Santo Domingo (the capital) and have settled in the Northeast, particularly New York City. They are mostly from the lower socioeconomic class in Santo Domingo but are moving up the economic ladder in the United States. They are becoming U.S. citizens in growing numbers. As long ago as 1975, 13 percent of the Hispanics in New York were Dominicans.[14]

Most immigrants from Central America arrived in the United States without legal documents. Many were refugees from the revolutions that plagued Central and South America in the late twentieth century. The newest Central American immigrants, however, tend to be "economic refugees" who are fleeing hopeless poverty in their homelands. As they seek economic prosperity in a "promised land," they bring with them new and varied cultural expressions that enrich the Hispanic presence in America.

These varied groups of Hispanics that come to the United States face problems of adjustment and the pressure of assimilation in a strange new environment. At times the clash of cultures is quite traumatic. The problem of adjustment is complicated by the issue of ethnicity. Particularly in recent times, arrivals from Cuba, Dominican Republic and Puerto Rico have had racial features ranging from very Negroid to very Caucasian.[15] The Negroid Hispanics are identified as black and thus face the same challenges as African-Americans. Mexicans who cross the border similarly range from those who are quite Native Indian to those who are very European in features. The majority are *mestizos* (mixed Indian and European). These are also exposed to the racial discrimination that plagues ethnic groups of color in the United States—a problem that for the most part was not a challenge to European immigrants. This challenge forced Hispanics to discover and celebrate their cultural roots and ethnic backgrounds.[16]

Most Hispanics, belong to one of four religious groupings: Catholic, evangelical Protestant, Pentecostal and African primal religions.[17] Although the vast majority are (or at least identify themselves as) Roman Catholic, a large and growing segment of the Hispanic population identify themselves as adherents of the other groups. Otto Maduro suggested in 1995 that this number is probably already beyond one-third of all Hispanics.[18] This shift especially holds true in major urban areas, particularly among those who have migrated from a rural environment.[19]

Gilbert Cadena gives us a demographic breakdown:[20] the 1990 CUNY National Survey of Religious Identification reported that 66 percent identified themselves as Catholic and 23 percent as Protestant or belonging to another Christian religious group. Among the Protestants, the breakdown was as follows: 7 percent were Baptists while Pentecostals, Jehovah's Witnesses and Methodists were about 2 percent each. Four percent were affiliated with other religious groups, and 6 percent had no religion.

Cadena also cites the Latino National Political Survey (1992) as the most comprehensive study of Hispanics to date.[21] This study reported that 60 to 82 percent identified themselves as being Catholic. The geographical breakdown is of interest:

> Foreign born Latinos had higher proportions of Catholic affiliations than U.S.-born Latinos. Mexican-origin individuals had the highest prevalence of Catholic affiliation followed by Cuban-origin and Puerto Rican-origin Latinos. For example, among Mexican-origin individuals, 82% of Mexican-born and 73% of Chicanos are Catholic. For Cubans, 80% of island-born and 64% of U.S.-born are Catholic. Among Puerto Ricans, 68% of island-born and 60% of U.S.-born are Catholic. Protestant affiliation ranges from less than 10% to over 20%. For example, 8% of Mexican-born and 16% of Chicanos are Protestant. Puerto Ricans have the highest rate of Protestantism with 23% island-born and 21% mainland-born compared to 14% of Cuban-born and 10% of Cuban Americans. Finally, Latinos having other religious affiliations or no religious preferences are as follows: Mexican-born (10%) and Chicana/o (11%); Puerto Rican-born (9%) and Puerto Rican American (19%); and Cuban-born (6%) and Cuban American (26%).[22]

Religiosidad Popular

Hispanic spirituality, as expressed in worship and other religious activities, is rooted in a complex cultural and historical phenomenon known as *religiosidad popular*, or popular religiosity. It has been defined as "the complexes of *spontaneous* expressions of faith which have been celebrated by the masses over a considerable period of time."[23] They are "spontaneous" because they arise out of the historic cultural world of the people and are not mandated by a church hierarchy.

This popular religiosity involves the very being and essence of what it means to be Hispanic. It is part of their cultural personality. In *religiosidad popular*, culture and religious sensibilities are combined—a combination that neither official Catholicism or

Protestantism is able to erase.[24]

Hispanics in the United States have come to the realization that for their way of life to survive, this aspect of their cultural spirituality cannot be allowed to expire. For this reason worship has become a medium in the fight for preservation. As analyzed by Virgilio Elizondo, this involves a battle against the Anglo-Saxon religious tradition and worldview:

> The beginning of the Americas reflects two radically distinct images/ myth representations of the Christian tradition. The United States was born as a secular enterprise with a deep sense of religious mission. The native religions were eliminated and supplanted by a new type of religion. Puritan moralism, Presbyterian righteousness and Methodist social consciousness coupled with deism and the spirit of rugged individualism to provide a sound basis for the new nationalism which would function as the core religion of the land. It was quite different in Latin America where the religion of the old European world clashed with native religious traditions. In their efforts to uproot the native religions, the conquerors found themselves assumed into them.[25]

Popular religiosity, therefore, involves expressions of faith that has its roots not only in the Spanish Christian tradition but in Amerindian and African traditions as well. In some instances the Spanish predominates, in others the Amerindian or the African is dominant. Thus contemporary Hispanic worship, whether Catholic or Protestant, cannot be understood or appreciated apart from an understanding of the religiocultural historic synthesis.

Amerindian. It has rightly been noted that the Amerindian contribution to the Hispanic heritage has been grossly underestimated. The impact of native peoples is still evident even in areas where they were decimated. "Indians were decimated but did not become extinct," says Juan José Arrom. "During the initial process or transculturation, together with their tangible and visible customs, they may have left us some of their invisible and innermost feelings."[26]

The Mexican tradition can serve to illustrate the deeply religious orientation of Amerindian peoples. Ricardo Ramirez is clear that the Mexican tradition is above all a *religious* one. Atheism did not exist in pre-Columbian America. Indians, like most non-Westerners, held to a worldview that was wholistically spiritual. The indigenous line of the Hispanic "is concerned through and through with the divine, with cosmic powers of good and evil, gods, goddesses, each with its own myths, with sacrifice, death and resurrection."[27] The Amerindian is fascinated with the transcendent. Divine qualities are attributed to all elements of nature, and all things have divine origins. Pre-Columbian spirituality therefore expressed itself in popular rituals that emphasized both the transcendence and the immanence of the divine. There was also "emphasis on the cosmic rituals expressing the harmonious unity of opposing tensions: male and female, suffering and happiness, self-immanence and transcendence, individual and group, sacred and profane, life and death."[28]

One other characteristic of Amerindian life that has influenced Hispanic popular religion is a strong concept of community. For the indigenous Indian, participation in the collective group was the basis of existence. "It was not the individuals who by coming together made up the community, but rather it was the community which . . . actually brought the individual person into existence."[29] Communal consciousness thus permeated all of life, including primal practices and rituals. Family, economics, politics, education, social life and religion were all communally oriented. Given this, we can see why *religiosidad popular* is not an individualistic matter between a person and God but a communal affair involving the divine and the community.

African. The African contribution to Hispanic heritage dates from the moment Africans appeared on Western shores in the sixteenth century. Their influence is evident in the mysterious and sensual rhythms of their music ("los ritmos misteriosos y sensuales de su música"), which was filled with spiritual feeling straight from the heart of Africa ("impregnada de espiritualismos propios del corazón de África").[30] The influence was evident just as much in dance, folklore and popular religiosity, particularly in the Hispanic islands of the Caribbean.

In the spirituality of many Hispanics, popular European or Mediterranean Christianity is syncretistically woven with African beliefs such as "the presence of the spirits of nature in the inexplicable and uncontrollable events of life."[31] Thus we find that much island popular religiosity belongs to a world in which the spirits (Spirit) and the marvelous play a significant role. It is quite common to find a Puerto Rican attending Mass on a Sunday morning, worshiping at a Pentecostal church the same afternoon and consulting a *curandera* or *espiritista* in the evening.[32]

As in the English-speaking Caribbean, African culture was brought across the Atlantic to Latin America by Yoruba slaves. It has been argued that there is no evidence of Yorubas being brought to Puerto Rico and thus African influence on Puerto Rican religion is minimal. But although manifestations of Yoruba culture on this island are limited given its small number of Africans as compared to its neighbors Hispaniola and Cuba, it is now quite clear that Puerto Rico received its share of Yoruba slaves, especially in the latter eighteenth and early nineteenth centuries.[33] Their influence on Puerto Rican religion is undeniable, even though less documented than in Puerto Rico's sister to the east, Cuba.

The African influence on religious life in Cuba is especially known through the practices of Santería (saint worship). Yoruba priests and priestesses of the Orishas intermingled their traditional practices with European Catholicism. There is considerable parallel with the Shango practices of Trinidad:

> Santería was the worship of the Yoruba god Ogun in the form of San Juan (St. John). Santería cultists worshipped Ogun as Ogun Arere, the warrior, Ogun Oke, the hunter, and Ogun Aguanille, the metal worker. While Ogun might have been the chief divinity of Santería belief, doubtless the cultists combined the worship of this Yoruba divinity with that of other gods; in this respect . . . the Cuban Santería would not have been different from Shango as it came to be practised in Trinidad.[34]

As in Trinidad, the African slaves learned enough about the Catholic saints to equate them with the Yoruba divinities. And the religious practices of Roman Catholicism were intermingled with religious devotion remembered from Africa to create a new synthesis called Santería.

Among the Cubans who have migrated to the United States since the Cuban revolution of 1959 are many priests and priestesses of Santería. The bulk of these came with the second wave of immigrants, which included a higher percentage of blacks than the first. With more devotees of the Orishas living in the United States, there has been an invigoration of all African-derived traditions. It has been suggested that "devotion to the *orishas* is fast becoming one of the preeminent models for the revival of African consciousness in the United States. As more and more people of African descent throughout the Americas look to find what is African in the designation African American, they are finding the traditions of the *orishas* to be their inspiration and guide."[35]

Joseph Murphy has described how Santería has helped the new immigrants, who find themselves "emmeshed in a new system of social organization and stratification."[36] Through the *ilé* (a mutual aid society), Santería provides a way Hispanics can leave behind externals and oppressive markers of identity and "reaffirm one family, one house in the spirit."[37]

This is demonstrated in a number of ways. Murphy notes that most *santeras* and *santeros* work as domestics and laborers. These jobs are rarely secure. Members of an *ilé* therefore turn to the spirits for help in facing the very practical problems stemming from unemployment, poverty and racism. The *ilé* is a close-knit community that provides material support for its members. Just as important are its services in health and healing—particularly the *santeras* and *santeros'* diagnostic skills and herbal treatments.

> The ilé has provided a fraternal and sororal support system for some of the most oppressed people on earth. It has acted as a family in a society where no family life was possible and as a lodge to ease the burdens of the cultural dissociations that its members have been forced to undergo. What gives meaning to these medical, social and cultural functions of the *ilé* is the service

rendered to the *orishas*. In the minds of its members, the core function of the *ilé* is to honor the spirits and receive from them in turn guidance and assistance in all of life's endeavors. The *orishas* offer their children spiritual experience and heavenly wisdom which is marked by progress in the initiatory hierarchy of the *ilé*. The *ilé* sets out a path of spiritual growth, a road *en santo*.[38]

A number of significant changes to Santería have occurred within the Cuban diaspora in the United States. Its features have been adapted to the new environment and to the needs of its followers both old and new. Whereas in Cuba followers were almost exclusively Afro-Cubans with Yoruba roots, in the United States we find many followers of Santería who are of non-African descent. White *santeros* and *santeras* have gained a prominence and visibility in the United States which they did not have on the island.[39] In reality, what we find as Santería in the United States is a version of the original Yoruba Orisha religion that was uprooted, syncretized, Cubanized and now Americanized.

Roman Catholic. Religiosidad popular has been influenced not only by the native Amerindians or the imported Yoruba Africans but also to a very large degree by the Catholic tradition from Spain, which gained a mystical twist during the centuries of Moorish domination.[40]

We may say that in many respects the *religiosidad popular* of Latin America and of the Hispanic peoples of the United States is a continuation and adaptation of the Mediterranean version of orthodox Catholicism as lived by the *pueblo* of the Iberian peninsula—a plant transplanted to a new but not altogether alien environment, grafted onto peoples whose cultures were not ultimately incompatible with it, and naturally growing and developing under the influence of its new circumstances, but still in continuity with its Iberian and Mediterranean origins.[41]

James Vidal notes that like every other region of European Christendom, Iberia had a rich popular religiosity—a way of worshiping and living the common faith that was not as intellectual as that of the official hierarchy and was more local in its orientation. This "religiosity . . . instinctively incorporated the archetypes and images of Mediterranean religion into the praxis and imagery of monotheistic Christianity."[42] Vidal suggests that when brought to the Americas, the Mediterranean religiosity "shared many archetypes and assumptions with the world view of the native civilizations, and that this made it much easier for the native Americans to accept it, and enter into it wholeheartedly."[43] Of course, as noted earlier, this resulted in quite a bit of syncretism—for example, the Yoruba slaves equated their African gods with the Catholic saints.

Yet much of Hispanic popular religion falls within the boundaries of "orthodox" European Christian faith. This includes many of the sacraments and symbols passed on by the conquistadors—incense lights, liturgical ornaments, vestments, rituals, statues and images, holy places and the like.[44] The place of saints and the Virgin (especially among those who revere the Virgin of Guadalupe) is also significantly high in popular religiosity. Interestingly, however, as Silva Nova Pena points out, "the place that the saints and the Virgin occupied as protectors, intercessors, and healers of suffering humanity is now replaced with the healing powers of the Holy Spirit."[45] The impact of the charismatic renewal movement on the Catholic Church has enriched contemporary popular religiosity.

Pentecostal. The interface between Hispanic Catholicism and Pentecostalism or evangelical Protestantism is surprising to many. Statistics show that a significant number of Hispanic youth in the United States (about 90 percent of them being baptized Catholics) refer to themselves as "Christians." By this they mean that they have some connection with evangelicalism or Pentecostalism.[46] But the interface does not only involve Catholics who are to some degree involved in Pentecostalism, but Pentecostals who are still involved in some Catholic popular religiosity. Justo González illustrates:

> In the same neighborhood there may be a Pentecostal church whose doctrine is staunchly anti-Catholic, but whose members come from the same strata of society as the majority of those in the Catholic church. Instead of the Mass, their worship will center on preaching, praise, *testimonios*, *coritos*, and

prayer for healing. The coritos, however, will most likely be sung to the accompaniment of a mariachi-style band, rather than Caribbean-style maracas and drums. Also, it is quite likely that some of the people who attend this church, and whose rhetoric is rabidly anti-Catholic, will have an image of the Virgin of Guadalupe at home.[47]

There is, however, a growing exodus from Catholicism to Pentecostalism. Numerous suggestions have been offered regarding the reasons for this shift. For example, it is proposed that "Pentecostalism may represent a perceived resource for the psychological, cultural, and social survival of a Hispanic who experiences both dominant society and Church authority as a threat to that survival." Besides, "the absolute certainty offered in [the] barrio churches is a greater defense against the risk and ambiguity which confronts the poor of modern society than the 'cultural coldness, the systematized, privileged, and secularized Christendom of North America.' "[48]

There seems to be a growing consensus that to a large degree the exodus is related to worship and popular religion. Indigenous Pentecostalism has created a world of popular religiosity that is every bit as impressive as Catholic *religiosidad popular*. Hispanic Pentecostalism, instead of dismantling the building blocks of the people's religious expression, creates an environment in which Hispanic converts can express their natural religiosity. Though it disallows processions and some other external religious manifestations linked to Catholicism, it provides the convert with an emotional form of worship that is analogous to the popular Catholic experience.[49] Allan Figueroa Deck summarizes the continuity between older expressions of Hispanic popular religion and contemporary Pentecostalism by noting that both include "strong affirmation of a transcendent God, small community context for prayer, emphasis on God's miraculous power, openness to mystery, orientation to healing of every kind (physical, psychological, social), and affective appeal to the working class and the poor based on the strong use of symbolism, imagery, ritual, and story (biblically and/or sacramentally based)."[50]

The growth of Pentecostalism is astounding. For a movement born at the beginning of the twentieth century, its rapid growth is a missiological phenomenon. It has been seen as the "Third Force" in Christendom alongside Roman Catholicism and mainline Protestantism.[51] However, among Hispanics throughout Latin America and in the United States it is "the Second Force." David Barrett in his 1982 *World Christian Encyclopedia* estimated the worldwide population of Pentecostal or charismatic Christians to be in excess of 150 million. More than 33 percent of this number are in Latin America or are Hispanics in the United States. In Mexico at that time, an estimated 70 percent of the six million Protestants were Pentecostals.[52]

Of the Hispanic groups focused on in this book, Puerto Ricans have the largest number of Pentecostals. Both in Puerto Rico and in New York, their numbers are phenomenal. As far back as 1960, Pentecostals had a greater total Hispanic membership in New York City than all the other Protestant denominations combined[53] in 240 churches. By 1983 that number had grown to 560 Hispanic Pentecostal congregations.[54] This growth is spurred on by the enormous growth in Puerto Rico itself and the constant migratory flow between the island and New York. Samuel Silva-Gotay gives us a comparative perspective on this growth:

The religious message of Pentecostalism and the deterioration of the quality of life since the economic crisis of 1972 made possible a second wave to the growth of Pentecostalism in Puerto Rico. There are statistics that suggest that evangelical Protestantism and Pentecostalism account for 30% of the general population and a majority in some barrios and small towns in Puerto Rico. Aguadilla, Puerto Rico, in the Northwestern corner of the island, for example, had a single Catholic church with a Presbyterian, Seventh Day Adventist and Pentecostal church as minority denominations for some 70 years. Today there are six different denominations and forty-four Pentecostal councils working in Aguadilla and about 100 congregations that increase their numbers daily by conducting evangelizing campaigns. It is probable that if the present sociological conditions persist and there is no change in the traditional mode of operation of Catholicism, Pentecostals will constitute the majority of believers on the island by the year 2025. This development would push aside the mainline Protestant denominations along with the Catholic church. Moreover, Puerto Rican Pentecostalism has a world-wide impact because the island churches have missions in 39 countries including the United States, Latin America, Africa and Asia.[55]

The sociopolitical dimension of indigenous Pentecostalism (as part of its *religiosidad popular*) is a powerful aspect of its attractiveness. It "represents the vehicle for liberation of all colonialized and oppressed peoples, not only in a spiritual sense but in all political, social, and economic contexts."[56] This is especially true as it touches the lives of urban Hispanics. Pentecostalism "produces self-esteem and self-appreciation at an individual level that translates into political strength and collective growth at a community level.[57] Because of this, "the individual is no longer doomed to accept his lot in life as what 'must be,' but is inspired to the knowledge that with God he can transcend all limitations."[58] No longer does he or she conform to the stereotyped image of the Hispanic—welfare cheat, drug addict, member of the street-corner beer crowd. The convert participates in a community of industrious leaders, articulate speakers and mutually supportive individuals. "Hispanic language and culture, belittled by white society, are a source of pride and identity within the Pentecostal church, reinforcing the shared sense of communal pride and understanding between Hispanic peoples."[59] This sociopolitical dimension to a great extent makes Pentecostal churches prototypes of the *comunidades de base* (base communities) popularized by Latin American liberation theologians.[60] Furthermore, the location of churches in urban barrios demonstrates their commitment to reach those who Puerto Rican liberation missiologist Orlando Costas refers to as "outside the gate"—"the forgotten, dispossessed, marginalized, and unattended people of our society."[61]

While all of the above is true, Vivian Garrison warns us against stereotyping, particularly Puerto Rican Pentecostals. They "are *not* the most deprived segment of this generally disadvantaged population."[62] It is true that "chronic, irrevocable economic hardship may characterize a few of the members, particularly women." However, "as a group they show no greater chronic economic disadvantage than Catholics in the same community."[63] Furthermore,

> the Puerto Rican Pentecostals are not drawn disproportionately from any specific age group, from the lowest socioeconomic stratum, from the most recent migrant population, or from among those whose family and other interpersonal relations show disorganization. They are no less, and possibly more, socioeconomically mobile as a group and are as involved in the life of the community as the Catholics from the same environment. They show no greater, and possibly lesser, rates of psychiatric disturbance.[64]

In conclusion, we must note that Hispanic Pentecostalism is not monolithic. Each group, particularly each national group, has its own *sazón* or flavor. Their popular religious expressions and worship services vary from community to community. However, some basic things remain constant. These include passion and enthusiasm; a sense of spirituality in which the Spirit is dominant; and an egalitarian expression of community in which they are at home *(en su casa)* among their own.[65]

Other Protestants. Protestant missions to Hispanic countries followed in the tradition of the European Reformation, and particularly the pedagogical emphasis of the evangelical movement. These evangelicals brought a distinct flavor to worship, with the focus on the preacher and the proclamation of the Word.[66] However, the impact of Pentecostalism in the twentieth century and the recognition of the value of *religiosidad popular* in the life of the Hispanic people are bringing about a paradigm shift among other Protestant groups. More and more Protestant groups are adopting non-Anglo practices as their norm. For example,

> when they celebrate a baptism they do so with a number of elements unknown in Anglo congregations, but quite common in the Mexican tradition—godparents, special dresses and foods, and practices of *compadrazgo*. In that same church, there may be a time set aside during the worship service for *coritos*, and they may also sing some songs taken from the mariachi Mass normally sung down the street. Meanwhile, at the other end of the country, in New York, similar combinations are taking place, although in a different context since the Mexican influence is not as powerful as the Puerto Rican or the Dominican.[67]

Maria Luisa Santillán Baert has pointed out that the United Methodist Church, for example, "has struggled to understand the uniqueness of a people that can give expression to their faith powerfully through their gifts and graces, and through their culture."[68] Thus in recent years that denomination "has begun to accept the validity and richness of the Hispanic culture as a bona fide, genuine, authentic, basis form of Christian expression that can enrich the life of the whole church."[69] Many United Methodist churches are adopting and adapting Hispanic celebrations such as *la quinceañera* (a ceremony or Mass for the fifteen-year-old girl in which she reaffirms her Christian faith, followed by a large party) and *las posadas*.

There is also a transformation taking place among Hispanic Presbyterians, as noted in Teresa Chávez Sauceda's article "Becoming a Mestizo Church."[70] As in the United Methodist Church, the *quinceañera* is becoming common:

> The Rev. Tomás Chávez, a Presbyterian pastor, has developed a Presbyterian quinceañera. In his accompanying discussion of the development of this liturgy, he traces the roots of this tradition to coming-of-age ceremonies among the Mayas, Aztecs, and Toltecs. At the age of fifteen, young boys became warriors and young girls were presented to the community as the potential mothers of future warriors. The separate ceremonies that marked their coming-of-age underscored the commitments and responsibilities imposed upon them as adult members of the community.[71]

Summary characteristics. Religiosidad popular is important to Hispanic life and worship for a number of reasons. First of all, it highlights the sense of community. *El pueblo* and *la raza* are essential to being Hispanic. Hispanic identity is more than a town, a people, a race. It is a community in which the *mysterium tremendum* is expressed[72] in ways that are indigenously relevant. This is not to say that Hispanics do not value their individual selves. But theirs is not the rugged individualism that characterizes the dominant American culture. Their individualism is embedded in the concept of the "uniqueness of each individual person and the ardent desire to be who you are and not to resemble anyone else—'Soy como soy y no me parezco a nadie.' "[73] It is expressed in the cultural trait of *person-*

alismo, in which "they relate to persons rather than to organized patterns of behavior efficiently carried out. This," says Joseph Fitzpatrick, "reflects itself in their reverence for the saints, their intimacy with heavenly patrons who act as their advocates."[74]

Second *religiosidad popular* is characterized by passion. It is not a passion that is irrational or anti-intellectual,[75] but a freedom for feelings and emotions to wholistically respond to the moving of the Spirit. Such popular religious events as Holy Week celebrations, passion plays, posadas, quinceañeras, Protestant preaching or Pentecostal worship service all testify to a deep, passionate Hispanic spirituality.

And third, at the heart of *religiosidad popular* is celebration—*fiesta*. To this we now turn.

Fiesta

The amalgamation of the Spanish with the Amerindian and African to form the Hispanic has resulted in a passionate spirit dubbed *fiesta*. All these cultures are cultures of passion. Their amalgamation intensifies that spirit. The fiesta (literally "feast") spirit is expressed in religious and nonreligious events. It pervades the life of the Hispanic person and community. The ubiquitous propensity for fiesta is highlighted in the following statement: "The Hispanic will find any occasion for getting together and find a pretext to stop the flow of time and commemorate people and events with festivals and ceremonies."[76] Fiestas are naturally spontaneous, creative and intensely participatory.[77]

For the Western mind it is difficult to associate fiesta with worship. We characterize fiesta with the secular and worship with the sacred. But in the non-Western worldview such distinctions are not as clear-cut. The following discussion by Jeanette Y. Rodriguez-Holguin is helpful:

> The separation of the holy and the profane is not apparent among Hispanics. Eliade is most helpful in this regard. He does say that there is a distinction between the sacred and the profane, but he also says that there exists in archaic religious systems a greater integration of this experience of both the

sacred and the profane. For instance, there is more congruence between nature and religious experience. Gonzalez provides an analysis that is congenial to Eliade's discussion. There is a comparable sense of wholeness or integration of the human experience of wants and needs.[78]

Hispanics thus cannot be understood, nor their world entered into, until one understands fiesta. "Through fiesta, man reflects on the totality of his life and comes to enjoy the fiesta much more; it is not an escape from the world of problems but a bringing of a whole day into the celebration of the fact that life is a gift."[79]

When fiesta is experienced in a Christian sense, it is done in conjunction with sacred time and space in relation to a sacred event.[80] It can involve ritual and religious drama in which the mighty deeds of God and the gospel are rehearsed and celebrated in community. For the Hispanic Christian, the most intense fiesta can be an experience in worship. Justo González's observation regarding the *lack* of fiesta in North American churches is apropos here:

> I find congregations where people just sit and stare—or stand and fidget—as the gospel is being read, and then when the organ finishes playing the postlude, they break forth in applause (presumably because they find the postlude more exciting than the gospel?). I am surprised to see people barely nod when they hear that Christ is risen from the dead, and then jump and shout when their team scores a touchdown. I find people complaining if the service is not over in exactly sixty minutes, and then get excited when a basketball game goes into overtime. I even find myself sitting in such worship services, sometimes in the middle of communion, looking forward to the benediction and the dinner that comes later. And we are supposed to be celebrating the Event of the Ages.[81]

Fiesta as celebration. A worship service that is indeed a fiesta is highly emotive and celebrative. It is warm and enthusiastic, marked by joyful spontaneity. Corporate interaction and participation are vital. It includes "tactile qualities such as music (in accord with the rhythm and modulation preferred by the particular Hispanic group), dance, applause, humor and laughter, *el abrazo* (the embrace). . . . The pace may be different as well; indeed a good celebration may destroy the 'less-than-an-hour' myth of ordinary U.S. celebrations."[82]

It seems clear that one of the main reasons Pentecostalism is growing rapidly in the Hispanic community is that its worship is consonant with the fiesta spirit. Protestant churches that were so anti-Catholic that they rejected not only the rites and ceremonies but the fiesta spirit as well had difficulty gaining acceptance in the Hispanic culture. Pentecostals and other charismatic movements, on the other hand, gain ready acceptance with their indigenous, spontaneous, emotional and enthusiastically festive worship services.[83] The Hispanic who worships in such a setting experiences a joyful satisfaction of fullness.

It is important to note that this celebration cannot be manufactured. "It is not something [achieved] by human effort."[84] Not only is it "[a] gift of grace that descends into every heart abundantly,"[85] but it is a natural, nonsuperficial response of the worshiper and the worshiping community. For this reason Hispanic worship as a fiesta in many instances is planned but not rehearsed.

> Oftentimes Hispanic worship seems chaotic. Indeed, there are some Hispanic pastors and other leaders who are remiss in that they do not even plan the celebration, but simply let it happen. But in most cases the difference between our worship and that of the dominant culture is that we think in terms of planning a party rather than rehearsing a performance. Certainly choirs and bands rehearse; but the service, as such, is never rehearsed. We plan, as one does for a fiesta, in order to make sure that necessary arrangements have been made. In the case of a fiesta, one arranges for enough food and chairs, for a mariachi or some other kind of music, and for parking. But one cannot actually plan all the details, as one does in a performance, because the success of the fiesta depends on the attitude and participation of those present, not just of the performers. Likewise, in worship the celebration is the people's fiesta, and therefore the pastor and other worship leaders can plan only up to a point, leaving the rest to the celebrants themselves—and, as many Hispanics would stress, to the guidance of the Holy Spirit.[86]

The fiesta spirit is not only expressed in celebrative acts that are vocal or involve movement; it is expressed in art—"contrasting color in the decor and vestments, in the fashion of the *zarape* (rainbow-hued woven fabric) and plastic arts that convey the presence of grace."[87] Works of art, particularly those taken from nature, are especially meaningful to Hispanics. Artworks are often created as symbols of their affinity with the cosmos and their search to live in harmony with nature.[88] "A work of art, like a symbol, not only expresses something beautiful, but transcends what is tangibly expressed."[89] Mexican-Americans are illustrative of this. They

> seem to have a natural disposition toward artistic expressions as conveying more deeply their feelings as well as truth itself. Among the pre-Hispanic peoples, truth could only be explained through *flor y canto* (flower and song) since words have different connotations according to past experiences of the persons hearing them. Colors express feelings; poetry combines truth and feeling. Dance is a form of worship which is frequently practiced on feast days outside the church. Therefore, during liturgical celebrations, Mexican Americans use flowers, colors, songs, dances, and poetry as symbols of their joy and their worship.[90]

Artistic expression is widely used in Catholic churches in processions, incense, images and the like. Protestant churches that seek to capture the indigenous spirit are using art more extensively in the worship *ambiente* (environment). Windows are decorated with colorful plastics; walls are hung with scriptural quotations, children's art and banners.[91] All this is done to mark in people's memory that worship is a fiesta of God's people.

In the Hispanic culture the most significant fiestas are connected with family. Family is more than the "closely knit, tightly defined, and exclusive family, as when we speak of the nuclear family in the dominant culture—a family where one main value is privacy."[92] In Hispanic cultures there is a strong emphasis on the extended family. The extended family includes all sorts of relatives, many of whose relationship is not clearly defined. This vast assemblage of people called family, who are related in a multiplicity of ways, are "a treasure, a heritage."[93] The connectedness is intensely expressed in fiesta celebrations, in which a sense of belonging is prominent.

When Hispanics come to worship, they come to a family fiesta. Hispanic worship is a festive celebration when the extended family gathers together to praise God and celebrate having one another as family. It is therefore just as festive as the birthday party or graduation celebration in the dominant culture. For Hispanics such emotional festivities should not be limited to secular family events but should extend to religious family events as well. In worship they offer to God their most joyous music, their best art, their warmest celebration of family community. It is done with the fullest emotion and the liveliest celebrative acts.

Fiesta as liberation. The concept of fiesta does not ignore the painfully oppressive situations of the marginal and downtrodden in the worshiping family. In the Hispanic worldview, a fiesta is not simply a party. There is an element of agony in the worship fiesta experience. The words of Virgilio Elizondo are often cited:

> The Latino does not party because things are going well, or because there are no problems or difficulties; he celebrates because he is alive. He celebrates because of his sense of the tragic, accepting the many different forces of life and yet realizing there is the ultimate happiness which has already begun. He does not allow himself to be swallowed up by the many tensions and problems, the moments of sickness and death that are part of life, but he rises above them and celebrates life.[94]

Although life is to be lived, appreciated and celebrated, the Hispanic affirms in worship a commonality with pain, frustration, oppression and marginalization. The worship experience is fiesta that serves as a liberating force to the masses.

I noted earlier that there is a segment of Hispanics who have strong economic and political influence in the United States. Most of these are from the first wave of Cuban immigrants to Miami. Others are found in major metropolitan cities like Los Angeles, San Antonio and Chicago. However, the masses of Hispanics are "exiles" who live a life of hopelessness, alienation, frustration and powerlessness.

The urban Hispanic, through years of racist conditioning, suffers from an ethnic stereotype that predetermines failure and self-hate. An Anglo-dominated system of colonialism has crippled the Hispanic soul and effectively isolated him from his own culture, history, and language. As a result of historical oppression, the Hispanic is caught in a cycle of despair—stripped of energy, motivation, and hope for a better future. He is alienated from his own people and from a society that has eroded any sense of self-respect or pride.[95]

In the urban barrios the powerlessness is aggravated as the social situation deteriorates. Low educational levels, unemployment and health problems demonstrate this, along with other social indices such as vulnerability to drugs and crime, teenage pregnancy, household squabbles and increasing numbers of broken homes. "They are victims of a powerful consumer society. They are reduced to a passive resistance"[96] as part of the underclass of the North American society.

Roberto Escamilla alerts us to the fact that the concept of liberation should not be only applied to the oppressed. Suburbanites need liberation. The affluent in suburbia "also are oppressed by their bondage to all kinds of selfish concerns."[97] They too must seek the same liberation that the oppressed yearn for.

The Roman Catholic Church, particularly in Latin America, has in recent decades attempted to address the problem of oppression and need for liberation among Hispanics. Liberation theology has been the theological foundation for this attempt. It is "a method of theological reflection that seeks to find the meaning of the gospel in the existential reality in which Latin Americans live." It asks, "Given the total, cultural, social, economic, and political realities of their lives, what is the meaning of the gospels in that total lived experience?"[98] Many Hispanics who have been influenced by liberation theology and have migrated to the United States have raised, and are still raising, the same questions in this society.

In some instances it is suggested that the shift by some Hispanic-American Catholics to Protestantism has to do with issues of liberation. Anneris Goris states that the shift in loyalty by some Dominicans from traditional Catholicism to Methodism may have little to do with theology and more to do with the sensitivity of the Methodists to their political, economic and social concerns.[99] Still, the truth is that both American Catholicism and Protestantism have failed to a large degree to address the oppression of Hispanic people.

> Religion can be [and has been] directed in such a way as to produce a narcotic effect and pacify people. Such a style is far from the needs of Hispanics, whether in North or South America. The theme of salvation has been too often presented exclusively in terms of the other world. This world is presented at times as evil, as the place where merit is produced. This world is where one suffers, where pain is endured, where one simply waits. Such religion leads to fatalism and convinces people that there is nothing to be done about existing conditions.[100]

As Hispanic people begin to demand more from the church, many churches are recapturing the liberating dimension of the fiesta spirit in worship. In worship, hope and liberation are celebrated. As the gospel is proclaimed and enacted, freedom, dignity, self-worth, comfort, strength, hope, joy and abundant life are provided. Healing, deliverance and empowerment are assured as worshipers participate in the redemptive drama of the gospel.[101]

Fiesta worship and celebrative liturgical events help to shape "the horizon of the participants: it can help them see beyond present rejection, persevere in the way in spite of hardship."[102] They are "fed the hope of shalom; they look forward to a new earth and new heavens. They anticipate the day when justice will be done at last, when God will wipe away all tears, take away their hunger, give them space to live and live well, and death will be done away with."[103]

But the fiesta celebration is not simply "pie in the sky by and by"; it is "a slice on the plate here and now." Hispanics come to worship to hear and participate in the good news of the gospel. In the barrio with its economic hardships, rundown apartments, overcrowded and underfunded schools and unsafe streets, they experience the bad news of an evil existence. They understand that suffering is integral to their existence. But they are not willing to allow it to destroy their lives. They are willing "to admit the reality of pain and to transcend its misery by celebrating life with a *fiesta*"[104] as they listen to the words of Jesus according to Luke:

> Blessed are you who are poor,
>   for yours is the kingdom of God.
> Blessed are you who are hungry now,
>   for you will be filled.
> Blessed are you who weep now,
>   for you will laugh. (Lk 6:20-21)

The concept of fiesta is summarized in the expression "¡Tenemos *vida!*" ("In spite of everything, we still have *life!*").[105] Worship is a festive affirmation that life is worth living. It is the moment when Hispanics come together as an extended family, bearing the burdens of daily life but celebrating in a joyful mood and with enthusiastic expression the present reign of God and the ultimate victory through Jesus Christ. This is done best in the spirit of a fiesta.

Hispanic Music

T*he spirit of the liturgical fiesta is probably best demonstrated in* Hispanic musical expressions—expressions that celebrate their continued struggle and hope, using their own music syncretized from their varied roots. These expressions are derivatives of Amerindian, African, Spanish and contemporary American traditions.

In a discussion of Hispanic spirituality, Eldin Villafañe speaks of a "musical élan" that permeates Hispanic culture. What he means by this is a particular quality, a "gift" from the African heritage, "that expresses and impresses all religious experiences with an emotional depth of transcendence, joy and liberation."[1] It is through music that Africa has made its greatest contribution to and left its most lasting mark on the Hispanic soul. Life at its most emotional depth is expressed through African musical idioms. "For it is that 'mysterious and sensual rhythm of his music' which has 'spilled-out' and touched deeply all areas of the Latin American personality and graced his/her value orientations with a particular 'élan.'"[2]

But this "élan" is not limited to the African influence. Hispanic music is rich because of its syncretistic character. Cross-rhythm patterns and polyrhythmic sounds are combined with the indigenous idioms of the Amerindians throughout Latin America, expressed in the spirit of a fiesta. Besides, we cannot ignore the traditions derived from Spain. Music with rich melody and harmony comes from the land of the conquistadors. In these pieces "one can discern the Hispanic cadences, and sometimes simple melodic lines that reflect the impact of seven hundred years of Moorish presence."[3] To all of these are now added diverse contemporary American idioms that have significantly affected and enhanced Hispanic liturgy, particularly in the United States.

Hispanic music is not only meant to stimulate the emotions of the participant; it is a means by which a people recapture their rich and varied history. Through music they return to their roots. In music they express their inner and total self—their yearnings, feelings, struggles, and historical passage.[4] Hispanics find it difficult to "check their musical hats at the door of the Church."[5] Familiar rhythms, instruments and melodies, deemed unacceptable for worship by the dominant culture, are of huge importance to the religious enterprise. Large numbers of Hispanics are rejecting liturgies that simply have "a coat of varnish that automatically gives an impression of Hispanicity."[6] Guitars, hymns translated from English to Spanish, and a few colorful stoles and vestments do not capture the spirit of Hispanic worship. The music, and the liturgy in general, must arise out of the soul, culture and history of the worshiper. Such music will of necessity celebrate Christian values within the historical cultural context of the people.

Hymnody
Increasingly, Hispanic congregations are rejecting traditional Gregorian chants and classical European music. They are also warming up less and less to the great English evangelical hymns of the seven-

teenth, eighteenth and nineteenth centuries. Spanish-language versions of classics like "Now Thank We All Our God" are increasingly met with ennui and resistance among a significant segment of the Hispanic community.[7] Many Hispanics find it difficult to put their soul into such musical expressions. It is clear that having the hymn in their language is not the problem. "What is missing is the 'sentimiento,' the 'feel,' the 'passion' which only authentic cultural expression can bring."[8] Hispanics more and more are seeking music in worship that is "an autochthonous expression of the depth of Hispanic anguish and aspirations."[9] There are still many, especially in the United States, who wish to culturally imitate the Anglos and be "accepted"; but many others are yearning for "real music" that "finds an echo in the soul."[10] And they are questioning.

> The question is: Why does [the Hispanic] not take *Polo Negrete* to church? Why does she not take *música caliente* to church? Why does she not take salsa, mambo, ranchera, or tango to church? Simply because she is afraid. Because there is a dichotomy in her. She has been taught that "Anglo" tradition is sacred and the other is profane. We do not mean to ignore the precious heritage of classical hymnology that we consider part of our evangelical culture, yet unfortunately many hymns are the personal experience of Christians in other times and other contexts and are out of place in our times, especially for Hispanics.[11]

Because of these feelings and concerns, a new Christian hymnology has arisen in the Hispanic community both in Roman Catholicism and in Protestantism. The new music "has roots in Latin folk and popular music and most of the time reflects the social realities of the southern continent."[12] "An avalanche" of hymns and songs continues to be poured out, expressing people's happiness, concerns and trials.[13]

Jose A. Rodriguez, a Hispanic Presbyterian, felt the need to make a contribution to the liturgical life of the church. So he collected more than ten thousand hymns and filed them in a computer. He notes that in hymns like these "our culture, spirituality and history are well expressed, and we continue to produce a vast number of hymns, making us less dependable in translating hymns in our language."[14]

As can be imagined, there are still Hispanics who prefer traditional Anglo hymns and frown on the new ethnic hymnody. And even though many pastors, music leaders and churches try to find a balance, they meet with significant resistance. Raquel Gutiérrez-Aichón illustrates from her personal experience:

> I wanted to introduce into our church some of the hymns that Dr. Roberto Escamilla would classify as truly Hispanic music, and that express our sense of celebration. It shocked my own mother, who was a very faithful Christian. She was alarmed to the point that one day after we arrived home from a Sunday service, she told me, "Just to think that after I prayed for years, that whatever talent you had you would dedicate to the Lord, you are the one now to bring the Devil to our services." It took some very careful explaining on my part to somehow be able to change (to some extent) her way of thinking. One of my strongest arguments was, of course, my growing concern to preserve our cultural heritage in our worship and our music as well. Our hymnody has been separate from the mainstream of all other music, and church music should be treated so as to be relevant to our culture. Our hymns and songs must be given expression in and by our culture.[15]

The *corito* is without question the most popular contemporary type of congregational song among Hispanics. It is an indigenous Pentecostal singing idiom that has gained wide acceptance in other Protestant churches, as well as in the Roman Catholic Church. *Coritos* are short songs of praise that tell a story or whose lyrics come directly from Scripture, especially the Psalms. They are set to lively music, usually with a Hispanic flavor. They are called "heart songs" because they relate the Hispanic's experience of the cost of discipleship; they often speak of suffering. It is also popular to focus on the Christian's personal love for Jesus.[16] These songs are usually memorized, and thus poor barrio congregations find them more appropriate and useful than songs found in expensive traditional hymnals.

Because of rising interest in *coritos* and other Hispanic songs, a number of songbooks are being produced. Two of interest were published by the United Methodists in 1979 and 1983: *Celebremos* and *Celebremos II*. The aim of the task force that produced them was to have a hymnal containing more indigenous Hispanic music. The songs are presented in both Spanish and English so that the non-Spanish-speaking worshiper could participate and be enriched both in message and in rhythm.[17]

Congregational singing is most important in Hispanic churches. A typical service in a contemporary church involves a lot of participatory singing. It is quite common to find congregations standing and singing continuously for fifteen to twenty minutes. The singing is full-throated, and often emotional. Many songs involve congregation interaction, as well as personal expressions of praise that involve raising the hands.

Hispanic churches do make use of choirs, vocal ensembles and solos, though few evangelical or Pentecostal churches have choirs that are as technically musically trained (in the European mode) as, say, a North American choir. Hispanic choirs do not exist primarily for performance purposes. Rather, their role is to encourage participation in the vocal musical component of the worship service.[18] At the heart of this is the philosophical understanding that worship is not a "spectator sport" but a participatory event.

> Let us describe a typical Sunday Hispanic/Caribbean service at the Cathedral [of the Holy Cross, in Boston]. . . . The liturgy has a taste of the "home" church [iglesia doméstica] where children feel free to walk and adults to move freely. The service begins close to 10 a.m. with a long procession of ministers snaking through the side and central aisles while the choir and congregation join in a rousing hymn. The choir is made up of 15 vocalists and instrumentalists. Its rhythmic heartbeat reflects two sets of Afro-Caribbean drums—congas and bongos—along with the ever popular güiro and maracas. Four guitars trained in island "picking" patterns, an electric bass and Yamaha synthesizer fill out the accompaniment. The voices are by and large untrained but possess a strength and sincerity typical of Puerto Rican "folk" music.[19]

Instrumentation

The instruments employed in worship, along with their rhythmic sounds, are possibly the most indigenous aspect of the fiesta spirit in Hispanic worship. Hispanics who wish to return to their roots seek to replace the organ with instruments that are more Latino. The most popular instruments reflect a combination of influences that shape their culture—African and Amerindian, as well as popular contemporary North American instrumentation that speaks to the Hispanic soul.

The piano, though European in origin, is popular in a number of churches. However, its cost and the lack of skilled players make it prohibitive for many others. Those congregations that utilize the instrument are increasingly adopting a new style of accompaniment characterized by the repetition of basic chords.[20] This approach is lively and fits in the fiesta cultural spirit.

The basic, most popular instrument utilized in Hispanic worship is the Spanish guitar. It is used to accompany all vocal music—hymns, *coritos* and special renditions. "It is unsurpassed in its versatility, convenience, popularity, and ease of mastery."[21] In recent decades, the introduction of electric guitars has enhanced the rhythmic aspect of some worship services.

Although the slaves in the United States were dedrummed, the slavemasters had less success in this enterprise in the Caribbean. Rhythm enhanced by drums was an embedded part of the cultural expression of plantation society. "Plantation music became so identified with drums that in many different places of the Americas, as far as Paraguay, Ecuador, Santo Domingo, and Puerto Rico, it was named *bomba* (or words with similar sounds) after an African word for drum."[22] Today it is quite common to find a variety of drums in worship services, including congas and bongos.

The *güiro*, an Indian rhythmic instrument, is also a common sight in Hispanic churches, particularly in the Caribbean. Quintero-Rivera notes that this is the only percussion instrument used in the original music of *jíbaros* (Puerto Rican peasants). "The instrument plays two functions in the rhythmic structure of this music. In the first place, following a basic pattern (which in times evokes, in fact, Indian rhythms) it establishes a rhythmic counterpoint to the guitar, which is of fundamental importance in the conformation of a poly-rhythmic texture."[23]

Other native instruments such as the *maracas* add to the rhythmic liveliness of a Hispanic worship service. It is not unusual to find tambourine used as well. Many congregants bring their own tam-bourines and during the singing beat them against their legs, against the palms of their hands, and over their heads.

Mariachi music from Mexico is sweeping churches across the Southwestern United States. It is not uncommon to find *coritos* being sung to the accompaniment of a mariachi-style band; this is a signif-icant change, particularly in Protestant worship. As Maria Luisa Santillán Baert points out, "Mariachi bands would not have been acceptable in worship, much less funeral services, a few years ago."[24]

Hispanics are tapping into their deep cultural roots to produce a worship service that is meaningful, relevant, lively and exciting. To do that they will not limit themselves to only certain types of instru-ments dictated by European tradition. Rather, they are willing to "baptize" all the instruments that speak to the depth of their soul, and use them in festive praise to God.

Preaching, Prayer & Response

N*ot much formal study has been dedicated to preaching, prayer* and response in Hispanic worship. Possibly this is because these don't stand out as they do in say, African-American worship. They are, rather, an integral part of the whole worship enterprise.

These three elements have in common a communicative dimension. For Hispanics, communication is not limited to speech and cognition. The whole person is involved. Because Hispanics give much importance to the person, they realize that people communicate "not brain to brain, but person to person,"[1] for the most part. The totality of the person is included, not merely informative words.

When communicating, the Latino will usually try to visualize and experience the world as a totality. This whole view includes emotions, gestures, sounds, words and situations. The Latino is very emotional, but when explaining emotion, a rational basis emerges.

Emotion is not seen as irrational but as complementary to the rational in the communication of the whole person. The Hispanic is both emotional and rational and appreciates the necessity of an interplay of both in the totality of healthy life experience and communication.[2]

Therefore whether in preaching, prayer or response by the worshiper, Hispanic worship is marked by a wholistic balance between the rational and the emotional.

Preaching

Even in Hispanic worship services the dictum is true that "worship that does not engage the mind fails to engage the entire human being."[3] Thus for many Hispanics, preaching and the sermon are still at the heart of the worship service. Congregations for the most part expect inspiring and powerful messages.

Not only is this true in Protestant circles, but Catholics, possibly influenced by Protestantism, are incorporating a livelier style of preaching into their liturgy. Allan Figueroa Deck supports this perception: "Hispanic exposure to powerful Protestant preaching that makes otherwise dead biblical images and stories come alive has added to the already vivid historical Catholic religious imagination."[4]

Preaching is not only expected to be powerful, but especially in Pentecostal and evangelical circles it is expected to be extensive. The preacher who has had an encounter with God will have much to proclaim and share with his or her congregants. It is typical for a sermon to last for at least forty-five minutes. On special occasions one does not expect the preacher to preach less than one hour, and an hour and a half is not uncommon. "Brief messages are rare," says Samuel Soliv017 Solián.[5] As a matter of fact, Hispanic Pentecostals come to church expecting to spend two to three hours worshiping.

In most Protestant worship services Scripture is fundamental in preaching—though it could be argued that the emotional and homiletical dimension overwhelms the cognitive and exegetical dimension in many charismatic churches. In Hispanic Catholicism the exposition of the Word has not been as dominant. Rosa María Icaza suggests that "in years past, because of the role that Spain played during the Protestant Reformation, and also because of the illiteracy of many Hispanics, Sacred Scripture had not nourished this people as the Word of God."[6] Many knew some Bible characters, stories and sayings, but they were seen as coming from "sacred history" rather than "sacred Scriptures." In recent years both Hispanic Catholic congregants and priests are rediscovering the power of the whole Word of God in the liturgy. Interestingly, Icaza points out, "Hispanics seem to identify closely with some passages or books of the Bible as expressing their own situations and concerns. Mexican Americans like particularly the book of Exodus; Puerto Ricans, the book of Maccabees; and Cubans, the Prophets."[7]

In Pentecostal churches especially, the manifestation of the Spirit takes precedence over the exposition of the Word in the worship experience. Worshipers come not so much to hear the Scriptures as to have an encounter with God. The preacher's role is not primarily to expound a text or passage but to move people emotionally, as well as to move them to action. At the end of the worship service, a typical worshiper needs to leave with a sense of "emotional release and spiritual rejuvenation."[8] The homiletical construct of the preacher's sermon can meet this felt need more than anything else in the service.

Prayer

Regarding the area of prayer in Hispanic liturgy, not much has been written. Yet students of Hispanic liturgy recognize that this aspect of worship is very significant in the experience of the worshiper. One author notes that "it is precisely in prayer and worship, as opposed to other areas of religious practice and theological theory, that Hispanics, whether Roman Catholic or Protestant, express the complexity, richness, and stunning originality of their particular religious heritage."[9]

The prayer time is a very open time. Prior to the prayer, congregants share their concerns. A visiting worshiper may be shocked at the things shared. Many Hispanics will speak of concerns that would be considered too personal and private to be discussed in a large group. But in this period of communion with God, just about all barriers are broken down, and the burdens of their hearts are poured out.

Periods of prayer may be spontaneous and prolonged. In some instances worshipers are invited to come to the front to seek God in prayer. In other instances "many lift their hands to heaven. Others cross themselves. Still others sway as if moved by an imperceptible breeze. Some mumble their prayers, producing a hum throughout the congregation. Others cry out in longing or in joy. Sometimes more than one person prays out loud. In many cases, it is impossible to tell all that is going on. But then, the same is true of any good fiesta."[10]

Response

The spirit of fiesta is well expressed in the response of the Hispanic within the worship service. Hispanics value periods of silence and are comfortable with it. It is "natural and refreshing," says Jill Martinez. But this silence "should not be confused with the imposed silence that oppresses. It is rather an experience of liberation."[11] For the most part, however, Hispanic worship is vocal, physical and interactive. The prevailing fiesta mood "provides the kind of informality and climate that makes it possible to 'hang loose' so as to be sufficiently relaxed and able to get in touch with another person."[12] This for the Hispanic is meaningfully expressed through the sense of touch.

Hispanics, like the early Christian believers, find that touching and other physical contact in worship are more powerful than words to express love and belonging—not a "kind of artificial sentimentality, but the authentic meaning of affirmation of the other person and the fact that we belong to one another because we belong to Christ."[13] Hispanics are not afraid to use their whole bodies to communicate the fiesta spirit. The handshake, the *abrazo* or embrace and the holy kiss are all integral to the worship service and are carried out with a level of comfort unknown in many Caucasian churches.

Because the Latino feels secure in his sexuality, he is not embarrassed or uncomfortable in physical contact. He feels the warmth and goodness of an *abrazo* with a woman; because he is secure, he is comfortable in the *abrazo* of another man, in the feeling of strength of a man. In Latin America it is very common to see men walking arm in arm with each other; there is a physical contact, a communication of bodily vibrations. The hippies in the United States have said this, but the Latino has been practicing it for a long time. There is a personal communication which goes beyond words.[14]

Many churches have formalized a period for physical contact as part of the worshipers' response within worship. This is called the "passing of the peace." But for Hispanics the "passing of the peace" begins from the time the worshiper enters the precincts of the church; they participate again in the ritual of friendship during the service, and they stay around and line up after the service to physically greet all their friends. In moments like these, time is not important. "There is no rush to beat the Baptists to the cafeteria line," says United Methodist writer Maria Luisa Santillán Baert.[15]

This expressiveness should not be surprising to anyone who recognizes the fiesta nature of Hispanic worship. In any fiesta celebration there are opportunities to congratulate and physically celebrate with the person or persons who are celebrating a birthday, graduation, baptism, confirmation or other significant milestone. This kind of expression is also natural at funerals as Hispanics express their sympathy and comfort the bereaved. With this expressiveness, "persons who have come in a joyful mood would find their joy increased. On the other hand, others who have come with a broken heart or bearing life's heavy burdens will experience the uplift that comes about when we know that someone else really cares."[16] The spirit of oneness that results from these encounters is a vital part of the worship experience of Hispanic peoples.

Another vital part of Pentecostal (and a growing number of other churches') worship service is the *testimonios*. During the service, members of the congregation are invited to give a word of testimony to the love and mercy of God. Typical testimonies involve expressions of thanksgiving for answered prayers, particularly for healing and economic provision. It is the period when the congregation as a whole shares in the joys of answered prayers and the burdens of prayers not yet answered. At this time congregants learn of the daily struggles of fellow worshipers. They are kept abreast of the needs, joys, sorrows, celebrations and concerns of the worshiping family. *Testimonios* are "a public witness to the ongoing ministry of the Holy Spirit in the life of the community."[17] It is a time when faith and hope are celebrated.

Dance

Dance as a component of Christian life and worship has been problematic for both Catholics and Protestants. European and Caucasian-American Catholics "have been imbued with a strain of Augustinianism that makes them uncomfortable with the sensual aspects of human existence."[18] Protestants, mostly because of Puritan roots or because of their interpretations of certain biblical injunctions, also have difficulty admitting dance as a part of worship.

Dance, however, has always been part and parcel of the total life of Amerindians and Africans. It was never limited to a recreational activity. The notion that it is scandalous to dance in worship would be foreign to the indigenous peoples of the Americas. In their religious services it was a form of prayer and communion with God.[19] It has been noted that dancing was part of the church liturgy throughout Latin America until the early twentieth century, when it became evident to some that such activity was against canon law.[20] But up to that time in Mexico, for example, indigenous dances were used in liturgical and nonliturgical settings.

Music and dance have been fundamental to the existence of Puerto Rican culture, influenced both by Africans and their dance movements and by some of the dances from Spain. Angel G. Quintero-Rivera discusses the *aguinaldo* and *seis* music that was common at Puerto Rican peasant celebrations. *Aguinaldo* has its roots in the Christmas offering and the Three Wise Men celebrations. *Seis* was liturgical music danced in Spain in the fourteenth and fifteenth centuries at the most important celebrations. "It was danced in the church, in front of the altar, as an offering to the Eucharistic sacrament."[21] In Puerto Rico, however, such dance was soon deemed lascivious by church authorities, and it was banned. *Seis* then took refuge in the popular dance sphere.

The negation of dance had an interesting cultural effect on some Hispanic circles and societies. It has been suggested that "wherever dancing was disallowed in the diaspora, as in Venezuela and Colombia, for instance, African religious traditions soon dissipated."[22]

These days there is a resurgence of dance as a religious expression in Hispanic worship. Both old and young worshipers are enthusiastically expressing themselves through music combined with gestures that involve the whole body. They are once again recapturing a way of responding to God that is wholistic.

Other Senses

Worship communication goes beyond the cognitive, bodily contact and gestures. All the senses are called into service to experience a fullness that cannot be captured otherwise. This is especially true in Catholic worship. Yet Protestant services too are increasingly appealing to all the senses of the worshiper.

Smells associated with incense have been common not only within Catholicism but in indigenous Indian religious ceremonies as well. The use of liturgical sounds such as bells is being recaptured. Visuals are a "feast for the eyes. Lavish artwork, brilliant colors, sensual curves, intricate designs, abundant flowers, and many flickering candles are ordinary embellishments for the people's prayer and worship."[23]

We have discovered that Hispanic liturgical fiesta demands enthusiasm, movement, spontaneity and expressiveness in sounds, smells and sight. In many churches there is a return to the folkways and consequently an "absence of the restraint, the gravitas, that generally characterizes the gatherings of those who exercise power."[24] In worship people move, sing, dance, cry with all their hearts. It is contagious and unavoidable. It is in praise to God in family community. It is a celebration—a fiesta!

Part 5

Conclusion

Rational &
Physical

R*obert C. Williams has said it well: "Worship is a special explora-*tion into awareness."[1] It encompasses the rational and nonrational; the verbal and nonverbal. Thus key components in worship would include the proclamation of the Word, music, dance, drama, prayer, silence and bodily contact. Such wholistic worship will "be construed always as embodying something more than the one-dimensional posture of admiration, honor, devotion, or idolization tendered a divine being"[2] at a simply cognitive level. Reverence, joy and adoration will be expressed in forms that involve the whole person, including the body.

Control of the Body
In many communities, such as those surveyed in this book, relevant worship involves the physical body. Mary Douglas in her seminal

work *Natural Symbols* makes a case for the idea that there is no such thing as natural behavior. "Every kind of action carries the imprint of learning." Actions are socially determined. She argues that the social body constrains the way the physical body is perceived. There is a constant exchange between the bodily experiences of the social and the physical. The forms that the physical body adopts in movement and repose, the care given it in grooming and feeding, correlate closely with the categories in which society is seen.[3] Douglas advances the hypothesis that "bodily control is an expression of social control—abandonment of bodily control in ritual responds to the requirements of a social experience which is being expressed."[4]

Formality in liturgical expressions would indicate "social distance, well-defined, public, insulated roles," while informality is more appropriate to "role confusion, familiarity, intimacy. Bodily control will be appropriate where formality is valued, and most appropriate where the valuing of culture above nature is most emphasized."[5] Where there is strong social control—whether in church or society—there will be strong bodily control. Where there is fluid social control, there will be flexibility and fluidity in physical expression.

Frank Senn, piggybacking on Douglas's anthropological studies, has applied her hypothesis to the difference between a highly liturgical church and a free church. The latter prefers more spontaneous and emotional expression in worship. In this structure the control of the individual by the social group and the grid is weak. The highly liturgical church has a highly articulated social structure which includes a more rigid control of the individual by the social group and grid. This structure manifests a "differentiation of social roles (clergy and laity) and an exaltation of the group over the individual. The result will be a high value placed on conscious and controlled participation in communal worship."[6]

When Douglas asks her clerical friends who emphasize controlled participation in worship why the new nonritual forms of religion are superior, she is answered by a "Teilhardist evolutionism which assumes that a rational verbally explicit, personal commitment to God is self-evidently more evolved and better than its alleged contrary, formal, ritualistic conformity." Besides, they argue, "the replacement of ritual conformity with rational commitment will give greater meaning to the lives of Christians." And if "Christianity is to be saved for future generations, ritualism[7] must be rooted out, as if it were a weed choking the life of the spirit."[8]

The basis for this so-called self-evident, evolved, better rational and cerebral worship is far from evident. Rather than being a natural evolution, it is a taming of the senses by the social body. We all begin life using all our senses—our whole body. It is only later that we are "tamed, and trimmed, groomed and inhibited by manners, etiquette, and the rational claims of a sensible society, become puritans, restraining our senses—only half alive, partly blind, dumb, deaf, and lame."[9]

Recapturing the Use of the Body

Worship must recapture the use of the body. For as Kenneth Dale remarks, "I *am* my body. My body reveals my inner self, my personality, my spiritual problems with remarkable accuracy, at least to the eye that is trained to look for this."[10] Rationalistic persons are reluctant to use their whole being, including their body, in worship. But worship must evoke all the ingredients of the human personality. The total human personality is our real self, and thus it is essential that we communicate liturgically through our bodies rather than simply cerebrally. Senn makes an important point:

> We know that something that is seen as well as heard is conveyed more powerfully than something that is only heard. The meaning of something conveyed kinetically, that is, through bodily motion, is more powerful still. Meaning conveyed through touch and taste is more impressive than meaning expressed kinetically, visually, or audibly. And finally, meaning involving several senses at once is obviously more impressionable than meaning involving only one.[11]

Wholistic worship cannot be limited to the intellectual sphere. In worship there needs to be an integral relationship between mind, body and spirit.

For rationalists, the paradigm of worship is the classroom. Liturgy reflects the mentality of the traditional lecture room, with the minister as a moral instructor and the congregation as students or spectators.[12] We sit in rows facing one direction and do what we are told. But even this model has been found to be inadequate and is being replaced by "student-centered teaching" in the academic environment, eliciting total involvement in the learning enterprise.[13] Instead of the lecture room model, Michael Marshall suggests the paradigmatic environment of the laboratory, the theater, the book of Revelation![14] These environments call for the use of one's whole being.

Such models can help us recapture the truth that worship is something *done*. It is an event. It is an activity. Kneeling to pray, extending the hand to receive the elements of Communion and to praise and bless, standing and sitting are all essential ingredients that have been tamed by the social body. Worship, with its movements, shape, poise and rhythm (not unlike a dance),[15] has too often been downgraded to a rational exercise and spectator sport in which the congregation passively listens to a dull and ineffective sermon.

Actions speak louder than words. As noted earlier, "meaning conveyed through touch and taste is more impressive than meaning expressed kinetically, visually, or audibly."[16] This basic psychological fact helps us understand why the liturgy was danced before it was sung and sung before it was spoken, and why touching and tasting have such "numinous and psychological powers."[17]

Our rationalistic attitude toward worship and our suppression of the physical stem from a heretical dualism of body and spirit. On the premise that the body is evil (or at least secondary to the spirit), the idea has been communicated that the body must be kept out of the way of worship as much as possible. We focus on the body in our daily secular life, but in worship we focus on the spirit and the mind. The clear implication is that worshipers must be different in worship than in daily life. Is it any wonder then that congregants are passive and withdrawn during the worship exercise? There is no connection with real life—with their real selves.[18]

I am not arguing that one's experience in worship must exactly replicate daily life. One of the immovable factors, the constants, in worship is the *mysterium tremendum*—that special encounter with God in a way that is different from our daily encounter. But besides the fact that this ultimate sense of the presence of God is not a rational experience, it seems to me that this experience can be fully realized only through the apt sign, symbol, ceremony that is enacted with one's whole personality, including the bodily self. Such a self cannot, or should not, be dichotomized into secular and sacred, or daily and weekly. We are whole beings whose actions must not be dichotomized either. The actions of our selves aid us in a deeper appreciation of the *mysterium tremendum*. Too often our liturgical texts are inadequate, trite, banal and insensitive. How much more eloquently can our liturgical action speak to us!

Elevation of the Rational

The powerful influence of the Enlightenment has caused us to miss the fact that throughout most of the history of worship there has been more concern with what was done than with what was said, with what was experienced than with what was preached. We therefore err when we continue the modern custom of centering the service on a sermon that is basically informational. Charles Kraft, anthropologist and communication professor at Fuller Theological Seminary School of World Mission, argues that this custom "is based on the Enlightenment assumption that what people need most is more information, and the way that information is gotten is via lecture."[19] It is also based on the assumption that what is most significant in worship is what we understand cognitively. But as Justo González reminds us, "I do not need to understand Dvorak's Fifth Symphony in order to enjoy it."[20]

The average Protestant worshiper expects the sermon to be the main event. Music, responses, prayers and readings are viewed as preliminaries that lead up to the sermon. People come to the "auditorium" ("a place of hearing," as many still call the sanctuary)[21] for the primary purpose of listening to a good sermon. The question is often heard from one who missed church: "What did the preacher say?" For many worshipers, attending the worship service is tantamount to "going to preaching."[22]

But even the preaching element of the service need not be solely a cerebral and intellectual affair devoid of emotive content. Frank A. Thomas, in his work *They Like to Never Quit Praisin' God: The Role of Celebration in Preaching*, states that much Western traditional preaching has been rationalistic in approach and orientation, focusing on the cerebral process and words, with little attention to the emotional process. "The goal of the sermon was to demonstrate truth, illustrate truth, logically deduce truth, and lead people to intellectually assent to truth. This by nature required an analytical objective style that sought to impart information or give instruction. This style required people to be generally passive in the process, waiting for the minister to convince them of the truth of the proposition."[23]

But the human mind has three components: the cognitive, the emotive and the intuitive. "The cognitive is the faculty for reason and rational thought. The emotive is the base for the arousal of feeling and affections. The intuitive is the capacity for direct knowing or learning beyond the conscious use of reasoning."[24] Most traditional homiletician assume the primary intent of preaching is cognitive. Sermons are not designed to arouse the worshiper. The sermon is meant to convince listeners of the logical argument based on propositional truth. The sermon is "concerned primarily with cognitive movement in deductive flow, with little appeal to emotive movement."[25] But it is this type of rational discourse that many churchgoers find boring, unproductive and out of touch with their real selves.

Recapturing the Emotive

Unlike these "dry-as-the-hills-of-Gilboa" discourses, African-American preaching takes account of the emotive element. The sermon, like the worship music, calls forth an emotional response. That's why black preaching is not a spectator event but a dialogue with call and response. Mongameli Mabona challenges us: "Let there be no participators and spectators in our worship. We are all participators in God's bounty and spectators of his works of loving kindness."[26]

Tragically, most of us seem to have agreed with modern ratio-nalists (contra millennia of tradition) who value reason and logic over the emotions and the physical. We need to be reminded that wholistic worship in ancient Israel was actively participatory. "Worshipers joined the sacrificial services," says Douglas Clark, "entered dramatically the stage for redemptive re-enactments of past events for renewal; and sang, chanted, and danced through antiphonal liturgies and elaborate ceremonies accompanied by musical instruments. Thus worship involved the whole person. Sensory reception and expression characterized the shared experi-ence."[27]

Although not much is recorded regarding the worship experi-ences of the primitive Christian church, it is fair to deduce that it was not simply a cerebral-rational encounter but a Pentecostal, Spirit-filled experience that rode the tension between structure and spontaneous action. Even as far back as the mid-second century, we find this mix in an account from Justin Martyr of the worship ser-vice in Rome, which included a fixed sequence of Scripture reading, sermon, common prayer concluded by a vigorous "amen," kiss of peace and Communion.[28] But here already the church began to descend into a rigid structuring of even physical movements, culmi-nating in the Tridentine Latin Mass in which the movements the priest were prescribed down to the last detail.

A number of Reformation traditions recaptured the spontaneous and physical traditions in worship. But it was not until the nine-teenth and twentieth centuries that there was a true revival of wor-ship that involved the whole being. The holiness movements, the Free Methodists and the Pentecostal movement are classic exam-ples. In the nineteenth century the North American camp meetings were characterized by spontaneity, accompanied by shouting, weeping, wailing, groaning out loud, even states of convulsion.[29]

An example of a denomination that arose at that time and has moved from that type of worship to a more cerebrally oriented worship is the Seventh-day Adventist Church. Early Adventism attempted to recapture the exuberance of worship in ancient Israel and the primitive church. In the 1840s and early 1850s Adventist worship was spontaneous, emotional, informal, physical and at times disorderly. There was much shouting, kissing, creeping and crawling, and all the physical and emotional manifestations that were characteristic of the Methodism from which it arose.[30] Ron Graybill has, I believe, convincingly demonstrated that Ellen White, cofounder of the SDA Church, was among the early Adventists who worshiped enthusiastically and physically.[31] She speaks of them praising God with loud voices and shouting. In her words, "it was a triumphant time." She advised, "None of you should keep silent in your meetings." The nonsilence in which she and James White were involved included clapping, loud singing, laughing aloud, and shouting "Hallelujah, praise the Lord," "Glory to God," "Amen."

Enthusiastic, physical, loud expressions in worship continued into the 1860s and 1870s but began to die out after that. Graybill suggests that the change came naturally as members became more educated and sophisticated. He also notes that cultural change played a role. Prior to the Civil War, Methodists, for example, were known as "shouting Methodists;" but post-Civil War Methodists were more sedate.

By the 1890s White was discouraging vocal expressions of enthusiastic worship. Her caution intensified in reaction to the turn-of-the-century fanatical Holy Flesh movement in Indiana. It seems that her concern here was linked more to the sect's theological heresy than to expressions in worship per se. At the same time, she was reflecting the cultural shift in white American Adventism. As Adventists became more evangelical, greater emphasis was placed on Scripture and preaching, and a cerebral moralist reductionism became evident in worship, to the point that worship was no longer a wholistically experienced event in most WASP Adventist churches.

Worshipers with African and Hispanic roots continue to a large degree to capture the true moods of worship—the moods of joyful, celebrative fiestas that involve the whole person. Their chantlike singing, plain talking, clapping, dancing, praying and dynamic proclamation of the Word all involve the whole being, not just the mind. They are intoxicating and powerful experiences.[32] These cultures recognize the importance of worshiping God with one's whole self. "Africans in particular have discovered the freedom to praise God with their whole selves," says Terry MacArthur, "their feet as well as their voices. I was taught to sit still in church. Africans are teaching us that our praise is less than full until we praise God with everything that we are and that includes shoulders, knees, and hips."[33] Another author states that "in Africa one praises God with one's muscles and bones and nerves, the whole bundle."[34] This makes all the more interesting Brenda Aghaowa's reflection on the predicament of blacks in a mostly white society. Drawing on the Ghanaian novel *The Torrent*, she observes:

> The novel describes a British-run secondary school in Ghana that endeavors to "turn bushboys from their 'savage' condition into 'civilized' people." In so doing, the students are taught to reject much of their own culture in favor of European norms, including the stricture that "one should worship God quietly and with physical restraint, not with emotional rejoicing and body movement."[35]

But today many missionaries as well as Africans (both in the homeland and in the diaspora) recognize that physical celebration and ecstasy in worship are most pleasing to God.

Dance

Dance is one of the most controversial physical expressions in the history of Christianity. In a worthwhile study on this topic, Debbie Roberts tells us that ancient peoples did not make a distinction between dance that was natural and dance that was spiritual. Dance was part of everyday life. They danced for worship as well as for warfare. It wasn't until the Christian era that dance was placed in the natural, nonspiritual category and was eliminated from religious ceremonies.[36]

A survey of Old Testament worship shows that dance was not alien to the Hebrew people's liturgy. Most celebrated is Miriam after the crossing of the Red Sea (Ex 15:20) and David before the ark (2 Sam 6:16-23); the former was a communal or folk dance, the latter a spontaneous solo performance. In the New Testament we find no reference to dancing in worship, but we do find it mentioned in Jesus' parable of the prodigal son (Lk 15:25).

In *The Mystery of Faith* Lawrence Johnson discusses the problem dance posed for the post-New Testament church because of its pagan connotations:

> Very popular among the pagans were nocturnal vigils, notorious for their ecstatic and often erotic dances, observed in honor of the various deities. To counteract these celebrations the Church substituted Christian vigils, among which were those observed on the feast of the martyrs. But traditional practices, especially when attractive and instinctive, did not automatically disappear. They were merely transferred to the new Christian observances. It was here that pastoral opinion was divided. Approving the continuation of the ancient ways was St. John Chrysostom (c.345-407) who congratulated his people: "These past days you have been received at the banq'uet of the holy martyrs . . . you have danced a beautiful dance." In Milan, St. Ambrose (c. 339-397), while rejecting the debauchery of pagan dances, admitted that "bodily dance in honor of God is to be called laudable for David danced in front of the ark." When pagan influences were absent, the dance could be transformed into a noble expression of Christian joy and praise. Others, however, immediately confronted with excesses inherited from paganism, strongly objected.[37]

Despite prohibitions by many of the church fathers and leaders, dancing in Christian ceremonies continued through medieval times. This is substantiated by the widespread legislation the church enacted to forbid the practice. "People danced in churches, at the tombs of the dead, on solemnities of the saints, and at other festivals of the year. The practice was so entrenched," says Johnson, "that ecclesiastical authorities often threatened with excommunication persons engaging in those dances and clerics permitting them."[38]

To a large degree, as Protestantism suppressed other arts it suppressed dance as well. This was particularly true in the Reformed tradition and the Radical Reformation on the Continent and in Puritanism in Great Britain and North America. "Any dancing," says Henry Mitchell, "especially among nineteenth-century Protestants, was an activity of the 'evil flesh,' rather than an art form."[39] It was not until the twentieth century that a revival of dance took place in religious settings in the United States and elsewhere. Even then these usually took place in nonliturgical settings, such as sacred dance concerts. But increasingly dance is being explored and incorporated in the celebration of the liturgy, as an integral part of the worship experience. Roberts predicts that dance as a mode of worship "will grow with magnitude and swiftness that will astound many conservative church members."[40] Dance, she believes, will be employed even in conservative churches and used as a test for evangelism.[41]

Dance, a form created by God, needs to be recaptured for use before God, and its emotive, physical and spiritual power must be tapped to the glory of God. In dance the worshiper can do what other elements of a services do not allow.

> Doctors know that through movement one can express what cannot be spoken. Dance can bring emotional release, the response desired. The body and mind are intertwined, and what affects one usually surfaces in the other. Our bodies reflect what is happening within us. Dance has effects like those of other forms of physical exercise. It causes the blood to circulate, activates thinking, quickens the heartbeat; one feels alive and vibrant.[42]

We need a worship that is wholistic, that incorporates and involves the whole person—cognitive, physical and emotional. Why can't God's people put as much energy—physical and emotional—into worship as they put into their sports or club activities?

Too many times " 'lit-orgy' passes for 'lit-urgy.' "[43] That's not what worship is all about. "Lit-orgy" focuses on self; "lit-urgy" has Christ as central. But Christ doesn't call only part of our being to worship. He wants it all!

Notes

Chapter 1: Introduction

[1]Brenda Eatman Aghaowa, *Praising in Black and White: Unity and Diversity in Christian Worship* (Cleveland: United Church Press, 1996), p. xii.

[2]For a very worthwhile treatment of multiethnicity in worship, see Alison Siewert, ed., *Worship Team Handbook* (Downers Grove, Ill.: InterVarsity Press, 1998). Especially see the articles by Alison Siewert, "Worship & Culture," pp. 17-20, and Sundee Frazier, "Multiethnic Windows on Worship," pp. 20-26. See also Mark Francis's excellent volume *Liturgy in a Multicultural Community* (Collegeville, Minn.: Liturgical, 1991).

[3]Cyprian Lamar Rowe, "The Case for a Distinctive Black Culture," in *This Far by Faith: American Black Worship and the African Roots* (Washington, D.C.: National Office for Black Catholics and the Liturgical Conference, 1977), p. 21.

[4]Stephen B. Bevans, *Models of Contextual Theology* (Maryknoll, N.Y.: Orbis, 1992), p. 7.

[5]Joseph Fitzpatrick, *One Church, Many Cultures: The Challenge of Diversity* (Kansas City, Mo.: Sheed & Ward, 1987), p. 28.

[6]H. Richard Niebuhr, *Christ and Culture* (New York: Harper & Row, 1951), p. 33.

[7]Karen Ward, "What Is Culturally-Specific Worship?" in *What Does "Multicultural" Worship Look Like?* ed. Gordon Lathrop (Minneapolis: Augsburg Fortress, 1996), p. 18; Fitzpatrick, *One Church*, p. 28.

[8]Richard R. Flores, "Chicanos, Culture and Borderlands: Reflections on Worship." *Modern Liturgy* 18, no. 9: 16. It may be worthwhile to note at this point the pluralism that characterizes all culture, particularly those that are open to being fluid and dynamic, like U.S. culture. Regarding this pluralism, Niebuhr notes, "The values a culture seeks to realize in any time or place are many in number. No society can even try to realize all its manifold possibilities; each is highly complex, made up of many institutions with many goals and interweaving interests. The values are many, partly because men are many. Culture is concerned with what is good for male and female, child and adult, rulers and ruled; with what is good for men in special vocations and groups, according to the customary notions of such good. Moreover, all the individuals have their special claims and interest; and everyone in his individuality is a complex being with desires of body and mind, with self-regarding and other-regarding motives, with relations to other men, nature and supernatural beings" (*Christ and Culture*, p. 38). If pluralism is a natural part of the cultural phenomenon in all societies, we can already begin to see the challenges we face in a growing, diverse, multicultural society.

[9]Fitzpatrick, *One Church*, p. 28.

[10]See Peter Schineller, *A Handbook of Inculturation* (New York: Paulist, 1990), p. 23; Ward, "What Is Culturally-Specific Worship?" p. 18.

[11]Mark Francis notes regarding this characteristic: "Aesthetic choices such as the juxtaposition of colors, dance movements, musical rhythm and tonality, as well as social conventions such as table manners, are all alternative choices people of a culture make along the course of their history and then share with future generations. There is nothing essentially 'more correct,' for example, about eating with a knife and fork instead of with one's hand or with chopsticks; in the Orient, looking directly at someone while talking to them can be considered aggressive and rude; and anyone who has driven in Italy knows that following traffic laws to the letter is considered aberrant behavior" (*Liturgy*, pp. 12-13).

[12]See Daniel Quinn, *Ishmael: An Adventure of the Mind and Spirit* (New York: Bantam, 1992), pp. 198-99.

[13]Iris Hamid, "Theology and Caribbean Development," in *With Eyes Wide Open*, ed. David Mitchell (Barbados: CA DEC, 1973), p. 128, cited in Raymond Ray Palackdrarrysing, "In Search of a Caribbean Theology," unpublished paper, United Theological College of the West Indies, Jamaica, 1976, p. 11.

[14]See David Abalos, "The Personal, Historical and Sacred Grounding of Culture: Some Reflections in the Creation of Latino Culture in the US from the Perspective of the Theory of Transformation," in *Old Masks, New Faces: Religion and Latino Identities*, ed. Anthony M. Stevens-Arroyo and Gilbert R. Cadena (New York: Bildner Center for Western Hemisphere Studies, 1995), p. 144.

[15]Ward, "What Is Culturally-Specific Worship?" p. 18.

[16]See Anthony B. Aarons, "Liturgical Reform in the Diocese of Jamaica: An Investigation into the Use of the Various Eucharistic Liturgies, 1662-1975," unpublished paper, United Theological College of the West Indies, Jamaica, 1981, p. 38.

[17]Siewert, "Worship & Culture," p. 17.

[18]Ibid.

[19]See Beverly Noble, "A Development of Liturgical Tradition Since 1962: A Study of the Anglican Church in Jamaica," unpublished paper, United Theological College of the West Indies, Jamaica, 1985, p. 35.

[20]See Robert E. Webber, *Worship Old and New: A Biblical, Historical and Practical Introduction*, rev. ed. (Grand Rapids, Mich.: Zondervan, 1994), p. 33.

[21]Ibid., p. 36.

[22]Ralph P. Martin, "History of Israelite and Jewish Worship," in *The Ministries of Christian Worship*, Library of Christian Worship 1 (Nashville: StarSong, 1994), p. 97.

[23]See Francis, *Liturgy*, p. 25.

[24]Webber, *Worship Old and New*, pp. 36-37.

[25]See Pedrito U. Maynard-Reid, *Poverty and Wealth in James* (Maryknoll, N.Y.: Orbis, 1987), pp. 54-58.

[26]Martin, "History of Israelite," p. 99.

[27]See Pedrito U. Maynard-Reid, *Complete Evangelism* (Scottsdale, Penn.: Herald, 1997), pp. 46-58.

[28]Francis, *Liturgy*, p. 21.

[29]Bevans, *Models*, p. 3.

[30]C. F. D. Moule, *Worship in the New Testament* (Richmond, Va.: John Knox Press, 1961), p. 9.

[31]Scholars believe that this is the same as the love feasts of Jude 12 and 2 Peter 2:13. See Philip Comfort, "The House Church and Its Worship," in *The Ministries of Chris-*

tian Worship, Library of Christian Worship 1 (Nashville: StarSong, 1994), p. 157.

[32]My focus in this section will be on the English-speaking territories. I will treat the Spanish-speaking territories in the next section. A study of the French-speaking countries like Haiti, Martinique and Guadalupe will have to wait for another appropriate moment.

Chapter 2: Worship Through the Ages

[1]H. Richard Niebuhr, *Christ and Culture* (New York: Harper & Row, 1951), pp. 45-82.

[2]Frank C. Senn, *Christian Worship and Its Cultural Setting* (Philadelphia: Fortress, 1983), p. 39. He goes on to say, "To be sure, there were those apologists of the second century such as Justin Martyr, Clement of Alexandria, and Origen who tried to build bridges between Christian revelation and Greek philosophy. But a more typical attitude was the kind displayed by Tertullian of Carthage who asked, *Quid Athenae Hierosolymis?* ('What has Athens to do with Jerusalem?')" p. 39.

[3]*Didache* 10.7, quoted in Ralph P. Martin, *Worship in the Early Church* (Grand Rapids, Mich.: Eerdmans, 1975), p. 138.

[4]Ferdinand Hahn, *The Worship of the Early Church* (Philadelphia: Fortress, 1973), p. 100.

[5]Quoted in Robert E. Webber, *Worship Old and New: A Biblical, Historical and Practical Introduction*, rev. ed. (Grand Rapids, Mich.: Zondervan, 1994), pp. 51-52.

[6]See Hahn, *Worship of the Early Church*, pp. 102-3.

[7]Quoted in Webber, *Worship Old and New*, p. 54.

[8]Ibid., p. 98.

[9]Ibid., p. 95.

[10]Senn, *Christian Worship*, p. 41.

[11]Ibid., p. 39.

[12]Webber, *Worship Old and New*, p. 103.

[13]See Joseph Fitzpatrick, *One Church, Many Cultures: The Challenge of Diversity* (Kansas City, Mo.: Sheed and Ward, 1987), p. 49.

[14]Webber, *Worship Old and New*, p. 99.

[15]Ibid., p. 101. Webber notes that this spirit of pragmatism is evident in their buildings and the development of their laws.

[16]See Fitzpatrick, *One Church*, pp. 54-59, for a discussion of the controversy over the Slavonic rites as an example of intercultural difference. In summary he notes that "the discussion of the Slavonic Rites is particularly helpful since it presents the problem in the context of political, social, economic, and religious conflicts of interest, all of which obscure and complicate the fundamental issue that people of a particular culture and language have a right to serve God and to express the word and life of Jesus within the context of their own way of life, providing there is nothing 'wrong' about their behavior" (p. 59).

[17]See Mark R. Francis, *Liturgy in a Multicultural Community* (Collegeville, Minn.: Liturgical, 1991), p. 40.

[18]Ibid., p. 41. Webber (*Worship Old and New*, p. 100) notes that the Gallican Rite was used throughout Europe, though varying considerably according to local customs. The Roman and Gallican rites seem to have influenced each other until the ninth century, when the latter was suppressed under Pepin and Charlemagne. After that the Roman liturgy became the standard approach to worship in the West.

[19]Senn, *Christian Worship*, p. 44. Senn notes that "increasing commerce resulted in the growth of towns, and the allure of the city contributed to the decay of the feudal system." Interestingly he also suggests that "economic well-being contributed to the decadence of the monasteries, the ecclesiastical hierarchy, and the liturgy" (ibid.).

[20]Ibid., pp. 44-45.

[21]Stephen B. Bevans, *Models of Contextual Theology* (Maryknoll, N.Y.: Orbis, 1992), p. 4.

[22]Senn, *Christian Worship*, p. 45.

[23]Webber, *Worship Old and New*, p. 109.

[24]Senn, *Christian Worship*, p. 46.

[25]Webber, *Worship Old and New*, p. 112.

[26]Ibid., pp. 114-19.

[27]Ibid., pp. 116-17.

[28]Ibid., p. 117.

[29]Quoted by Webber, *Worship Old and New*, p. 117 (from James Hastings Nichols, *Corporate Worship in the Reformed Tradition* {Philadelphia: Westminster, 1968], p. 122).

[30]As an aside here, Senn notes that church musicians in the eighteenth century imported into the services the sentimental style of the Italian operatic aria as plainsong chant, the chorale and the polyphonic motet fell out of use. Again, in the arena of music, the liturgy was adapting to the prevailing culture. See Senn, *Christian Worship*, pp. 46-47.

[31]Fitzpatrick states that "certainly one of the most creative and daring adaptations of Catholic belief and practice to another culture occurred with the development of the Chinese Rites, the adaptations of Catholic belief and practice to the language and culture of the people of China in the 15th and 16th centuries" (*One Church*, p. 61).

[32]James F. White notes that "The Council of Trent (1545-1563) sought to bring about a conservative reform by radical means. The fathers of Trent were concerned to end avarice, corruptions, and superstitions in worship, but their minds were directed to defending the status quo whenever possible, partly because the lack of liturgical scholarship allowed them to believe, for example, that St. Peter had composed the Roman canon and that to change existing practices was to abolish that which was apostolic. Furthermore, changes would be seen as conceding that the Protestant Reformers were right after all" ("Roman Catholic Worship from the Council of Trent to Vatican II," in *Twenty Centuries of Christian Worship*, Library of Christian Worship 2 [Nashville: StarSong, 1994], p. 72).

[33]Senn, *Christian Worship*, p. 47.

[34]Ibid.

[35]James F. White, *Christian Worship in Transition* (Nashville: Abingdon, 1990), pp. 78-85. See also Senn, *Christian Worship*, pp. 48-53.

[36]See Webber, *Worship Old and New*, pp. 122-23.

[37]Senn, *Christian Worship*, p. 49.

[38]Ibid.

[39]Don M. Wardlaw, "Tension in the Sanctuary," *Duke Divinity School Review* 43 (Winter 1978): 6. But he goes on to say, "Let's be realistic. Not all the worshipers hail the new wine as savior of the wedding feast. While many of our most loyal clergy and

laity have not slept through the liturgical revolution, neither have they joined it. All along they simply have preferred the way things were. To them the careful symmetries of eighteenth and nineteenth century music, architecture and thought constructs more aptly represent the Presence than do syncopated rhythms, circled and swaying congregations, and bright audio-visuals" (p. 7).

[40]See Webber, *Worship Old and New*, p. 125.

Chapter 3: Constancy & Diversity

[1]Lutheran World Federation, "Cartigny Statement on Worship and Culture: Biblical and Historical Foundations," in *The Ministries of Christian Worship*, Library of Christian Worship 7 (Nashville: StarSong, 1994), p. 206.

[2]Don M. Wardlaw, "Tension in the Sanctuary," *Duke Divinity School Review* 43 (Winter 1978): 12.

[3]Some have questioned whether music is a core element in worship. But our survey of liturgy showed that music did not become a central part of worship until the Davidic era.

[4]Frank C. Senn, *Christian Worship and Its Cultural Setting* (Philadelphia: Fortress, 1983), p. vii.

[5]See Lutheran World Federation, "Cartigny Statement," p. 205; Peter Schineller, *A Handbook of Inculturation* (New York: Paulist, 1990), p. 19.

[6]Stephen B. Bevans, *Models of Contextual Theology* (Maryknoll, N.Y.: Orbis, 1992), p. 1.

[7]Ibid., p. 2.

[8]Ibid., p. 20.

[9]John D. Witvliet, "Christian Cultural Engagement and Liturgical Inculturation," in *The Ministries of Christian Worship*, Library of Christian Worship 7 (Nashville: StarSong, 1994), p. 184; see Ricardo Ramirez, "Reflections on the Hispanicization of the Liturgy," *Worship* 57 (January 1983): 26.

[10]James F. White, *Introduction to Christian Worship*, rev. ed. (Nashville: Abingdon, 1990), p. 42.

[11]Mark R. Francis, *Liturgy in a Multicultural Community* (Collegeville, Minn.: Liturgical, 1991), p. 12. See also Brian Wren, *What Language Shall I Borrow? God-Talk in Worship: A Male Response to Feminist Theology* (New York: Crossroad, 1990), where he aims to show that every naming of God is borrowed from human experience. The principle of his argument is very apropos in this context. See Peter Schineller, "A Roman Catholic Approach to Liturgical Inculturation," in *The Ministries of Christian Worship*, Library of Christian Worship 7 (Nashville: StarSong, 1994), p. 180.

[12]Senn, *Christian Worship*, p. 65.

[13]Senn in makes an interesting point: "Those who have grown up with electric media are used to having their senses massaged or revitalized. Our culture itself has become highly sensate. Attendant to this has been a lower ability to concentrate on one medium for an extended period of time, especially a hot one. This has upset parents and teachers who are straying travelers from the age of Gutenberg and the printing press. Colleges and universities find that students have difficulty concentrating on lectures and heavy reading, so they are moving toward learning models which require 'participation or completion by the audience,' that is, models in which the student must organize and appropriate the data. This has serious impli-

cations for the language of worship. It suggests that worship will communicate better in our culture if it is a multimedia event which stimulates a number of senses at once" (*Christian Worship*, p. 57).

[14]Thomas H. Schattauer, "How Does Worship Relate to Cultures in North America?" in *What Does "Multicultural" Worship Look Like?* ed. Gordon Lathrop (Minneapolis: Augsburg Fortress, 1996), p. 10.

[15]Brenda Eatman Aghaowa, *Praising in Black and White: Unity and Diversity in Christian Worship* (Cleveland, Ohio: United Church Press, 1996), p. 28.

[16]Rebecca Slough, "Worship and Multicultural Diversity," in *The Ministries of Christian Worship*, Library of Christian Worship 7 (Nashville: StarSong, 1994), p. 193; Karen Ward, "What Is Culturally-Specific Worship?" in *What Does "Multicultural" Worship Look Like?* ed. Gordon Lathrop (Minneapolis: Augsburg Fortress, 1996), p. 21.

[17]Mark Bangert, "How Does One Go About Multicultural Worship?" in *What Does "Multicultural" Worship Look Like?* ed. Gordon Lathrop (Minneapolis: Augsburg Fortress, 1996), p. 25.

[18]Aghaowa, *Praising in Black and White*, p. 29; see Francis, *Liturgy*, p. 11.

[19]Winston George Chase, "A Critical Assessment of the Liturgy of the Moravian Church in Jamaica During the Period 1965-1975," unpublished paper, Faculty of Arts and General Studies, University of the West Indies, Jamaica, n.d., pp. 25-26.

[20]See Pamela O'Gorman, "The Intoduction of Jamaican Music into the Established Churches," *Jamaica Journal* 9, no. 1 (1975): 44.

[21]Ramirez, "Reflections," pp. 26-27. For an interesting discussion of how country, gospel and other music of the South are truly indigenous, see Jack Renard Pressau, "Songs of Salvation: Yesteryear's Music for Yesterday's Faith," *Duke Divinity School Review* 43 (Winter 1978): 54-67.

[22]R. Schreiter, *Constructing Local Theology* (Maryknoll, N.Y.: Orbis, 1985), p. 2, quoted in Bevans, *Models*, p. 6.

[23]Ricardo Ramirez points out that the Mexican American Cultural Center makes an important distinction between "incarnation" and "adaptation." The latter hints of external imposition of a particular mode of liturgy (see "Liturgy from the Mexican American Perspective," *Worship* 57 [July 1977]: 294).

[24]Edward P. Wimberly, "The Dynamics of Black Worship: A Psychosocial Exploration of the Impulses That Lie at the Roots of Black Worship," in *The Black Christian Worship Experience*, Black Church Scholar Series 4, ed. Melva Wilson Costen and Darius L. Swann (Atlanta: ITC Press, 1992), p. 200.

[25]Paul Brown, *In and for the World: Bringing the Contemporary into Christian Worship* (Minneapolis: Fortress, 1992), p. 51. He noted earlier that too often the language of worship is a sort of "Christianese," that is, "a label sometimes applied to worship language that is strongly different from ordinary language; it is liturgical dialect. Clergypersons, sad to say, and other church professionals usually speak it best and most often. . . . Laypersons who may not be fluent in the special dialect themselves will still defend its use, perhaps out of habit or custom, or perhaps because they, like their clergy, assume that it reflects the special not-of-this-world nature of the church" (pp. 42-43).

[26]See H. Richard Niebuhr, *Christ and Culture* (New York: Harper & Row, 1951), p. 43.

[27]Thea Bowman, "Justice, Power and Praise," in *Liturgy and Social Justice*, ed. Edward

M. Grosz (Collegeville, Minn.: Liturgical, 1989), p. 32. See Ramirez, "Reflections," p. 28.

[28]Moses Oladele Taiwo, "Victory over the Demons," *Ministry* (April 1991): 26.

[29]Michael Marshall, *Renewal in Worship* (Wilton, Conn.: Morehouse-Barlow, 1985), p. 24.

[30]Senn, *Christian Worship*, p. 93.

[31]It is sad that we miss this point and perpetuate sacred cows such as a set hour for divine worship—an hour originally chosen to fit milking habits in rural communities. Two hundred years after the Industrial Revolution we have not adjusted to the traveling and work habits of an urban society and its culture. The same applies to the inappropriateness of a cathedral style of worship in a small inner-city church. The latter borrows and imports everything secondhand in a faded and jaded form from the cathedral-church setting. Picture three women and a boy dressed in strange gowns accompanied by an incompetent organist. A few people sit far apart in uncomfortable pews singing "Now Thank We All Our God," pitched too high— starting with three top Cs! Everything in such a scenario, from beginning to end, says Marshall, is out of key and plainly absurd. For him this "claustrophobic religiosity" is perhaps the greatest enemy to true worship (*Renewal in Worship*, pp. 44-46). How much more relevant it would be if the inner-city culture were "baptized," Christianized, incarnated and expressed in worship!

[32]Ward, "What Is Culturally-Specific Worship?" p. 23.

Chapter 4: "We Had Church Today!"

[1]Joseph B. Bethea, "Worship in the Black Church," *Duke Divinity School Review* 43 (Winter 1978): 46.

[2]George Ofori-atta-Thomas, "The African Inheritance in the Black Church Worship," in *The Black Christian Worship Experience*, ed. Melva Wilson Costen and Darius L. Swann, Black Church Scholar Series 4 (Atlanta: ITC Press, 1992), p. 45. See Joseph M. Murphy, *Working the Spirit: Ceremonies of the African Diaspora* (Boston: Beacon, 1994), p. 146.

[3]Murphy, *Working the Spirit*, p. 146.

[4]Quoted in Lerone Bennett Jr., *The Shaping of Black America: The Struggles and Triumphs of African-Americans, 1619 to the 1990s* (New York: Penguin, 1995), p. 163.

[5]Quoted in Delores S. Williams, "Rituals of Resistance in Womanist Worship," in *Women at Worship: Interpretations of North American Diversity*, ed. Marjorie Procter-Smith and Janet R. Walton (Louisville, Ky.: Westminster John Knox, 1993), p. 221. Melva Wilson Costen notes that these overturned pots were also propped up with a rock or large stick, or suspended from one or more large tree limbs. The congregants would then sing as softly as possible around the inverted pot (*African American Christian Worship* [Nashville: Abingdon, 1993], p. 38).

[6]Costen, *African American Christian Worship*, p. 50.

[7]Ibid.

[8]See Bennett, *Shaping of Black America*, pp. 117, 162; John E. Brandon, "Worship in the Black Experience," in *The Black Christian Worship Experience*, ed. Melva Wilson Costen and Darius L. Swann, Black Church Scholar Series 4 (Atlanta: ITC Press, 1992), p. 112.

[9]Cited in Portia K. Maultsby, "The Use and Performance of Hymnody, Spirituals

and Gospels in the Black Church," in *The Black Christian Worship Experience*, ed. Melva Wilson Costen and Darius L. Swann, Black Church Scholar Series 4 (Atlanta: ITC Press, 1992), p. 149.

[10]Henry H. Mitchell, "The Continuity of African Culture" in *This Far by Faith: American Black Worship and the African Roots* (Washington, D.C.: National Ofice for Black Catholics and the Liturgical Conference, 1977), p. 17.

[11]See Albert Pero, "Worship and Theology in the Black Context," in *Theology and the Black Experience*, ed. A. Pero and A. Moro (Minneapolis: Augsburg, 1988), p. 239.

[12]Costen, *African American Christian Worship*, pp. 15-16.

[13]Quoted in C. Eric Lincoln and Lawrence H. Mamiya, *The Black Church in the African American Experience* (Durham, N.C.: Duke University Press, 1990), p. 124.

[14]James T. Campbell, *Songs of Zion: The African Methodist Episcopal Church in the United States and South Africa* (New York: Oxford University Press, 1995), p. 64.

[15]Lincoln and Mamiya, *Black Church*, p. 124.

[16]Cyprian Lamar Rowe, "The Case for a Distinctive Black Culture," in *This Far by Faith: American Black Worship and the African Roots* (Washington, D.C.: National Office for Black Catholics and the Liturgical Conference, 1977), p. 24.

[17]Quoted in Costen, *African American Christian Worship*, p. 115.

[18]Rowe, "Case for a Distinctive Black Culture," p. 23.

[19]Lincoln and Mamiya, *Black Church*, p. 76.

[20]Ibid., p. 79.

[21]Ibid., p. 125.

[22]Bethea, "Worship in the Black Church," p. 49.

[23]Brenda Eatman Aghaowa, *Praising in Black and White: Unity and Diversity in Christian Worship* (Cleveland: United Church Press, 1996), p. 30.

[24]Lincoln and Mamiya, *Black Church*, p. 106.

[25]Charles Hamilton, *The Black Preacher in America* (New York: William Morrow, 1972), pp. 19-28 ; quoted in Lincoln and Mamiya, *Black Church*, p. 106.

[26]Pedrito U. Maynard-Reid (incorrectly attributed to Melva Costen), "African-American Worship," in *The Ministries of Christian Worship*, Library of Christian Worship 7 (Nashville: StarSong, 1994), p. 229.

[27]See Pedrito U. Maynard-Reid, *Poverty and Wealth in James* (Maryknoll, N.Y.: Orbis, 1987), pp. 55-56; J. Wendell Mapson Jr., *The Ministry of Music in the Black Church* (Valley Forge, Penn.: Judson, 1984), p. 19.

[28]Maynard-Reid, "African American Worship," p. 229.

[29]William B. McClain, "The Black Religious Experiences in the United States," in *This Far by Faith: American Black Worship and the African Roots* (Washington, D.C.: National Office for Black Catholics and the Liturgical Conference, 1977), p. 31.

[30]Aghaowa, *Praising in Black and White*, p. 39.

[31]Karen Ward, "What Is Culturally-Specific Worship?" in *What Does "Multicultural" Worship Look Like?* ed. Gordon Lathrop (Minneapolis: Augsburg Fortress, 1996), pp. 19-20.

[32]Aghaowa, *Praising in Black and White*, pp. 30-32.

[33]Ofori-atta-Thomas, "African Inheritance," p. 58; C. Michael Hawn, "Vox Populi: Developing Global Song in the Northern World," in *The Ministries of Christian Worship*, Library of Christian Worship 7 (Nashville: StarSong, 1994), p. 211.

[34]Aghaowa, *Praising in Black and White*, p. 41.

[35]Henry H. Mitchell,"The Continuity of African Culture," in *This Far by Faith: American Black Worship and the African Roots* (Washington, D.C.: National Office for Black Catholics and the Liturgical Conference, 1977), p. 12.

[36]Hawn, "Vox Populi," p. 212.

[37]See Mongameli Mabona, "Black People and White Worship," in *The Challenge of Black Theology in South Africa*, ed. Basil Moore (Atlanta: John Knox, 1973), p. 107; here it is noted that nowhere in the African traditional religion is a person encouraged "to cultivate high moral excellence or self-perfection by entering into himself!"

[38]W. E. B. Du Bois, *The Souls of Black Folk* (New York: Fawcett, 1961), p. 3.

[39]Ibid., p. 139.

[40]James H. Cone, *The Spirituals and the Blues: A Interpretation* (Maryknoll, N.Y.: Orbis, 1991), p. 82.

[41]Williams, "Rituals of Resistance," p. 221.

[42]See Harold Dean Trulear, "The Lord Will Make a Way Somehow: Black Worship and the Afro-American Story," *Journal of the Interdenominational Theological Center* 13, no. 1 (fall 1985): 89-90; Annie Ruth Powell, "Hold onto Your Dream: African-American Protestant Worship," in *Women at Worship; Interpretations of North American Diversity*, ed. Marjorie Procter-Smith and Janet R. Walton (Louisville, Ky.: Westminster John Knox Press, 1993), p. 44.

[43]Aghaowa, *Praising in Black and White*, p. 43.

[44]Manning Marable Blackwater states that "black Christianity, as well as the totality of the black religious experience within America, cannot be understood outside the development of white racism and capitalist exploitation" (Manning Marable Blackwater, *Historical Studies in Race, Class Consciousness and Revolution* [Dayton, Ohio: Black Praxis, 1981], p. 34, quoted in Hans A. Baer and Merrill Singer, *African-American Religion in theTwentieth Century* [Knoxville: University of Tennessee Press, 1992], p. xxii).

[45]Aghaowa, *Praising*, p. 43.

[46]Ibid.

[47]Mapson, *Ministry of Music*, p. 19. See James H. Cone, "Sanctification, Liberation and Black Worship," *Theology Today* 35 (July 1978): 140.

[48]Walter L. Pearson, "Why I Have Hope," *Adventist Review*, February 1997, p. 9.

[49]Bethea, "Worship in the Black Church," p. 50.

[50]Lincoln and Mamiya, *Black Church*, p. 229; see also p. 235.

[51]Ibid., p. 226.

[52]McClain, "Black Religious Experiences," p. 33.

[53]Maynard-Reid, "African-American Worship," p. 230.

[54]Robert C. Williams, "Worship and Anti-Structure in Thurman's Vision of the Sacred," in *The Black Christian Worship Experience*, ed. Melva Wilson Costen and Darius L. Swann, Black Church Scholar Series 4 (Atlanta: ITC Press, 1992), p. 172; Aghaowa, *Praising in Black and White*, p. 73.

[55]Williams, "Worship and Anti-structure," p. 172.

[56]McClain, "Black Religious Experiences," p. 30.

[57]Pero, "Worship and Theology," p. 242; cf. Arthaniel Edgar Harris Sr., "Worship in the AME Zion Church," *AME Zion Quarterly Review* 98, no. 2 (July 1986): 33-34.

[58]Aghaowa, *Praising in Black and White*, p. 43.

[59]Cone, "Sanctification," pp. 139-42.
[60]Bethea, "Worship in the Black Church," p. 44.

Chapter 5: African-American Music

[1]James H. Cone, "Sanctification, Liberation and Black Worship," *Theology Today* 35 (July 1978): 145. But note C. Eric Lincoln and Lawrence H. Mamiya, *The Black Church in the African American Experience* (Durham, N.C.: Duke University Press, 1990), p. 346: "Singing is second only to preaching as the magnet of attraction and the primary vehicle of spiritual transport for the worshiping congregation." Compare Cone, "Sanctification," p. 144.

[2]Lincoln and Mamiya, *Black Church*, p. 348.

[3]J. Wendell Mapson Jr., *The Ministry of Music in the Black Church* (Valley Forge, Penn.: Judson, 1984), p. 22; see also p. 16.

[4]Ibid., p. 11.

[5]Grayson W. Brown, "Music in the Black Spiritual Tradition," in *This Far by Faith: American Black Worship and the African Roots* (Washington, D.C.: National Office for Black Catholics and the Liturgical Conference, 1977), p. 89.

[6]William B. McClain, preface to *Songs of Zion* (Nashville: Abingdon, 1981), p. ix.

[7]Cone, "Sanctification," p. 144.

[8]Ibid.

[9]Don Cusic, *The Sound of Light: A History of Gospel Music* (Bowling Green, Ohio: Bowling Green State University Popular Press, 1990), p. 86.

[10]Melva Wilson Costen, *African American Christian Worship* (Nashville: Abingdon, 1993), p. 98.

[11]John E. Brandon, "Worship in the Black Experience," in *The Black Christian Worship Experience*, ed. Melva Wilson Costen and Darius L. Swann, Black Church Scholar Series 4 (Atlanta: ITC Press, 1992), p. 114.

[12]See Eileen Southern, *The Music of Black Americans: A History* (New York: W. W. Norton, 1971), p. 90; and Eileen Southern, *The Music of Black Americans: A History*, 3rd ed. (New York: W. W. Norton, 1997), pp. 84-89. There was significant negative reaction to the loudness of blacks' singing (especially at camp meetings), as reported by John F. Watson in his *Methodist Error: Or, Friendly Christian Advice to Those Methodists Who Indulge in Extravagant Religious Emotions and Bodily Exercises* (1819). These "noisy" and excessively exuberant worship services were a cause of discomfort for the Methodist church fathers. Commenting on the camp meeting, Watson wrote: "Here ought to be considered too, a most exceptional error, which has the tolerance at least of the rulers of our camp meetings. In the *blacks'* quarter, the coloured people get together, and sing for hours together, short scraps of disjointed affirmations, pledges, or prayers, lengthened out with long repetition *choruses*. These are all sung in the merry chorus-manner of the southern harvest field, or husking-frolic method, of the slave blacks" (pp. 63-64; quoted in Southern, *Music of Black Americans*, 3rd ed., p. 85).

[13]Quoted in Mapson, *Ministry of Music*, p. 12.

[14]Portia K. Maultsby, "The Use and Performance of Hymnody, Spirituals and Gospels in the Black Church," in *The Black Christian Worship Experience*, ed. Melva Wilson Costen and Darius L. Swann, Black Church Scholar Series 4 (Atlanta: ITC Press, 1992), p. 153.

[15]C. Michael Hawn, "Vox Populi: Developing Global Song in the Northern World," in *The Ministries of Christian Worship*, Library of Christian Worship 7 (Nashville: StarSong, 1994), p. 211.

[16]Brenda Eatman Aghaowa, *Praising in Black and White: Unity and Diversity in Christian Worship* (Cleveland, Ohio: United Church Press, 1996), p. 44. Lincoln and Mamiya have pointed out that "the transition from congregational hymns to songs for specialized soloists and ensembles [especially during the latter part of the nineteenth and early part of the twentieth centuries] had important sociological consequences. While the former united worshipers through the collective activity of singing and declaring theological and doctrinal commonalities, the new style [of Thomas Dorsey and others] required the congregation to assume the role of audience. In essence, worshipers became bystanders who witnessed the preaching and personal testimonies of singers. At best the congregation was to share in those attestations by affirmative 'amens,' nodding, humming, clapping, swaying, or occasionally by singing along on choruses and vamps. One unexpected consequence was that black worshipers and concert goers often became the audience to a new homiletical gospel experience" (*Black Church*, pp. 361-62).

[17]Cusic, *Sound of Light*, p. 92.

[18]Ibid.

[19]Quoted in Maultsby, "Use and Performance of Hymnody," p. 153.

[20]Ibid.

[21]Quoted in James T. Campbell, *Songs of Zion: The African Methodist Episcopal Church in the United States and South Africa* (New York: Oxford University Press, 1995), p. 41.

[22]Ibid.

[23]Ibid. See Southern, *Music of Black Americans*, 1971 ed., p. 90. Interestingly, Bishop Payne in his book *Recollection of Seventy Years* (Nashville, 1888) also reports tension over the introduction of trained choirs in the worship service: "The first introduction of choral singing into the A.M.E. Church took place in Bethel, Philadelphia, Pa., between 1841 and 1842. It gave great offense to the older members, especially those who had professed personal sanctification. Said they: 'You have brought the devil into the Church, and therefore we will go out.' So, suiting the action to the word, many went out of Bethel, and never returned" (quoted in Southern, *Music of Black Americans*, 3rd ed., pp. 128-29).

[24]Jon Michael Spencer, *Protest and Praise: Sacred Music of Black Religion* (Minneapolis: Fortress, 1990), p. 135.

[25]Ibid.

[26]Ibid., p. 136.

[27]See Paul Oliver, "Spirituals," in *The New Grove Gospel, Blues and Jazz*, ed. Paul Oliver, William Bolcom and Max Harrison (New York: W. W. Norton, 1986), p. 2.

[28]See Costen, *African American Christian Worship*, p. 100.

[29]Lincoln and Mamiya, *Black Church*, p. 374. For example, of the 285 songs in the African-American hymnal *Songs of Zion* (Nashville: Abingdon, 1981), only two are from Wesley. In contrast, ninety-eight are Negro spirituals or Afro-American liberation songs.

[30]Noted in Lincoln and Mamiya, *Black Church*, p. 374.

[31]Costen, *African American Christian Worship*, pp. 98-99.

[32]Lincoln and Mamiya, *Black Church*, p. 375.

[33]Mapson, *Ministry of Music*, p. 47.

[34]Oliver, "Spirituals," p. 7; Campbell, *Songs of Zion*, p. 42.

[35]Campbell, *Songs of Zion*, p. 42.

[36]Costen, *African American Christian Worship*, p. 99; Mapson, *Ministry of Music*, p. 37. Mapson notes that during the 1800s illiteracy was prevalent and the use of hymnals was virtually nonexistent.

[37]Oliver notes that many spirituals fall into this category and points out that they were "sung with inflections, extended syllables and quarter-tones that [were] the wonder and despair of the few people who tried to notate them" ("Spirituals," p. 4).

[38]Lincoln and Mamiya, *Black Church*, p. 350.

[39]Ibid.

[40]Costen, *African American Christian Worship*, p. 96.

[41]James H. Cone, *The Spirituals and the Blues: A Interpretation* (Maryknoll, N.Y.: Orbis, 1991), p. 30.

[42]E. Franklin Frazier notes that "we are not unaware of the interpretations which often reflect the biases of whites" (*The Negro Church in America* [New York: Schocken, 1974], p. 19).

[43]W. E. B. Du Bois, *The Souls of Black Folk* (New York: Fawcett, 1961), p. 186.

[44]Ibid., p. 179.

[45]Cone, *Spirituals and the Blues*, p. 20.

[46]Gayraud S. Wilmore, *Black Religion and Black Radicalism: An Interpretation of the Religious History of African Americans*, 3rd ed. (Maryknoll, N.Y.: Orbis, 1998), p. 255.

[47]John Lovell, *Black Song: The Forge and the Flame* (New York: Macmillan, 1972), p. 119, quoted in Wilmore, *Black Religion*, p. 262.

[48]Du Bois, *Souls of Black Folk*, p. 186.

[49]Costen notes that "the preponderance of the use of personal pronouns in Spirituals can be attributed to a number of factors. The African understanding of one's personal interrelationship with others as all of the community experiences struggle, is one factor. The 'I' technically communicates that 'we'—'all of us'—share in the struggle. There is also the possible intent of the singer to seek affirmation as a person of importance in an oppressive arena" (*African American Christian Worship*, p. 96).

[50]For more on the double meaning of *spiritual* see Cone, *Spirituals and the Blues*, pp. 80-81, and his use of Earl Conrad, *Harriet Tubman* (New York: P. S. Erickson, 1969); Lerone Bennett Jr., *The Shaping of Black America: The Struggles and Triumphs of African-Americans, 1619 to the 1990s* (New York: Penguin, 1975), p. 164.

[51]Lincoln and Mamiya, *Black Church*, p. 367.

[52]Ibid.

[53]Ibid.; cf. Costen, *African American Christian Worship*, p. 97. It is important to note here Grayson W. Brown's advice: "Our use of choirs must never be such that it invites the congregation to return again to audience status. Choirs are always used as back-ups for the whole community, so that everyone is about the business of praising the Lord in song" ("Music in the Black Spiritual Tradition," p. 92).

[54]Stephen Cushman identifies five distinct repertories in gospel music: (1) "Rural White (1830-1865)," the "shape-note" revival music of the South and Midwest, (2)

"Rural Black (1830-1900)," call/response songs and spirituals, (3) "Northern Urban White (1875-1975)," songs such as those in Philip P. Bliss's *Gospel Songs* and Bliss and Sankey's *Gospel Hymns and Sacred Songs*, (4) "Urban Black (1900-1945)," (5) "Urban Commercial Synthesis (1970-Present)" ("Gospel Songs," in *Music and the Arts in Christian Worship*, Library of Christian Worship 4, bk. 1 [Nashville: StarSong, 1994], pp. 353-54). My discussion focuses on the latter two.

[55]See Southern, *Music of Black Americans*, 1971 ed., p. 402, and her 3rd ed., p. 452.

[56]See Oliver, "Spirituals," pp. 191, 199; William B. McClain, "The Black Religious Experiences in the United States," in *This Far by Faith: American Black Worship and the African Roots* (Washington, D.C.: National Office for Black Catholics and the Liturgical Conference, 1977), pp. 30-31, 35.

[57]McClain, preface, p. x.

[58]See Cusic, *Sound of Light*, p. 91.

[59]Jon Michael Spencer, "African-American Song," in *Music and the Arts in Christian Worship*, Library of Christian Worship 4, bk. 1 (Nashville: StarSong, 1994), p. 359; Lincoln and Mamiya, *Black Church*, p. 361.

[60]Costen, *African American Christian Worship*, p. 102.

[61]Eileen Southern insightfully notes that "many spirituals convey to listeners the same feeling of rootlessness and misery as do the blues. The spiritual is religious, however, rather than worldly and tends to be more generalized in its expression than specific, more figurative in its language than direct, and more expressive of group feelings than individual ones. Despite these differences it is nevertheless often difficult to distinguish between the two kinds of songs. Some songs have such vague implications that scholars classify them as 'blues-spiritual' " (*Music of Black Americans*, 3rd ed., p. 333).

[62]Ibid., p. 103.

[63]Ibid.

[64]Lincoln and Mamiya, *Black Church*, pp. 363-64.

[65]Ibid., p. 377.

[66]Michael G. Hayes, "The Function of Praise Songs in African-American Worship," in *Music and the Arts in Christian Worship*, Library of Christian Worship 4 (Nashville: StarSong, 1994), p. 348.

[67]Ibid.

[68]Spencer, "African-American Song," p. 360.

[69]Pedrito U. Maynard-Reid (incorrectly attributed to Melva Costen), "African-American Worship," in *The Ministries of Christian Worship*, Library of Christian Worship 7 (Nashville: StarSong, 1994), p. 229 .

[70]Brown, "Music in the Black Spiritual Tradition," p. 90.

Chapter 6: The Spoken Word

[1]C. Eric Lincoln and Lawrence H. Mamiya, *The Black Church in the African American Experience* (Durham, N.C.: Duke University Press, 1990), p. 136.

[2]W. E. B. Du Bois, *The Souls of Black Folk* (New York: Fawcett, 1961), p. 134. As a take-off on these I am arguing in these chapters that three things characterize the worship of African Americans: music, the spoken word and the response.

[3]Ibid.

[4]Wyatt Tee Walker, *The Soul of Black Worship: A Trilogy—Preaching, Praying, Singing*

(New York: Martin Luther King Fellows Press, 1984), p. 6.

[5]Melva Wilson Costen, *African American Christian Worship* (Nashville: Abingdon, 1993), p. 47.

[6]Gayraud S. Wilmore, *Black Religion and Black Radicalism: An Interpretation of the Religious History of African Americans*, 3rd ed. (Maryknoll, N.Y.: Orbis, 1998), p. 27.

[7]E. Franklin Frazier, *The Negro Church in America* (New York: Schocken, 1974), p. 24.

[8]George Ofori-atta-Thomas, "The African Inheritance in the Black Church Worship," in *The Black Christian Worship Experience*, ed. Melva Wilson Costen and Darius L. Swann, Black Church Scholar Series 4 (Atlanta: ITC Press, 1992), p. 57.

[9]Harold Dean Trulear, "The Lord Will Make a Way Somehow: Black Worship and the Afro-American Story," *Journal of the Interdenominational Theological Center* 13, no. 1 (fall 1985): 100.

[10]Ibid.

[11]William C. Turner, "The Musicality of Black Preaching: A Phenomenology," *Journal of Black Sacred Music* 2, no. 1 (spring 1988): 21.

[12]Henry H. Mitchell, "The Continuity of African Culture," in *This Far by Faith: American Black Worship and the African Roots* (Washington, D.C.: National Office for Black Catholics and the Liturgical Conference, 1977), p. 13.

[13]Brenda Eatman Aghaowa, *Praising in Black and White: Unity and Diversity in Christian Worship* (Cleveland: United Church Press, 1996), p. 40.

[14]Costen, *African American Christian Worship*, p. 105.

[15]Frank A. Thomas, *They Like to Never Quit Praisin' God: The Role of Celebration in Preaching* (Cleveland: United Church Press, 1997), p. 11.

[16]Henry H. Mitchell makes it clear that "every sermon must make *sense*; it must be manifestly reasonable" (*Celebration and Experience in Preaching* [Nashville: Abingdon, 1990], p. 21).

[17]Ibid.

[18]Ibid., pp. 67-68.

[19]Ibid., p. 37.

[20]Walker, *The Soul of Black Worship*, p. 13.

[21]William B. McClain, *The Soul of Black Worship* (Madison, N.J.: Multi-ethnic Center, Drew University, 1980), p. 23.

[22]Aghaowa, *Praising in Black and White*, p. 42.

[23]McClain, *Soul of Black Worship*, pp. 22-23.

[24]James Weldon Johnson, *God's Trombones* (New York: Viking, 1927), pp. 4-5, quoted in James H. Cone, *The Spirituals and the Blues: A Interpretation* (Maryknoll, N.Y.: Orbis, 1991), p. 37.

[25]McClain, *Soul of Black Worship*, pp. 21-22.

[26]Ibid., p. 32.

[27]See Thomas, *They Like to Never Quit Praisin' God*, p. 3.

[28]Lincoln and Mamiya point out that in responses to the survey question "Do your sermons reflect any of the changes in black consciousness (black pride, black is beautiful, black power, etc.) since the civil rights movement?" age and education were strongly related variables. "Younger clergy and/or those with more education tended to reflect more positive attitudes toward emphasizing aspects of black consciousness in their sermons. Older and less educated pastors tended to respond negatively." The authors also say that "the variable of denomination is also

strongly related to sermon content reflecting black consciousness"—Pentecostals versus Methodist and Baptists, for example, the former being less intentional in incorporating such consciousness in their sermons. "Clergy who decline to include black consciousness-type content in their sermons expressed the conviction that their job is only 'to preach the Christian Gospel' or that there is too much emphasis on race' " (*Black Church*, pp. 175-76). See C. Eric Lincoln, *The Black Church Since Frazier* (New York: Schocken, 1974), for a brief study of the contemporary black church's relationship to black theology.

[29]Walker, *Soul of Black Worship*, p. 16.
[30]Ibid., pp. 16-17.
[31]Frazier, *Negro Church*, p. 24.
[32]McClain, *Soul of Black Worship*, p. 29.
[33]Costen, *African American Christian Worship*, p. 105.
[34]McClain, *Soul of Black Worship*, p. 29.
[35]Jon Michael Spencer, *Protest and Praise: Sacred Music of Black Religion* (Minneapolis: Fortress, 1990), p. 243.
[36]Frazier, *Negro Church*, p. 25.
[37]Lincoln and Mamiya, *Black Church*, p. 343.
[38]Spencer, *Protest and Praise*, p. 229.
[39]Ibid., p. 228.
[40]See Thomas, *They Like to Never Quit Praisin' God*, p. 105; Turner, "Musicality of Black Preaching," p. 22.
[41]Turner, "Musicality of Black Preaching," p. 22.
[42]Ibid.
[43]Spencer, *Protest and Praise*, pp. 229-30.
[44]Ibid., p. 235.
[45]Ibid., p. 242.
[46]Walter L. Pearson, "Why I Have Hope," *Adventist Review*, February 1997, p. 9.
[47]McClain, *Soul of Black Worship*, p. 25.
[48]James H.Cone, "Sanctification, Liberation and Black Worship," *Theology Today* 35 (July 1978): 144.
[49]Walker, *Soul of Black Worship*, p. 33.
[50]Costen, *African American Christian Worship*, pp. 41-42.
[51]Ibid., p. 107.
[52]Ibid., p. 42.

Chapter 7: The Response

[1]Melva Wilson Costen, *African American Christian Worship* (Nashville: Abingdon, 1993, p. 18).
[2]Ibid., p. 77.
[3]Ibid., pp. 91-92.
[4]William B. McClain, "The Black Religious Experiences in the United States," in *This Far by Faith: American Black Worship and the African Roots* (Washington, D.C.: National Office for Black Catholics and the Liturgical Conference, 1977), p. 33.
[5]George Ofori-atta-Thomas, "The African Inheritance in the Black Church Worship," in *The Black Christian Worship Experience*, ed. Melva Wilson Costen and Darius L. Swann, Black Church Scholar Series 4 (Atlanta: ITC Press, 1992), pp. 54-55.

[6]Ibid., pp. 55-56.

[7]See C. Eric Lincoln and Lawrence H. Mamiya, *The Black Church in the African American Experience* (Durham, N.C.: Duke University Press, 1990), p. 353.

[8]Henry H. Mitchell, "The Continuity of African Culture," in *This Far by Faith: American Black Worship and the African Roots* (Washington, D.C.: National Office for Black Catholics and the Liturgical Conference, 1977), p. 13.

[9]Delores S. Williams, "Rituals of Resistance in Womanist Worship," in *Women at Worship: Interpretations of North American Diversity*, ed. Marjorie Procter-Smith and Janet R. Walton (Louisville, Ky.: Westminster John Knox, 1993), p. 221.

[10]Costen, *African American Christian Worship*, p. 52.

[11]Jon Michael Spencer, *Protest and Praise: Sacred Music of Black Religion* (Minneapolis: Fortress, 1990), p. 142.

[12]W. E. B. Du Bois, *The Souls of Black Folk* (New York: Fawcett, 1961), p. 135.

[13]Quoted in Lincoln and Mamiya, *Black Church*, p. 354, cf. p. 353; see also Costen, *African American Christian Worship*, pp. 53-54; Du Bois, *Souls of Black Folk*, p. 134; Spencer, *Protest and Praise*, p. 135.

[14]Quoted in James T. Campbell, *Songs of Zion: The African Methodist Episcopal Church in the United States and South Africa* (New York: Oxford University Press, 1995), p. 62.

[15]Spencer, *Protest and Praise*, p. 143.

[16]Lincoln and Mamiya, *Black Church*, pp. 352-53.

[17]Joseph M. Murphy, *Working the Spirit: Ceremonies of the African Diaspora* (Boston: Beacon Press, 1994), p. 153.

[18]James H. Cone, "Sanctification, Liberation and Black Worship," *Theology Today* 35 (July 1978): 146.

[19]Harold Dean Trulear, "The Lord Will Make a Way Somehow: Black Worship and the Afro-American Story," *Journal of the Interdenominational Theological Center* 13, no. 1 (fall 1985): 99; cf. Spencer, *Protest and Praise*, p. 149.

[20]Brenda Eatman Aghaowa, *Praising in Black and White: Unity and Diversity in Christian Worship* (Cleveland, Ohio: United Church Press, 1996), p. 96, from Cheryl Townsen Gilkes, "The Black Church as a Therapeutic Community: Suggested Areas for Research into the Black Religious Experience," *Journal of the Interdenominational Theological Center* 8, no. 1 (fall 1980): 29-44.

[21]Lincoln and Mamiya, *Black Church*, p. 365.

[22]See Edward P. Wimberly, "The Dynamics of Black Worship: A Psychosocial Exploration of the Impulses That Lie at the Roots of Black Worship," in *The Black Christian Worship Experience*, ed. Melva Wilson Costen and Darius L. Swann, Black Church Scholar Series 4 (Atlanta: ITC Press, 1992), p. 201.

[23]Trulear, *The Lord Will Make a Way*, p. 91.

[24]Ibid., p. 92.

[25]See Costen, *African American Christian Worship*, p. 65.

[26]Albert Pero, "Worship and Theology in the Black Context," in *Theology and the Black Experience*, ed. A. Pero and A. Moro (Minneapolis: Augsburg, 1988), p. 240.

[27]Hans A. Baer and Merrill Singer, *African-American Religion in the Twentieth Century: Varieties of Protest and Accommodation* (Knoxville: University of Tennessee Press, 1992), pp. 84-85.

[28]Cone, "Sanctification," p. 141.

[29]Trulear, *The Lord Will Make a Way*, p. 99.

Chapter 8: An Adventure of the Spirit

[1]The region is actually composed of many language groups and dialects. Most prominent are Spanish (Cuba, Dominican Republic and Puerto Rico), French (Haiti, Martinique, Guadaloupe, St. Martin and French Guyana) and Dutch (Netherlands Antilles, St. Maarten and Suriname).

[2]Note Belfield A. Castello, "The Search for an Existential Context for the Caribbean Church," (University of the West Indies, Jamaica, 1978), p. 28; Castello cites Lambres Comitas and David Lowenthal, *Slaves, Free Men, Citizens*, West Indian Perspectives (New York: Doubleday/Anchor, 1973), p. 277. See also Bob Plant et al., *Worship Around the World* (Don Mills, Ontario: CANEC Publishing & Supply House, 1980), p. 77.

[3]I borrowed this basic outline from Garrick A. B. Anthony, "The Folk Research Center, St. Lucia: A Case Study" (Antigua, 1975), p. 3, who thus divides the St. Lucia society.

[4]See George Eaton Simpson, *Religious Cults of the Caribbean: Trinidad, Jamaica and Haiti* (Rio Piedras, Puerto Rico: Institute of Caribbean Studies, University of Puerto Rico, 1970), pp. 12-13, 160; and Angelica Pollak-Eltz, "The Shango Cult and Other African Rituals in Trinidad, Grenada and Carriacou and Their Possible Influence on the Spiritual Baptist Faith," *Caribbean Quarterly* 39, nos. 3-4 (September-December 1993): 15.

[5]Pedrito Maynard-Reid, "Caribbean Worship," in *The Ministries of Christian Worship*, Library of Christian Worship (Nashville: StarSong, 1994), p. 214; see C. M. Jacobs, *Joy Comes in the Morning: Elton George Griffith and the Shouter Baptists* (Port-of-Spain, Trinidad and Tobago: 1996), p. 451.

[6]Ibid.; see also Althea Spencer, "Caribbean Church Music: An Introduction," unpublished paper, United Theological College of the West Indies, Jamaica, 1980-1981, p. 17.

[7]R. Ligon, *A True and Exact History of the Island of Barbados*, (Portland, Ore.: F. Cass, 1998), p. 47, cited in Dale Bisnauth, *History of Religions in the Caribbean* (Kingston, Jamaica: Kingston Publishers, 1989), p. 82.

[8]Bisnauth, *History of Religions*, p. 82.

[9]Cited in ibid.

[10]Ibid.

[11]S. Gwynn, *Mungo Park and the Quest for the Niger*, (London: John Lane, 1934), p. 139, cited in ibid.

[12]Eudora Thomas, *A History of the Shouter Baptists in Trinidad and Tobago* (Trinidad: Calalous, 1987), p. 31.

[13]Bisnauth, *History of Religions*, p. 83; see also Thomas, *History of the Shouter Baptists*, pp. 30-31.

[14]Bisnauth, pp. 89-90.

[15]See John Barton Hopkin, "Music in the Jamaican Pentecostal Churches," *Jamaica Journal*, no. 42 (September 1988)): 24-25; Bisnauth, *History of Religions in the Caribbean*, p. 165.

[16]Arthur C. Dayfoot, "The Shaping of the West Indian Church: Historical Factors in the Formation of the Pattern of Church Life in the English-Speaking Caribbean

1492-1870," Th.D. thesis, Toronto School of Theology, 1982, p. 283, citing C. F. Pascoe, *Two Hundred Years of the S.P.G.: An Historical Account . . . 1701-1900* (1901), p. 211.

[17]Dayfoot, *Shaping of the West Indian Church*, p. 284.

[18]Angelina Pollak-Eltz, "The Shango Cult and Other African Rituals in Trinidad, Grenada and Carriacou and Their Possible Influence on the Spiritual Baptist Faith," *Caribbean Quarterly* 39, nos. 3-4 (September-December 1993): 12.

[19]Quoted in Thomas, *History of the Shouter Baptists*, p. 22.

[20]Joseph M. Murphy, *Working the Spirit: Ceremonies of the African Diaspora*, (Boston: Beacon Press, 1994), p. 118.

[21]*An Account of Jamaica and Its Inhabitants* (Longman: London, 1808), pp. 250-51, quoted in Sister Donatine Prince, "Music and Liturgy in the Roman Catholic Church in Jamaica," unpublished paper, St. Michael's Seminary, 1979, p. 7.

[22]Murphy, *Working the Spirit*, p. 124.

[23]Quoted in ibid.

[24]William James Garner, *A History of Jamaica from Its Discovery by Christopher Columbus to the Year 1872* (1873; London: T. Fisher Unwin, 1909), p. 465, cited in Murphy, *Working the Spirit*, p. 124.

[25]Murphy, *Working the Spirit*, p. 124.

[26]Ibid., p. 122.

[27]Dayfoot, "Shaping of the West Indian Church," p. 519, n. 7.

[28]Hopkin, "Music in the Jamaican Pentecostal Churches," p. 25.

[29]Maynard-Reid, "Caribbean Worship," p. 214.

[30]Joanne Stephens, "The Changing Perspective of the Roman Catholic Church Towards Music Used in the Liturgy in Trinidad," unpublished paper, University of the West Indies, 1984, p. 12.

[31]Ibid., p. 13.

[32]Note Z. Albert-Perez, "Helping WI Church to Understand the Cults of Africa," *Sunday Guardian*, Trinidad, July 31, 1966, n.p.

[33]Stephen D. Glazier, "Caribbean Religions as Peripheral Cults: A Reevaluation," unpublished paper, University of Connecticut, 1979, p. 9.

[34]George Eaton Simpson, *Religious Cults: Trinidad, Jamaica and Haiti* (Rio Piedras, Puerto Rico: Institute of Caribbean Studies, University of Puerto Rico, 1970), p. 94.

[35]Ibid. See also George Eaton Simpson, "The Acculturative Process in Trinidadian Shango," *Anthropological Quarterly* 37 (1964): 21.

[36]Interview with Rawle Gibbons, Creative Arts Center, University of the West Indies, St. Augustine, Trinidad, July 3, 1997.

[37]See Pollak-Eltz, "Shango Cult."

[38]The Kele religion in St. Lucia was also introduced by indentured Yoruba laborers. It is similar to the Orisha in Trinidad and Grenada but developed independent of it (ibid., p. 12).

[39]Pollak-Eltz (ibid.) mentions that today Cuban Santería is the most prominent of the Yoruba-derived religions in the Americas and has most influenced the Trinidadian Orisha religion. Books on Santería are widely distributed in Trinidad. She also points out that since 1981 international conferences on Yoruba religion have been held in the United States, Cuba and Brazil. They have been attended by adherents from Trinidad and Grenada, Umbandists from Brazil and *santeros* from Venezuela.

Trinidadian followers of Orisha are much in contact with Yoruba leaders in Brazil, Puerto Rico and Nigeria.

[40]Simpson, *Religious Cults*, p. 11.

[41]Gibbons, interview.

[42]Ibid.

[43]Quoted in Shereen Ali, "Shango in Trinidad: Many Rivers to Cross." *Trinidadian Guardian*, July 25, 1995, p. 5.

[44]Ibid.

[45]Ibid.

[46]Simpson, *Religious Cults*, p. 77.

[47]Ibid., p. 110.

[48]George Eaton Simpson, "Baptismal, 'Mourning' and 'Building' Ceremonies of the Shouters in Trinidad," *Journal of American Folklore* 79, no. 314 (October-December 1966): 538; Murphy, *Working the Spirit*, p. 114.

[49]See Simpson, "Baptismal," p. 538.

[50]Bisnauth, *History of Religions in the Caribbean*, p. 178.

[51]Walter F. Pitts Jr., *Old Ship of Zion: The Afro-Baptist Ritual in the African Diaspora* (New York: Oxford University Press, 1993), p. 10.

[52]Murphy, *Working the Spirit*, p. 125.

[53]Ibid.

[54]Simpson, *Religious Cults*, p. 157.

[55]Pitts, *Old Ship of Zion*, p. 99.

[56]Simpson, *Religious Cults*, p. 173; see also Murphy, *Working the Spirit*, pp. 132-40, for an excellent detailed description of a typical service of the Mount Zion Tabernacle of God church on the outskirts of Kingston.

[57]Cited in Pitts, *Old Ship of Zion*, p. 99.

[58]Simpson, *Religious Cults*, pp. 173-74.

[59]Bisnauth, *History of Religions in the Caribbean*, p. 179.

[60]Simpson, *Religious Cults*, p. 167.

[61]Bisnauth, *History of Religions in the Caribbean*, p. 178.

[62]See Prince, "Music and Liturgy," p. 36, and Leslie Chang, "An Introduction to the Cumina Cult," unpublished paper, United Theological College of the West Indies, Jamaica, 1973, p. 9.

[63]Pollak-Eltz, "Shango Cult," p. 21.

[64]Ibid., p. 22. See also Simpson, "Baptismal," pp. 537-38; Simpson, *Religious Cults*, p. 11; Thomas, *History of the Shouter Baptists*, p. 32.

[65]Pitts, *Old Ship of Zion*, p. 102.

[66]Simpson ("Acculturative Process," p. 24) says in a footnote that this law did not affect the Orisha movement but its repeal furthered the cause of the Spiritual Baptists.

[67]Jacobs, *Joy Comes in the Morning*, pp. 451-53. Jacobs further asks, "Could . . . the concept of the Black Divinity, their pride in African and things African, have been the Caribbean precursors of a kind of theological Afrocentrism?" (pp. 452-53).

[68]Interview with Mother Monica Randoo, Cocorite, Trinidad, July 3, 1997.

[69]Simpson, "Baptismal," p. 537, also as per interview with Mother Monica.

[70]*Constitution and Government of the West Indian United Spiritual Baptist Order* (San Fernando, Trinidad: Vangard), p. 3.

[71]Stephen D. Glazier, *Marchin' the Pilgrims Home: Leadership and Decision-Making in an Afro-Caribbean Faith* (Westport, Conn.: Greenwood, 1983), p. 45.

[72]See Pitts, *Old Ship of Zion*, pp. 103-4; Thomas, *History of the Shouter Baptists*, pp. 31-32. See also Glazier, *Marchin'*, pp. 44-47, for more details on the worship ceremonies summarized here.

[73]Glazier, *Marchin'*, p. 47.

[74]Randoo, interview.

[75]Pitts, *Old Ship of Zion*, p. 101, citing George E. Simpson, *Black Religion in the New World* (New York: Columbia University Press, 1976), pp. 121-22.

[76]Bisnauth, *History of Religions in the Caribbean*, p. 190.

[77]Margaret D. Rouse-Jones, "Changing Patterns of Denominational Affiliations in Trinidad and Tobago: An Exploratory Study," in *Social and Occupational Stratification in Contemporary Trinidad and Tobago*, ed. Ryan Selway (St. Augustine, Trinidad and Tobago: Institute of Social and Economic Research, University of the West Indies, 1991), pp. 354-55.

[78]Barry Chevannes, "Towards an Afro-Caribbean Theology: Principles for the Indigenisation of Christianity in the Caribbean," *Caribbean Quarterly* 37 (March 1991): 45.

[79]See Rouse-Jones, "Changing Patterns," p. 364. Margaret Rouse-Jones, the head librarian of the University of the West Indies (Trinidad campus) and a researcher on Caribbean Pentecostalism, is herself a Pentecostal. Interview with Margaret D. Rouse-Jones, Library, University of the West Indies, St. Augustine, July 2, 1997.

[80]See Anthony L. LaRuffa, "Culture Change and Pentecostalism in Puerto Rico," *Social and Economic Studies* 18 (September 1969)): 281.

[81]Hopkin, "Music in the Jamaican Pentecostal Churches," p. 25.

[82]Ibid.

[83]See ibid., pp. 25-26, 35.

[84]Christopher Harlan Walker, "Caribbean Charismatics: The Pentecostal Church as Community on the Island of Tobago," Ph.D. diss., University of North Carolina, 1987, pp. 146, 175-76.

[85]Ibid., pp. 117-18.

[86]Ibid., p. 148.

[87]For example, Rouse-Jones, interview.

[88]Rouse-Jones, "Changing Patterns," p. 365.

[89]Frank E. Manning is noteworthy here: "Looking to the future, one might predict that Pentecostalism will become increasingly more indigenous, particularly on the symbolic/cultural level. As this happens Pentecostalism will sever its ties with metropolitan sponsors. . . . The model for this type of evolutionary (involutionary?) development has been set by such contemporary cults as Jamaican Pocomania and Trinidadian Spiritual Baptism, both of which had their initial inspiration in the nineteenth century from American Protestantism but later syncretized with African-creole residues. In another century Pentecostalism may join the Caribbean's syncretic cults. . . ." (Manning, "Pentecostalism: Christianity and Reputation," in *Perspectives on Pentecostalism: Case Studies from the Caribbean and Latin America* ed. Stephen D. Glazier [Washington, D.C.: University Press of America, 1980], pp. 182-86, quoted in Walker, "Caribbean Charismatics," p. 180).

[90]Spencer, "Caribbean Church Music," p. 17.

[91]Knolly Clarke, "Liturgy and Culture in the Caribbean: What Is to Be Done?" in *Troubling of the Waters*, ed. Idris Hamid (San Fernando, Trinidad: Rahamian, 1973), p. 146.

[92]Kortright Davis, *The Caribbean Church—to Change or to Stay? Just a Simple Survey* (Barbados: Caribbean Group for Social and Religious Studies, 1982), p. 19; see also Raymond Ray Palackdrarrysing, "In Search of a Caribbean Theology," (United Theological College of the West Indies, Jamaica, 1976), p. 11.

[93]See Plant et al., *Worship Around the World*, p. 78.

[94]Prince, "Music and Liturgy," p. 35.

Chapter 9: Caribbean Music

[1]Donatine Prince, "Music and Liturgy in the Roman Catholic Church in Jamaica," unpublished paper, University of the West Indies, Jamaica, 1979, pp. 36-37.

[2]See Althea Spencer, "Caribbean Church Music: An Introduction," unpublished paper, United Theological College of the West Indies, Jamaica, 1980-1981, p. 27.

[3]J. Wendell Mapson Jr., *The Ministry of Music in the Black Church* (Valley Forge, Penn.: Judson, 1984), p. 13.

[4]Quoted in Prince, "Music and Liturgy," p. 7.

[5]Ibid.

[6]Ibid., p. 8, quoted from *Jamaica Journal*, June 1970, p. 36.

[7]See Verena Reckord, "Rastafarian Music: An Introductory Study," *Jamaica Journal* 11, no. 1 (August 1977), for insight on the influence of Rasta music on Jamaican music.

[8]Spencer, "Caribbean Church Music," p. 18.

[9]Russ Smith, "The Soul of the Caribbean," *The Other Side* 28 (May-June 1992): 40.

[10]Note J. H. Kwabena Nketia, "African Roots of Music in the Americas," *Jamaica Journal* 43 (1980): 14.

[11]Spencer, "Caribbean Church Music," p. 26.

[12]Pedrito U. Maynard-Reid, "Caribbean Worship," in *The Ministries of Christian Worship*, Library of Christian Worship 7 (Nashville: StarSong, 1994), p. 215.

[13]Iris Hamid, *In Search of New Perspectives* (Bridgetown, Barbados: Caribbean Ecumenical Consultation for Development, 1971), p. 18, cited in Donovan L. Grant, "Toward a Ministry of Music: An Examination of the Ministry of Music in the Roman Catholic Church of Jamaica and the United Church of Jamaica and Grand Cayman," unpublished paper, University of the West Indies, Jamaica, 1985, p. 8.

[14]See interview with Mother Monica Randoo, Cocorite, Trinidad, July 3, 1997.

[15]During the interview with Rawle Gibbons (Creative Arts Center, University of the West Indies, St. Augustine, Trinidad, July 3, 1997), Funse Aiye Jinai offered these comments.

[16]See Joanne Stephens, "The Changing Perspective of the Roman Catholic Church Towards Music Used in the Liturgy in Trinidad," unpublished paper, University of the West Indies, St. Augustine, 1984, p. 13.

[17]John Barton Hopkin, "Music in the Jamaican Pentecostal Churches," *Jamaica Journal*, no. 42 (September 1988): 22-40.

[18]Ibid., p. 31.

[19]See Joseph G. Moore, "Music and Dance as Expressions of Religious Worship in Jamaica," in *African Religious Groups and Beliefs: Papers in Honor of William R. Bas-*

com, ed. Simon Ottenberg (Merrut, India: Folklore Institute, 1982), p. 267.

[20]Hopkin, "Music in the Jamaican Pentecostal Churches," pp. 29-30.

[21]Spencer, "Caribbean Church Music," p. 28.

[22]Pamela O'Gorman, "The Introduction of Jamaican Music into the Established Churches," *Jamaica Journal* 9, no. 1 (1975): 42.

[23]Cited in Richard O. Ramsey, "The Relationship Between the Church Music and Songs Used in the Main-line Churches in Jamaica and the Jamaican Culture and Social Classes," unpublished paper, United Theological College of the West Indies, Jamaica, n.d., p. 9.

[24]Prince, "Music and Liturgy," p. 12.

[25]See Moore, "Music and Dance," pp. 266, 282; also Joseph M. Murphy, *Working the Spirit: Ceremonies of the African Diaspora* (Boston: Beacon Press, 1994), pp. 132-40, for good insights on the use of Sankey hymns.

[26]Hopkin, "Music in the Jamaican Pentecostal Churches," p. 30.

[27]Ibid., p. 26.

[28]Ibid., p. 29.

[29]See Beverly B. Noble, "A Development of Liturgical Tradition Since 1962: A Study of the Anglican Church in Jamaica," unpublished paper, United Theological College of the West Indies, Jamaica, 1985, p. 36; Raymond Ray Palackdrarrysing, "In Search of a Caribbean Theology," unpublished paper, United Theological College of the West Indies, Jamaica, 1976, pp. 12-13; Grant, "Towards a Ministry of Music," p. 8.

[30]See O'Gorman, "Introduction of Jamaican Music," p. 41.

[31]All songs can be found in *Sing a New Song*, vol. 3, ed. Patrick Prescod (Bridgetown, Barbados: Caribbean Conference of Churches/Cedar Press, 1981).

[32]See Ramsey, "Relationship Between the Church Music," p. 8. Majorie Whylie, to whom Ramsey is indebted for his ideas here, also notes that we need a reeducation in concepts such as "white = purity."

[33]See Grant, "Towards a Ministry," p. 20; Ramsey, "Relationship Between the Church Music," pp. xvi-xviii.

[34]Cited in Ramsey, "Relationship Between the Church Music," p. 18.

[35]O'Gormann, "Introduction of Jamaican Music," p. 41.

[36]Cited in ibid., p. 43.

[37]Barry Chevannes, "Towards an Afro-Caribbean Theology: Principles for the Indigenisation of Christianity in the Caribbean," *Caribbean Quarterly* 37 (March 1991): 46.

[38]See Anthony B. Aarons, "Liturgical Reform in the Diocese of Jamaica: An Investigation into the Use of the Various Eucharistic Liturgies, 1662-1975," unpublished paper, United Theological College of the West Indies, Jamaica, 1981, p. 41.

Chapter 10: The Word & the Response

[1]See Ashley Smith, "The Christian Minister as a Political Activist," *Caribbean Journal of Religious Studies* 2 (September 1979): 28. Smith notes that because of this expectation many ministers find it almost impossible to not regard themselves as more than merely human.

[2]John Barton Hopkin, "Music in the Jamaican Pentecostal Churches," *Jamaica Journal*, no. 42 (September 1988): 26.

[3]William W. Watty, foreword to *The Carribean Pulpit: An Anthology*, ed. C. H. L. Gayle and W. W. Watty (Kingston, Jamaica: C. H. L. Gayle, 1983), p. v.

[4]Ibid.

[5]Hopkin, "Music in the Jamaican Pentecostal Churches," p. 26.

[6]See ibid.

[7]Christopher Harlan Walker, "Caribbean Charismatics: The Pentecostal Church as Community on the Island of Tobago," Ph.D. diss., University of North Carolina, 1987, p. 114.

[8]Hopkin, "Music in the Jamaican Pentecostal Churches," p. 27.

[9]Ibid.

[10]Ibid.

[11]Ibid.

[12]Ibid., p. 34.

[13]Ibid., p. 28.

[14]Quoted in George Eaton Simpson, *Religious Cults of the Caribbean: Trinidad, Jamaica and Haiti* (Rio Piedras, Puerto Rico: Institute of Caribbean Studies, University of Puerto Rico, 1970), p. 13; see also Angelina Pollak-Eltz, "The Shango Cult and Other African Rituals in Trinidad, Grenada and Carriacou and Their Possible Influence on the Spiritual Baptist Faith," *Caribbean Quarterly* 39, nos. 3-4 (September-December 1993): 13.

[15]Ibid., p. 14.

[16]From an interview with Rawle Gibbons, Creative Arts Center, University of the West Indies, St. Augustine, Trinidad, July 3, 1997.

[17]Idris Hamid, *In Search of New Perspectives* (Bridgetown, Barbados: Caribbean Consultation for Development, 1971), p. 8, quoted in Donovan L. Grant, "Towards a Ministry of Music: An Examination of the Ministry of Music in the Roman Catholic Church of Jamaica and the United Church of Jamaica and Grand Cayman," unpublished paper, University of the West Indies, Jamaica, 1985, p. 8.

[18]Cited in Donatine Prince, "Music and Liturgy in the Roman Catholic Church in Jamaica," unpublished paper, University of the West Indies, Jamaica, 1979, p. 29.

[19]Hopkin, "Music in the Jamaican Pentecostal Churches," p. 28.

[20]Simpson, *Religious Cults*, pp. 176-77.

[21]Raymond Ray Palackdrarrysing, "In Search of a Caribbean Theology," unpublished paper, United Theological College of the West Indies, Jamaica, 1976, p. 13.

Chapter 11: In the Spirit of a Fiesta

[1]See Allan Figueroa Deck, "The Spirituality of the United States Hispanics: An Introductory Essay," *U.S. Catholic Historian* 9 (winter 1990): 138; Justo L. González, "Hispanic Worship: An Introduction," in *Alabadle! Hispanic Christian Worship*, ed. Justo L. González (Nashville: Abingdon, 1996), p. 9; Otto Maduro, "Directions for a Reassessment of Latina/o Religion," in *Enigmatic Powers: Syncretism with African and Indigenous Peoples' Religions Among Latinos*, ed. Anthony M. Stevens-Arroyo and Andrés I. Pérez y Mena (New York: Bildner Center for Western Hemisphere Studies, 1995), pp. 53-54; Joan Moore, "The Social Fabric of the Hispanic Community Since 1965," in *Hispanic Catholic Culture in the U.S.: Issues and Concerns*, ed. Jay P. Dolan and Allan Figueroa Deck (Notre Dame, Ind.: University of Notre Dame Press, 1994), p. 6.

[2]Francis Buckley, "Popular Religiosity and Sacramentality: Learning from Hispanics a Deeper Sense of Symbol, Ritual and Sacrament," *The Living Light* 27 (summer 1991): 353; see also Eldin Villafañe, *The Liberating Spirit: Toward an Hispanic American Pentecostal Social Ethic* (Grand Rapids, Mich.: Eerdmans, 1993), p. 8; James R. Vidal, "Towards an Understanding of Synthesis in Iberian and Hispanic American Popular Religiosity," in *An Enduring Flame: Studies on Latino Popular Religiosity,* ed. Anthony M. Stevens-Arroyo and Ana María Diaz-Stevens (New York: Bildner Center for Western Hemisphere Studies, 1994), p. 69; Frank C. Senn, *Christian Worship and Its Cultural Setting,* (Philadelphia: Fortress, 1983), p. 53.

[3]David Abalos, "The Personal, Historical and Sacred Grounding of Culture: Some Reflections in the Creation of Latino Culture in the US from the Perspective of the Theory of Transformation," in *Old Masks, New Faces: Religion and Latino Identities,* Anthony ed. M. Stevens-Arroyo and Gilbert R. Cadena (New York: Bildner Center for Western Hemisphere Studies, 1995), p. 168.

[4]Deck, "Spirituality of the United States Hispanics," p. 138.

[5]See Moises Sandoval, "The Church Among the Hispanics in the United States," in *The Church in Latin America, 1492-1992,* ed. Enrique Dussel (Maryknoll, N.Y.: Orbis, 1992), pp. 231, 236-37; Ricardo Ramirez, "The American Church and Hispanic Migration: An Historical Analysis, Part I," *Migration Today* 6 (February 1978): 17-18.

[6]Yolanda Tarango, "The Church Struggling to Be Universal: A Mexican American Perspective," *International Review of Mission* 78 (April 1989): 168.

[7]Allan Figueroa Deck, *The Second Wave: Hispanic Ministry and the Evangelization of Cultures.* (New York: Paulist, 1989), p. 10.

[8]Leo Grebler, Joan W. Moore and Ralph C. Guzman, *The Mexican-American People: The Nation's Largest Minority* (New York: Free Press, 1970), p. 487.

[9]Phillip E. Lampe, "Religion and the Assimilation of Mexican Americans," *Review of Religious Research* 18 (Spring 1977): 248.

[10]See Migene González-Wippler, "Santería: Its Dynamics and Multiple Roots," in *Enigmatic Powers: Syncretism with African and Indigenous Peoples' Religions Among Latinos,* ed. Anthony M. Stevens-Arroyo and Andrés I. Pérez y Mena (New York: Bildner Center for Western Hemisphere Studies, 1995), p. 105; Ana María Diaz-Stevens, "Analyzing Popular Religiosity for Socio-religious Meaning," in *An Enduring Flame: Studies on Latino Popular Religiosity,* ed. Anthony M. Stevens-Arroyo and Ana María Diaz-Stevens (New York: Bildner Center for Western Hemisphere Studies, 1994), p. 22.

[11]Moore, "Social Fabric," p. 27.

[12]See ibid.; Joseph Fitzpatrick, *One Church, Many Cultures: The Challenge of Diversity* (Kansas City, Mo.: Sheed & Ward, 1987), pp. 128-29.

[13]See Fitzpatrick, *One Church,* p. 129.

[14]Ibid., p. 129.

[15]Gilbert R. Cadena notes that "racially, Latinos identify themselves as white, Black and Latino. For Latino U.S. citizens, 56% of Mexicans identified racially as white, 43% as Latino and less then one percent as Black. Among Puerto Ricans, 58% identified as white, 38% as Latino, and 4% as Black, among Cubans, 92% identified as white, 4% as Latino, and 4% as Black" ("Religious Ethnic Identity: A Socio-religious Portrait of Latinos and Latinas in the Catholic Church," in *Old Masks, New Faces: Religion and Latino Identities,* ed. Anthony M. Stevens-Arroyo and Gilbert R.

Cadena [New York: Bildner Center for Western Hemisphere Studies, 1995], p. 46).
See also Moore, "Social Fabric," p. 8.

[16]It has been suggested that the stimulus for this was the emergence of black consciousness among African-Americans and the civil rights movement. Racism pushed the strong effort to search out their identity and background in Africa. Fitzpatrick notes that "as the emphasis on Black identity found expression in literature, drama, poetry, and art, the Blacks as a people developed an organizational strength and gained many benefits for them as a people and as a distinct group of citizens in the U.S.A." (*One Church*, p. 147). In an interesting footnote, Fitzpatrick points to Michael Novak (who is now associated with the American Enterprise Institute and the new conservative right) in his 1971 work *The Rise of the Unmeltable Ethnic*, where he is indignant at what he describes as powerful pressures to give up one's ethnic identity and become Anglo-Saxon (Fitzpatrick, *One Church*, p. 147). These very sentiments are being expressed by Hispanics.

[17]See Alex D. Montoya, "Worship in Evangelical Hispanic Churches," in *The Ministries of Christian Worship*, Library of Christian Worship 7 (Nashville: StarSong, 1994), p. 221.

[18]Maduro, "Directions for a Reassessment," p. 56.

[19]Cf. Diaz-Stevens, "Analyzing," p. 28; Anthony M. Stevens-Arroyo, "Discovering Latino Religion," in *Discovering Latino Religion: A Comprehensive Social Science Bibliography*, ed. Anthony M. Stevens-Arroyo and Segundo Pantoja (New York: Bildner Center for Western Hemisphere Studies, 1995), p. 15.

[20]Cadena, "Religious Ethnic Identity," pp. 33-59.

[21]Ibid., pp. 38-39.

[22]Ibid.

[23]Jeanette Y. Rodriguez-Holguin, "Hispanics and the Sacred," *Chicago Studies* 29 (August 1990): 138.

[24]Allan Figuero Deck, "Hispanic Catholic Prayer and Worship," in *Alabadle! Hispanic Christian Worship*, ed. Justo L. González (Nashville: Abingdon, 1996), p. 40.

[25]Virgilio Elizondo, "Popular Religion as the Core of Cultural Identity in the Mexican American Experience," in *An Enduring Flame: Studies on Latino Popular Religiosity*, ed. Anthony M. Stevens-Arroyo and Ana María Diaz-Stevens (New York: Bildner Center for Western Hemisphere Studies, 1994), p. 119. See also Villafañe, *Liberating Spirit*, p. 112.

[26]Cited in Villafañe, *Liberating Spirit*, p. 8.

[27]Ricardo Ramirez, "Liturgy from the Mexican American Perspective," *Worship* 57 (July 1977): 294.

[28]Elizondo, "Popular Religion," p. 119.

[29]Villafañe, *Liberating Spirit*, p. 8.

[30]Luis M. Soler, *Historia de la esclaritud negra en Puerto Rico* (Rio Piedras, Puerto Rico: Editorial Universidad de Puerto Rico, 1970), p. 23, cited in Villafañe, *Liberating Spirit*, p. 10.

[31]Samuel Silva-Gotay, "The Ideological Dimensions of Popular Religiosity and Cultural Identity in Puerto Rico," in *An Enduring Flame: Studies on Latino Popular Religiosity*, ed. Anthony M. Stevens-Arroyo and Ana María Diaz-Stevens (New York: Bildner Center for Western Hemisphere Studies, 1994), p. 138.

[32]Diaz-Stevens, "Analyzing," p. 27. She goes on to say that that same person, before

going to bed, will kneel before her or his home altar, favorite saints or icons amidst lighted candles and holy water.

[33]González-Wippler, "Santería," pp. 104-5.

[34]Dale Bisnauth, *History of Religions in the Caribbean* (Kingston, Jamaica: Kingston Publishers, 1989), p. 165.

[35]Joseph M. Murphy, *Working the Spirit: Ceremonies of the African Diaspora* (Boston: Beacon Press, 1994), p. 82.

[36]Ibid., p. 88.

[37]Ibid.

[38]Ibid.

[39]Mercedes Cros Sandoval, "Afro-Cuban Religion in Perspective," in *Enigmatic Powers: Syncretism with African and Indigenous Peoples' Religions Among Latinos*, ed. Anthony M. Stevens-Arroyo and Andrés I. Pérez y Mena (New York: Bildner Center for Western Hemisphere Studies, 1995), pp. 92-93.

[40]Senn, *Christian Worship*, p. 53.

[41]Vidal, "Towards an Understanding of Synthesis," p. 87.

[42]Ibid., p. 70.

[43]Ibid.

[44]See Carlos Rosas, "Mexican Americans Sing Because They Feel Like Singing," *Pastoral Music* 1 (June-July 1977): 17; Rosa Maria Icaza, "Spirituality of the Mexican American People," *Worship* 63 (May 1989): 233.

[45]Silva Novo Pena, "Religion," in *The Hispanic American Almanac: A Reference Work on Hispanics in the United States*, ed. Nicolas Kanellos (Detroit: Gale Research, 1993), p. 380.

[46]Allan Figueroa Deck and Joseph Armando Nuñez, "Religious Enthusiasm and Hispanic Youths," *America*, October 23, 1982, p. 232.

[47]González, "Hispanic Worship," pp. 12-13.

[48]Kenneth Davis, "Brevia from the Hispanic Shift: Continuity Rather Than Conversion?" in *An Enduring Flame: Studies on Latino Popular Religiosity*, ed. Anthony M. Stevens-Arroyo and Ana María Diaz-Stevens (New York: Bildner Center for Western Hemisphere Studies, 1994), p. 208.

[49]Pena, "Religion," p. 380; Silva-Gotay, "Ideological Dimensions of Popular Religiosity," p. 156; Stevens-Arroyo, "Discovering Latino Religion," p. 15.

[50]Deck, "Hispanic Catholic," p. 40.

[51]Villafañe, *Liberating Spirit*, p. 85.

[52]Quoted in Allan Figueroa Deck, "The Challenge of Evangelical/Pentecostal Christianity to Hispanic Catholicism," in *Hispanic Catholic Culture in the U.S.: Issues and Concerns*, ed. Jay P. Dolan and Allan Figueroa Deck (Notre Dame, Ind.: University of Notre Dame Press, 1994), p. 410.

[53]Vivian Garrison, "Sectarianism and Psychosocial Adjustment: A Controlled Comparison of Puerto Rican Pentecostals and Catholics," in *Religious Movements in Contemporary America*, ed. Irving I. Zaretsky and Mark P. Leone (Princeton, N.J.: Princeton University Press, 1974), p. 301.

[54]Villafañe, *Liberating Spirit*, pp. 100-101.

[55]Silva-Gotay, "Ideological Dimensions of Popular Religiosity," p. 166.

[56]Raymond Rivera, "The Political and Social Ramifications of Indigenous Pentecostalism," in *Prophets Denied Honor: An Anthology on the Hispano Church of the United*

States, ed. Antonio M. Stevens-Arroyo (Maryknoll, N.Y.: Orbis, 1980), p. 340.

[57]Ibid.

[58]Ibid.

[59]Ibid.

[60]Samuel Solcontainsán, "Hispanic Pentecostal Worship," in *Alabadle! Hispanic Christian Worship*, ed. Justo L. González (Nashville: Abingdon, 1996), p. 47.

[61]Quoted in ibid.

[62]Garrison, "Sectarianism," p. 313.

[63]Ibid.

[64]Ibid., p. 327.

[65]See Fitzpatrick, *One Church*, p. 156; Solcontainsán, "Hispanic Pentecostal Worship," pp. 45, 55; Villafañe, *Liberating Spirit*, p. 128.

[66]Montoya, "Worship in Evangelical Hispanic Churches," p. 221.

[67]González, "Hispanic Worship," p. 13.

[68]Maria Luisa Santillán Baert, "Worship in the Hispanic United Methodist Church," in *Alabadle! Hispanic Christian Worship*, ed. Justo L. González (Nashville: Abingdon, 1996), p. 58.

[69]Ibid., pp. 58-59.

[70]Teresa Chávez Sauceda, "Becoming a Mestizo Church," in *Alabadle! Hispanic Christian Worship*, ed. Justo L. González (Nashville: Abingdon, 1996), pp. 96-97.

[71]Ibid., p. 97. See also Miguel Angel Darino, "What Is Different About Hispanic Baptist Worship?" in *Alabadle! Hispanic Christian Worship*, ed. Justo L. González. (Nashville: Abingdon, 1996), pp. 81-82, for a discussion on the awakening among Hispanic Baptists.

[72]Rodriguez-Holguin, "Hispanics and the Sacred," p. 138.

[73]Roberto Escamilla, "Worship in the Context of the Hispanic Culture," *Worship* 51 (July 1977): 291.

[74]Fitzpatrick, *One Church*, pp. 133-34.

[75]Villafañe, *Liberating Spirit*, pp. 112-13.

[76]Quoted in ibid., p. 12.

[77]Ibid., p. 129.

[78]Rodriguez-Holguin, "Hispanics and the Sacred," p. 142. I would use the term *secular* instead of *profane*. Secular and religious, or holy, are two dimensions of the spiritual. Profane is its antithesis.

[79]Escamilla, "Worship in the Context," p. 293, citing Virgilio Elizondo *Christianity and Culture: An Introduction to Pastoral Theology and Ministry for the Bicultural Community* (Huntington, Ind.: Our Sunday Visitor, 1975), pp. 172-73.

[80]See Ruben R. Armendariz, "Las Posadas (A Hispanic Christmas Service)," in *The Ministries of Christian Worship*, Library of Christian Worship 5 (Nashville: StarSong, 1994), p. 195.

[81]González, "Hispanic Worship," p. 20.

[82]Ramirez, "Liturgy from the Mexican American Perspective," pp. 297-98.

[83]See Montoya, "Worship in Evangelical Hispanic Churches," pp. 221-23; cf. Anthony L. LaRuffa, "Culture Change and Pentecostalism in Puerto Rico," *Social and Economic Studies* 18 (September 1969): 278.

[84]Roberto Escamilla, "Fiesta Worship," *The Interpreter* 20 (June 1976): 4.

[85]Ibid.

[86]González, "Hispanic Worship," pp. 20-21.
[87]Ramirez, "Liturgy from the Mexican American Perspective," p. 298.
[88]Icaza, "Spirituality of the Mexican American People," p. 243.
[89]Ibid., p. 242.
[90]Ibid., pp. 242-43.
[91]González, "Hispanic Worship," p. 23.
[92]Ibid., p. 22.
[93]Jill Martinez, "Worship and the Search for Community in the Presbyterian Church (U.S.A.): The Hispanic Experience," *Church and Society* 76 (March-April 1986): 44.
[94]Elizondo, *Christianity and Culture*, p. 172.
[95]Rivera, "Political and Social Ramifications," pp. 339-40.
[96]Orlando E. Costas, "Survival, Hope and Liberation in the Other American Church: An Hispanic Case Study," in *One Faith, Many Cultures: Inculturation, Indigenization and Contextualization*, ed. Ruy O. Costa (Maryknoll, N.Y.: Orbis, 1988), p. 143.
[97]Escamilla, "Fiesta Worship," p. 3.
[98]Fitzpatrick, *One Church*, p. 140.
[99]Anneris Goris, "Rites for a Rising Nationalism: Religious Meaning and Dominican Community Identity in New York City," in *Old Masks, New Faces: Religion and Latino Identities*, ed. Anthony M. Stevens-Arroyo and Gilbert R. Cadena (New York: Bildner Center for Western Hemisphere Studies, 1995), p. 137.
[100]Ricardo Ramirez, "Reflections on the Hispanicization of the Liturgy," *Worship* 57 (January 1983): 28.
[101]See Villafañe, *Liberating Spirit*, p. 104; Costas, "Survival, Hope and Liberation," p. 143.
[102]Timothy Matovina, "Liturgy, Popular Rites and Popular Spirituality," *Worship* 63 (July 1989): 350.
[103]Costas, "Survival, Hope and Liberation," p. 143.
[104]Escamilla, "Worship in the Context," p. 292.
[105]Ibid., p. 291.

Chapter 12: Hispanic Music

[1]Eldin Villafañe, *The Liberating Spirit: Toward an Hispanic American Pentecostal Social Ethic* (Grand Rapids, Mich.: Eerdmans, 1993), p. 117.
[2]Ibid., p. 11.
[3]Raquel Gutiérrez-Achón, "An Introduction to Hispanic Hymnody," in *Alabadle! Hispanic Christian Worship*, ed. Justo L. González (Nashville: Abingdon, 1996), p. 109.
[4]Virgilio P. Elizondo, *Christianity and Culture: An Introduction to Pastoral Theology and Ministry for the Bicultural Community* (Huntington, Ind.: Our Sunday Visitor, 1975), p. 168.
[5]Celeste Burgos and Ken Meltz, "How Shall We Sing the Lord's Song in a Foreign Land?: Theological and Cultural Implications of Hispanic Liturgical Music," *Faith and Forms* 22 (spring 1989): 17.
[6]Ricardo Ramirez, "Reflections on the Hispanicization of the Liturgy," *Worship* 57 (January 1983): 26-27.
[7]Burgos and Meltz, "How Shall We Sing," p. 17.
[8]Ibid.

[9]Villafañe, *Liberating Spirit*, p. 117.

[10]Miguel Angel Darino, "What Is Different About Hispanic Baptist Worship?" in *Alabadle! Hispanic Christian Worship*, ed. Justo L. González (Nashville: Abingdon, 1996), p. 83.

[11]Ibid., p. 84.

[12]Gutiérrez-Achón, " Introduction to Hispanic Hymnody," p. 102.

[13]Ibid.

[14]Jose A. Rodriguez, "Hispanic Hymns in the New Hymnal," *Reformed Liturgy and Music* 24 (spring 1990): 82.

[15]Gutiérrez-Achón, "Introduction to Hispanic Hymnody," pp. 104-5. Two articles by Carlos A. Lopez express the sentiments of those who oppose the new hymnody and prefer the more traditional fare: "Hymn Singing in the Hispanic Tradition," *Reformed Liturgy and Music* 21 (summer 1987): 156-57; and "Hispanic-American Song," in *Music and the Arts in Christian Worship*, Library of Christian Worship 4, bk. 1 (Nashville: StarSong, 1994), pp. 360-62. Illustrative of this is the following: "The young new pastors are heavily favoring contemporary music and words, either compositions imported from Latin American countries, or produced in the Southwest, Florida—by Cubans—and/or other areas with heavy concentrations of Hispanic parishioners, such as Chicago, New York, Philadelphia, and so forth. Hymns are also selected because of either the music or the words. Favorite hymns become favorite because the music is easy to learn and the words easy to remember. 'Coritos' are popular. The theology is usually shallow, but there are exceptions. One finds many mainline denomination Hispanic churches using guitars and singing 'coritos' these days. This goes hand in hand with a return of emotionalism and the preaching on moral issues emphasizing conversion experiences. It is 'the Old Time Religion' all over again" ("Hymn Singing," p. 157). Cf. also Alex D. Montoya, "Music in Evangelical and Pentecostal Hispanic Churches," in *The Ministries of Christian Worship*, Library of Christian Worship 7 (Nashville: StarSong, 1994), p. 222.

[16]Samuel Soliván, "Hispanic Pentecostal Worship," in *Alabadle! Hispanic Christian Worship*, ed. Justo L. González (Nashville: Abingdon, 1996), pp. 52-53; Montoya, "Music in Evangelical and Pentecostal," p. 222.

[17]Maria Luisa Santillán Baert, "Worship in the Hispanic United Methodist Church," in *Alabadle! Hispanic Christian Worship*, ed. Justo L. González (Nashville: Abingdon, 1996), p. 67.

[18]Montoya, "Music in Evangelical and Pentecostal," p. 223.

[19]Burgos and Meltz, "How Shall We Sing," p. 18.

[20]Montoya, "Music in Evangelical and Pentecostal," p. 223.

[21]Ibid.

[22]Angel G. Quintero-Rivera, "The Camouflaged Drum: Melodization of Rhythms and Maroonaged Ethnicity in Caribbean Peasant Music," *Caribbean Quarterly* 40, no. 1 (March 1991): 27.

[23]Ibid., p. 33. Interestingly, Quinto-Rivera notes that "since the Indian presence was, from early times in our history very weak in the Caribbean, and since 'Hispanic' Caribbean peasant music uses almost no drums (with which the African influence has been identified in the Americas), but mainly guitar-type instruments, this peasant music has generally been characterized as basically Spanish" (ibid., p. 29).

[24]Baert, "Worship in the Hispanic United Methodist Church," p. 64.

Chapter 13: Preaching, Prayer & Response

[1]Virgilio P. Elizondo, *Christianity and Culture: An Introduction to Pastoral Theology and Ministry for the Bicultural Community* (Huntington, Ind.: Our Sunday Visitor, 1975), p. 166.

[2]Ibid., pp. 166-67.

[3]Justo L. González, "Hispanic Worship: An Introduction," in *Alabadle! Hispanic Christian Worship*, ed. Justo L. González (Nashville: Abingdon, 1996), p. 24.

[4]Allan Figueroa Deck, "Hispanic Catholic Prayer and Worship," in *Alabadle! Hispanic Christian Worship*, ed. Justo L. González (Nashville: Abingdon, 1996), p. 30.

[5]Samuel Soliván, "Hispanic Pentecostal," in *Alabadle! Hispanic Christian Worship*, ed. Justo L. González (Nashville: Abingdon, 1996), p. 54.

[6]Rosa Maria Icaza, "Spirituality of the Mexican American People," *Worship* 63 (May 1989): 234.

[7]Ibid., pp. 234-35.

[8]Alex D. Montoya, "Worship in Evangelical Hispanic Churches," in *The Ministries of Christian Worship*, Library of Christian Worship 7 (Nashville: StarSong, 1994), p. 222.

[9]Deck, "Hispanic Catholic," p. 29.

[10]González, "Hispanic Worship," pp. 23-24.

[11]Jill Martinez, "Worship and the Search for Community in the Presbyterian Church (U.S.A.): The Hispanic Experience," *Church and Society* 76 (March-April 1986): 45.

[12]Roberto Escamilla, "Fiesta Worship," *The Interpreter* 20 (June 1976): 4.

[13]Ibid.

[14]Elizondo, *Christianity and Culture*, p. 167.

[15]Maria Luisa Santillán Baert, "Worship in the Hispanic United Methodist Church," in *Alabadle! Hispanic Christian Worship*, ed. Justo L. González (Nashville: Abingdon, 1996), p. 70.

[16]Escamilla, "Fiesta Worship," p. 2.

[17]Soliván, "Hispanic Pentecostal," p. 53.

[18]Deck, "Hispanic Catholic," p. 39.

[19]Ibid.

[20]Elizondo, *Christianity and Culture*, p. 169.

[21]Angel G. Quintero-Rivera, "The Camouflaged Drum: Melodization of Rhythms and Maroonaged Ethnicity in Caribbean Peasant Music," *Caribbean Quarterly* 40, no. 1 (March 1991): 33.

[22]Jon Michael Spencer, *Protest and Praise: Sacred Music of Black Religion* (Minneapolis: Fortress, 1990), p. 142.

[23]Deck, "Hispanic Catholic," p. 36.

[24]Gustavo Benavides, "Resistance and Accommodation in Latin American Popular Religiosity," in *An Enduring Flame: Studies on Latino Popular Religiosity*, ed. Anthony M. Stevens-Arroyo and Ana María Diaz-Stevens (New York: Bildner Center for Western Hemisphere Studies, 1994), p. 55.

Chapter 14: Rational & Physical

[1]Robert C. Williams, "Worship and Anti-structure in Thurman's Vision of the

Sacred," in *The Black Christian Worship Experience*, ed. Melva Wilson Costen and Darius L. Swann, Black Church Scholar Series 4 (Atlanta: ITC Press, 1992), p. 162.

[2]Ibid.

[3]Mary Douglas, *Natural Symbols: Explorations in Cosmology* (London: Barrie and Jenkins, 1973), p. 93.

[4]Ibid., p. 99.

[5]Ibid., p. 100.

[6]Frank C. Senn, *Christian Worship and Its Cultural Setting*, (Philadelphia: Fortress, 1983), pp. 73-74.

[7]Douglas takes ritualism to signify a heightened appreciation of symbolic action which is manifested in a couple of ways: (1) "belief in the efficacy of instituted signs" and (2) "sensitivity to condensed symbols" (*Natural Symbols*, p. 26). She disagrees with sociologists who use the term *ritualist* for one who "performs external gestures without inner commitment to the ideas and values expressed." This she believes is a "distractingly partisan use of the term," derived from the antiritualist assumption in the long history of religious revivalism. She argues that *ritual* should be kept neutral. Among the reasons given is that "anthropologists need to communicate with sociologists and zoologists. They are in the habit of using ritual to mean action and belief in the symbolic order without reference to the commitment or non-commitment of the actors" (ibid., p. 20).

[8]Ibid., p. 22.

[9]Michael Marshall, *Renewal in Worship* (Wilton, Conn.: Morehouse-Barlow, 1985), pp. 70-71.

[10]Kenneth J. Dale, "Body and Mind in Worship (In Pursuit of Wholeness)," *Japan Christian Quarterly* 49 (winter 1983): 59.

[11]Senn, *Christan Worship*, p. 75.

[12]Ibid., pp. 46, 68; Miguel Angel Darino, "What Is Different About Hispanic Baptist Worship?" in *Alabadle! Hispanic Christian Worship*, ed. Justo L. González (Nashville: Abingdon, 1996), p. 85.

[13]In teacher-centered teaching the professor is the focus of all significant communication in the classroom. Chairs and desks are arranged in neat rows facing the instructor. Students sit attentively waiting for pearls of wisdom from the professor's lips, and they take notes profusely. In student-centered teaching, seats are arranged in a circle; many voices are heard, all are learners, all are participants, all are involved. See Jonathan Zophy, "Student-Centered Teaching." *Perspectives*, February 1991, pp. 20-21.

[14]Marshall, *Renewal in Worship*, p. 31.

[15]Ibid., p. 35.

[16]Senn, *Christian Worship*, p. 75.

[17]Ibid.

[18]See ibid., pp. 75-76, for some insightful thoughts on this dichotomy.

[19]Charles H. Kraft, *Christianity with Power: Your Worldview and Your Experience of the Supernatural* (Ann Arbor, Mich.: Servant, 1989), pp. 42-43.

[20]Justo L. González, "Hipsanic Worship: An Introduction," in *Alabadle! Hispanic Christian Worship*, ed. Justo L. González (Nashville: Abingdon, 1996), p. 25.

[21]Don M. Wardlaw, "Tension in the Sanctuary," *Duke Divinity School Review* 43 (winter 1978): 15.

[22]Ibid.

[23]Frank A. Thomas, *They Like to Never Quit Praisin' God: The Role of Celebration in Preaching* (Cleveland, Ohio: United Church Press, 1997), p. 5.

[24]Ibid., pp. 8-9.

[25]Ibid., p. 10. Henry H. Mitchell notes that over "more than two thousand years, the word *emotion* itself has suffered from gross misrepresentation. All too often the term seems to connote only the lower emotions: fear, lust, hate, prejudice, and paranoid distrust. We confuse 'emotion and emotionalism, defining the quality by its extreme' (Craddock, *Authority*, p. 85)" (*Celebration and Experience in Preaching* [Nashville: Abingdon, 1990], p. 28).

[26]Mongameli Mabona, "Black People and White Worship," in *The Challenge of Black Theology in South Africa*, ed. Basil Moore (Atlanta: John Knox, 1973), p. 107. I've often told my classes and seminars that the church is filled with what I call "neckback" (Jamaican for the back of one's neck) Christians. We walk into church gazing at another's neckback, go through the service, and leave worship still gazing at a fellow worshiper's neckback without any interaction. Thea Bowman makes a similar point: "So often we attempt to do liturgy without bonding. You come into a silent church—and I'm not talking about the silence of prayer—you come into this silent church: nobody looks at you, nobody acknowledges your presence, nobody welcomes you, nobody includes you, nobody smiles at you, nobody touches you. I've seen people come to church, stay in church, and leave church without any human contact. Sometimes we come together in the same church without becoming one people" ("Justice, Power and Praise," in *Liturgy and Social Justice*, ed. Edward M. Grosz [Collegeville, Minn.: Liturgical, 1989], p. 27).

[27]Douglas R. Clark, "Worship Patterns in the Psalms," paper presented at the West Coast Religion Teachers Conference, April 1991, p. 6.

[28]See also Bruce Johanson, "To Draw Near to a Faithful Soul: Worship-Appropriate Features of 1 Thessalonians," paper presented at the West Coast Religion Teachers Conference, April 1991, p. 1.

[29]Robert E. Webber, *Worship Old and New: A Biblical, Historical and Practical Introduction*, rev. ed. (Grand Rapids, Mich.: Zondervan, 1994), p. 112.

[30]See Ronald Bissell, "Worship in Early Seventh-day Adventist Church," paper presented at the West Coast Religion Teachers Conference, April 1991, p. 2, 13; Ronald Graybill, "Glory, Glory," *Adventist Review*, October 1, 1987, p. 13; special section on "Early Adventures in Maine" in *Spectrum* 17, no. 5 (August 1987): 15-50.

[31]Ronald D. Graybill, "Enthusiasm in Early Adventist Worship," *Ministry*, October 1991, pp. 10-12.

[32]Marshall says, "It is not an accident that at the first Pentecost the spirit-filled apostles were mistakenly regarded by many as drunk. In all ecstatic experiences and whenever and wherever men and women are released through the transcendence of worship, there is always the possibility of confusing and overlapping phenomena" (*Renewal in Worship*, p. 7).

[33]Terry MacArthur, "Towards Global Worship: Beyond the Headlines," in *The Ministries of Christian Worship*, Library of Christian Worship 7 (Nashville: StarSong, 1994), p. 203.

[34]Henry H. Mitchell, "The Continuity of African Culture," in *This Far by Faith: American Black Worship and the African Roots* (Washington, D.C.: National Office for Black

Catholics and the Liturgical Conference, 1977), p. 13.

[35]Brenda Eatman Aghaowa, *Praising in Black and White: Unity and Diversity in Christian Worship* (Cleveland, Ohio: United Church Press, 1996), p. 28.

[36]Debbie Roberts, *Rejoice: A Biblical Study of the Dance* (Bedford, Tex.: Revival, 1982), p. xiii. See Shereen Ali, "Shango in Trinidad: Many Rivers to Cross," *Trinidadian Guardian*, July 25, 1995, p. 5.

[37]Lawrence J. Johnson, *The Mystery of Faith: The Ministers of Music* (Washington, D.C.: National Association of Pastoral Musicians, 1983), p. 84.

[38]Ibid, p. 85.

[39]Mitchell, *Celebration and Experience*, p. 27

[40]Roberts, *Rejoice*, p. xiii.

[41]Ibid.

[42]Ibid., p. 7; see Martha A. Kirk, "A Mexican Dance," in *Music and the Arts in Christian Worship*, Library of Christian Worship 4, bk. 2 (Nashville: StarSong, 1994), p. 762.

[43] Paul Hoon, *The Integrity of Worship* (Nashville: Abingdon, 1971), p. 298, quoted in Wardlaw, "Tension in the Sanctuary," p. 8.

Bibliography

Aarons, Anthony B. "Liturgical Reform in the Diocese of Jamaica: An Investigation into the Use of the Various Eucharistic Liturgies—1662-1975." Paper presented at the United Theological College of the West Indies, Jamaica, 1981.

Abalos, David. "The Personal, Historical and Sacred Grounding of Culture: Some Reflections in the Creation of Latino Culture in the U.S. from the Perspective of the Theory of Transformation." In *Old Masks, New Faces: Religion and Latino Identities.* Edited by Anthony M. Stevens-Arroyo and Gilbert R. Cadena, pp. 143-72. New York: Bildner Center for Western Hemisphere Studies, 1995.

Aghaowa, Brenda Eatman. *Praising in Black and White: Unity and Diversity in Christian Worship.* Cleveland, Ohio: United Church Press, 1996.

Albert-Perez, Z. "Helping WI Church to Understand the Cults of Africa." *Sunday Guardian,* July 31, 1966, n.p.

Ali, Shereen. "Shango in Trinidad: Many Rivers to Cross." *Trinidadian Guardian,* July 25, 1995, pp. 5-6.

Anthony, Garrick A. B. *The Folk Research Center, St Lucia: A Case Study.* Antigua, 1975.

Armendariz, Ruben R. "Las Posadas: A Hispanic Christmas Service." In *The Ministries of Christian Worship* 5. Nashville: Star Song, 1994.

Bach-y-Rita, George. "The Mexican American: Religious and Cultural Influences." In *Mental Health and Hispanic Americans: Clinical Perspectives.* Edited by Rosina M. Becerra, Marvin Karno and Javier I. Escobar, pp. 29-40. New York: Grune & Stratton, 1993.

Baer, Hans A., and Merrill Singer. *African-American Religion in the Twentieth Century: Varieties of Protest and Accommodation.* Knoxville: University of Tennessee Press, 1992.

Baert, Maria Luisa Santillán. "Worship in the Hispanic United Methodist Church." In *!Alabadle!:Hispanic Christian Worship.* Edited by Justo L. Gonzàlez, pp. 57-72. Nashville: Abingdon, 1996.

Bangert, Mark. "How Does One Go About Multicultural Worship?" In *What does "Multicultural" Worship Look Like?* Edited by Gordon Lathrop, pp. 24-33. Minneapolis: Augsburg Fortress, 1996.

Bascom, William R. "The Focus of Cuban Santeria." In *Peoples and Cultures of the Caribbean: An Anthropological Reader.* Edited by Michael M. Horowitz, pp. 522-27. Garden City, N.Y.: Natural History Press, 1971.

Benavides, Gustavo. "Resistance and Accommodation in Latin American Popular Religiosity." In *An Enduring Flame: Studies on Latino Popular Religiosity.* Edited by Anthony M. Stevens-Arroyo and Ana María Diaz-Stevens, pp. 37-67. New York: Bildner Center for Western Hemisphere Studies, 1994.

Benavides, Gustavo. "Syncretism and Legitimacy in Latin American Religion." In *Enigmatic Powers: Syncretism with African and Indigenous Peoples' Religions Among*

Latinos. Edited by Anthony M. Stevens-Arroyo and Andrés I. Pérez y Mena, pp. 19-46. New York: Bildner Center for Western Hemisphere Studies, 1995.

Bennett, Lerone Jr. *The Shaping of the Black America: The Struggles and Triumphs of African-Americans, 1619 to the 1990s.* New York: Penguin, 1975.

Bethea, Joseph B. "Worship in the Black Church." *Duke Divinity School Review* 43 (winter 1978):44-53.

Bevans, Stephen B. *Models of Contextual Theology.* Maryknoll, N.Y.: Orbis, 1992.

"Bibliography for Singing in Worship." In *Music and the Arts in Christian Worship.* Library of Christian Worship 4, bk. 1. Nashville: Star Song, 1994.

Bisnauth, Dale. *History of Religions in the Caribbean.* Kingston, Jamaica: Kingston, 1989.

Bissell, Ronald. "Worship in the Early Seventh-day Adventist Church." Paper presented at the West Coast Religion Teachers Conference, April 1991.

Boehm, Mike. "Musical Resources for the Hispanic Community." *Pastoral Music* 10 (February-March 1986):24-25.

Bowman, Thea. "Justice, Power and Praise." In *Liturgy and Social Justice.* Edited by Edward M. Grosz. Collegeville, Minn.: Liturgical Press, 1989.

Brandon, John E. "Worship in the Black Experience." In *The Black Christian Worship Experience.* Black Church Scholar 4. Edited by Melva Wilson Costen and Darius L. Swann, pp. 109-16. Atlanta: ITC, 1992.

Bromiley, Geoffrey W. "History of New Testament Worship." In *The Ministries of Christian Worship.* Library of Christian Worship 1. Nashville: Star Song, 1994.

Brown, Paul B. *In and for the World: Bringing the Contemporary into Christian Worship.* Minneapolis: Fortress, 1992.

Brown, Grayson W. "Music in the Black Spiritual Tradition." In *This Far by Faith: American Black Worship and the African Roots,* pp. 88-93. Washington, D.C.: National Office for Black Catholics and the Liturgical Conference, 1977.

Buckley, Francis "Popular Religiosity and Sacramentality: Learning From Hispanics a Deeper Sense of Symbol, Ritual and Sacrament." *The Living Light* 27 (summer 1991):351-60.

Burgos, Celeste, and Ken Meltz. " 'How Shall We Sing the Lord's Song in a Foreign Land?': Theological and Cultural Implications of Hispanic Liturgical Music." In *Faith and Forms* 22 (spring 1989):16-18.

Burma, John H. *Mexican-Americans in the United States: A Reader.* New York: Schenkman, 1970.

Cadena, Gilbert R. "Religious Ethnic Identity: A Socio-Religious Portrait of Latinos and Latinas in the Catholic Church." In *Old Masks, New Faces: Religion and Latino Identities.* Edited by Anthony M. Stevens-Arroyo and Gilbert R. Cadena, pp. 33-59. New York: Bildner Center for Western Hemisphere Studies, 1995.

Campbell, James T. *Songs of Zion: The African Methodist Episcopal Church in the United States and South Africa.* New York: Oxford University Press, 1995.

Canizaves, Raul Jose. "Santeria: From Afro-Caribbean Cult to World Religion." *Caribbean Quarterly* 40, no. 1 (1994):59-63.

Carrasco, David. "A Perspective for a Study of Religious Dimensions on Chicano Experience: *Bless Me, Ultima* as a Religious Text." *Aztlaan* 13 (spring-fall 1982):195-222.

Castello, Belfield A. "The Search for an Extential Context for the Caribbean Church."

Paper presented at the University of the West Indies, Jamaica, 1978.

Chambers, Edward. "The Church: The Best Hope for Change and Social Justice." *La Raza* 3 (summer 1977):45-47.

Chandran, J. Russell, and John Robb Flemming. "East Asia Theological Commission on Worship." *South East Asia Journal of Theology* 4 (April 1963):26-44.

Chang, Leslie. "An Introduction to the Cumina Cult." Paper presented at the United Theological College of the West Indies, Jamaica, 1973.

Chase, Winston George. "A Critical Assessment of the Liturgy of the Moravian Church in Jamaica During the Period 1965-1975." Paper presented at the Faculty of Arts and General Studies, University of the West Indies, Jamaica, n.d.

Chevannes, Barry. "Towards an Afro-Caribbean Theology: Principles for the Indigenisation of Christianity in the Caribbean." *Caribbean Quarterly* 37, no. 1 (1991):45-54.

Clark, Douglas R. "Worship Patterns in the Psalms." Paper presented at the West Coast Religion Teachers Conference, April 1991.

Clarke, Knolly. "Liturgy and Culture in the Caribbean: What Is to Be Done?" In *Troubling of the Waters*. Edited by Iris Hamid, pp. 141-57. Trinidad: Rahaman, 1973.

Comfort, Philip. "The House Church and Its Worship." In *The Ministries of Christian Worship*. Library of Christian Worship 1. Nashville, Tenn.: Star Song, 1994.

Cone, James. H. *The Spirituals and the Blues: A Interpretation*. Maryknoll, N.Y.: Orbis, 1991.

————. "Sanctification, Liberation and Black Worship." *Theology Today* 35 (July 1978):139-52.

Constitution and Government of the West Indian United Spiritual Baptist Order. San Fernando, Trinidad: Vangard, n.d.

Cook, Scott. "The Prophets: A Revivalistic Folk Religious Movement in Puerto Rico." In *Peoples and Cultures of the Caribbean: An Anthropological Reader*. Edited by Michael M. Horowitz, pp. 560-79. Garden City, N.Y.: Natural History Press, 1971.

Costas, Orlando E. "Survival, Hope and Liberation in the Other American Church: An Hispanic Case Study." *One Faith, Many Cultures: Inculturation, Indigenization and Contextualization*. Edited by Ruy O. Costa, pp. 136-44. Maryknoll, N.Y.: Orbis, 1988.

Costen, Melva Wilson. "A Response to Dr. Williams' Paper." In *The Black Christian Worship Experience*. Black Church Scholar 4. Edited by Melva Wilson Costen and Darius L. Swann, pp. 175-76. Atlanta: ITC, 1992.

————. "Books and Articles on Afro-American Worship: An Annotated Bibliography." In *The Black Christian Worship Experience*. Black Church Scholar 4. Edited by Melva Wilson Costen and Darius L. Swann, pp. 237-56. Atlanta: ITC, 1992.

————. *African American Christian Worship*. Nashville: Abingdon, 1993.

Costen, Melva Wilson, and Darius Leander Swann, eds. *The Black Christian Worship Experience*. Black Church Scholar 4. Atlanta: ITC, 1992.

Cushman, Stephen. "Gospel Songs." In *Music and the Arts in Christian Worship*. Library of Christian Worship 4, bk. 1. Nashville: Star Song, 1994.

Cusic, Don. *The Sound of Light: A History of Gospel Music*. Bowling Green, Ohio: Bowling Green State University Popular Press, 1990.

Dale, Kenneth J. "Body and Mind in Worship: In Pursuit of Wholeness." *Japan Christian Quarterly* 49 (winter 1983):58-60.

250 ──────────────────── Diverse Worship

Darino, Miguel Angel. "What Is Different About Hispanic Baptist Worship?" In *!Ala-badle!: Hispanic Christian Worship.* Edited by Justo L. Gonzàlez, pp. 73-88. Nashville: Abingdon, 1996.

Davis, Kenneth. "Brevia from the Hispanic Shift: Continuity Rather Than Conversion?" In *An Enduring Flame: Studies on Latino Popular Religiosity.* Edited by Anthony M. Stevens-Arroyo and Ana María Diaz-Stevens, pp. 205-10. New York: Bildner Center for Western Hemisphere Studies, 1994.

Davis, Kortright. *The Caribbean Church: To Change or to Stay? Just a Simple Survey.* Barbados: CGRS, 1982.

Dayfoot, Authur C. "The Shaping of the West Indian Church: Historical Factors in the Formation of the Pattern of Church Life in the English-Speaking Caribbean 1492-1870." Th.D. thesis, Toronto School of Theology, 1982.

Deck, Allan Figueroa. "Fundamentalism and the Hispanic Catholic." *America,* January 26, 1985, pp. 64-66.

──────. *The Second Wave: Hispanic Ministry and the Evangelization of Cultures.* New York: Paulist, 1989.

──────. "The Spirituality of the United States Hispanics: An Introductory Essay." *U.S Catholic Historian* 9 (winter 1990):137-46.

──────. "The Challenge of Evangelical/Pentecostal Christianity to Hispanic Catholicism." In *Hispanic Catholic Culture in the U.S.: Issues and Concerns.* Edited by Jay P. Dolan and Allan Figueroa Deck, pp. 409-39. Notre Dame, Indiana: University of Notre Dame Press, 1994.

──────. "Hispanic Catholic Prayer and Worship." In *!Alabadle!:Hispanic Christian Worship.* Edited by Justo L. Gonzàlez, pp. 29-42. Nashville: Abingdon, 1996.

Deck, Allan Figueroa, and Joseph Armando Nunez. "Religious Enthusiasm and Hispanic Youths." *America,* October 23, 1982, pp. 232-34.

DePeya, Hazel An Gibbs, ed. *Call Him by His Name Jesus.* San Fernando, Trinidad: Fishnet, 1996.

Diaz-Stevens, Ana María. "Analyzing Popular Religiosity for Socio-Religious Meaning." In *An Enduring Flame: Studies on Latino Popular Religiosity.* Edited by Anthony M. Stevens-Arroyo and Ana María Diaz-Stevens, pp. 17-36. New York: Bildner Center for Western Hemisphere Studies, 1994.

Douglas, Mary. *Natural Symbols: Explorations in Cosmology.* London: Barrie & Jenkins, 1973.

DuBois, W. E. B. *The Soul of Black Folk.* New York, Fawcett, 1961.

Dunn, James D. G. *Unity and Diversity in the New Testament: An Inquiry into the Character of Earliest Christianity.* London: SCM Press, 1977.

Earl, Riggins R. Jr. "Under Their Own Vine and Fig Tree: The Ethics of Social and Spiritual Hospitality in Black Church Worship." In *The Black Christian Worship Experience.* Black Church Scholar 4. Edited by Melva Wilson Costen and Darius L. Swann, pp. 181-93. Atlanta: ITC, 1992.

Elizondo, Virgilio P. *Christianity and Culture: An Introduction to Pastoral Theology and Ministry for the Bicultural Community.* Huntington, Ind.: Our Sunday Visitor, 1975.

──────. "Popular Religion as the Core of Cultural Identity in the Mexican American Experience." In *An Enduring Flame: Studies on Latino Popular Religiosity.* Edited by Anthony M. Stevens-Arroyo and Ana María Diaz-Stevens, pp. 113-32. New York: Bildner Center for Western Hemisphere Studies, 1994.

Escamilla, Roberto. "Fiesta Worship." *The Interpreter* 20 (June 1976):n.p.
———. "Worship in the Context of the Hispanic Culture." *Worship* 51 (July 1977):290-93.
Fitzpatrick, Joseph. *One Church Many Cultures: The Challenge of Diversity.* Kansas City: Sheed & Ward, 1987.
Flores, Richard R. "Chicanos, Culture and Borderlands: Reflections on Worship." *Modern Liturgy* 18, no. 9: 16-17.
Francis, Mark R. *Liturgy in a Multicultural Community.* Collegeville, Minn.: Liturgical Press, 1991.
———. "A History of Cultural Adaptation in Christian Worship." In *The Ministries of Christian Worship.* Library of Christian Worship 7. Nashville: Star Song, 1994.
———. "Liturgical Adaptation in the Roman Catholic Church in the Twentieth Century." In *The Ministries of Christian Worship.* Library of Christian Worship 7. Nashville: Star Song, 1994.
Frazier, Sundee. "Multiethnic Windows on Worship." In *Worship Team Handbook.* Edited by Alison Siewart, pp. 20-26. Downers Grove, Ill.: InterVarsity, 1998.
Frazier, E. Franklin. *The Negro Church in America.* New York: Schochen, 1974.
Garrison, Vivian. "Sectarianism and Psychosocial Adjustment: A Controlled Comparison of Puerto Rican Pentecostals and Catholics." *Religious Movements in Contemporary America.* Edited by Irving I. Zaretsky and Mark P. Leone, pp. 298-329. Princeton, N.J.: Princeton University Press, 1974.
Gibbons, Rawle. Interview by author. Creative Arts Center, University of the West Indies, Jamaica, July 3, 1997.
Glazier, Stephen D. "Caribbean Religions as Peripheral Cults: A Reevaluation." Paper presented at the University of Connecticut, 1979.
———. *Marchin' the Pilgrims Home: Leadership and Decision-Making in an Afro-Caribbean Faith.* Westport, Conn.: Greenwood, 1983.
González, Justo L. "Hispanic Worship: An Introduction." In *¡Alabadle!: Hispanic Christian Worship.* Edited by Justo L. Gonzàlez, pp. 9-27. Nashville: Abingdon, 1996.
González, Justo L., ed. *¡Alabadle!: Hispanic Christian Worship.* Nashville: Abingdon, 1996.
González-Wippler, Migene. "Santería: Its Dynamics and Multiple Roots." In *Enigmatic Powers: Syncretism with African and Indigenous Peoples' Religions Among Latinos.* Edited by Anthony M. Stevens-Arroyo and Andrés I. Pérez y Mena, pp. 99-111. New York: Bildner Center for Western Hemisphere Studies, 1995.
Goris, Anneris. "Rites for a Rising Nationalism: Religious Meaning and Dominican Community Identity in New York City." In *Old Masks, New Faces: Religion and Latino Identities.* Edited by Anthony M. Stevens-Arroyo and Gilbert R. Cadena, pp. 117-41. New York: Bildner Center for Western Hemisphere Studies, 1995.
Grant, Donovan L. "Towards a Ministry of Music: An Examination of the Ministry of Music in the Roman Catholic Church of Jamaica and the United Church of Jamaica and Grand Cayman." Paper presented at the University of the West Indies, Jamaica, 1985.
Graybill, Ronald D. "Glory, Glory." *Adventist Review,* October 1, 1987, pp. 12-13.
———. "Enthusiasm in Early Adventist Worship." *Ministry,* October 1991, pp. 10-12.
Grebler, Leo, Joan W. Moore, and Ralph C. Guzman. *The Mexican-American People: The Nation's Largest Minority.* New York: Free Press, 1970.

Gutiérrez-Achón, Raquel. "An Introduction to Hispanic Hymnody." In *!Alabadle!: Hispanic Christian Worship*. Edited by Justo L. Gonzàlez, pp. 101-10. Nashville: Abingdon, 1996.

Guzman, Anibal. " 'Martyrdom and Hope': Five Hundred Years of Christian Presence in Latin America and the Caribbean." *International Review of Mission* 82 (January 1993):11-17.

Hahn, Ferdinand. *The Worship of the Early Church*. Philadelphia: Fortress, 1973.

Harris, Arthaniel Edgar Sr. "Worship in the AME Zion Church." *AME Zion Quarterly Review* 98, no. 2 (July 1986):33-36.

Hascall, John. "Native American Liturgy." *Liturgy* 7, no. 1 (1988):34-39.

————. "Native American Worship." In *The Ministries of Christian Worship*. Library of Christian Worship 7. Nashville: Star Song, 1994.

Hawn, C. Michael. "Vox Populi: Developing Global Song in the Northern World." In *The Ministries of Christian Worship*. Library of Christian Worship 7. Nashville: Star Song, 1994.

Hayes, Michael G. "The Function of Praise Songs in African-American Worship." In *Music and the Arts in Christian Worship*. Library of Christian Worship 4, bk 1. Nashville: Star Song, 1994.

Hernández, Edwin I. "Persistence of Religion Through Primary Group Ties Among Hispanic Seventh-day Adventist Young People." *Review of Religious Research* 32 (December 1990):157-72.

————. "Relocating the Sacred Among Latinos: Reflections on Methodology." In *Old Masks, New Faces: Religion and Latino Identities*. Edited by Anthony M. Stevens-Arroyo and Gilbert R. Cadena, pp. 61-76. New York: Bildner Center for Western Hemisphere Studies, 1995.

Hopkin, John Barton. "Music in the Jamaican Pentecostal Churches." *Jamaica Journal* 42 (September 1988):22-40.

Hovda, Robert W., ed. *This Far by Faith: American Black Worship and the African Roots*. Washington, D.C.: National Office for Black Catholics and the Liturgical Conference, 1977.

Hughes, Cornelius G. "Views from the Pews: Hispanic and Anglo Catholics in a Changing Church." *Review of Religious Research* 33 (June 1992):364-75.

Icaza, Rosa Maria. "Spirituality of the Mexican American People." *Worship* 63 (May 1989):232-46.

Jacobs, C. M. *Joy Comes in the Morning: Elton George Griffith and the Shouter Baptists*. Port-of-Spain, Trinidad & Tobago: n.p., 1996.

Johanson, Bruce. "To Draw Near to a Faithful God: Worship-Appropriate Features of 1 Thessalonians." Paper presented at the West Coast Religion Teachers Conference, April 1991.

Johnson, Lawrence J. *The Mystery of Faith: The Ministers of Music*. Washington, D.C.: National Association of Pastoral Musicians, 1983.

Kirk, Martha A. *Dancing with Creation: Mexican and Native American Dance in Christian Worship and Education*. San Jose, Calif.: Resource Publications, 1983.

————. "A Mexican Dance." In *Music and the Arts in Christian Worship*. Library of Christian Worship 4, bk. 2. Nashville: Star Song, 1994.

Kraft, Charles H. *Christianity with Power: Your Worldview and Your Experience of the Supernatural*. Michigan: Servant, 1989.

Lampe, Phillip E. "Religion and the Assimilation of Mexican Americans." *Review of Religious Research* 18 (spring 1977):243-53.

LaRuffa, Anthony L. "Culture Change and Pentecostalism in Puerto Rico." *Social and Economic Studies* 18 (September 1969):273-81.

Leonard, Richard C. "Old Testament Vocabulary of Worship." In *The Ministries of Christian Worship*. Library of Christian Worship 1. Nashville: Star Song, 1994.

————. "New Testament Vocabulary of Worship." In *The Ministries of Christian Worship*. Library of Christian Worship 1. Nashville: Star Song, 1994.

Lincoln, C. Eric. *The Black Church Since Frazier*. New York: Schochen, 1974.

Lincoln, C. Eric, and Lawrence H. Mamiya. *The Black Church in the African American Experience*. Durham, N.C.: Duke University Press, 1990.

Lindblade, Sondra. "The Emergence of a Multicultural Society." In *The Ministries of Christian Worship*. Library of Christian Worship 7. Nashville: Star Song, 1994.

Lopez, Carlos A. "Hymn Singing in the Hispanic Tradition." *Reformed Liturgy and Music* 21 (summer 1987):156-57.

————. "Hispanic-American Song." In *Music and the Arts in Christian Worship*. Library of Christian Worship 4, bk. 1. Nashville: Star Song, 1994.

Lutheran World Federation. "Cartigny Statement on Worship and Culture: Biblical and Historical Foundations." In *The Ministries of Christian Worship*. Library of Christian Worship 7. Nashville: Star Song, 1994.

Mabona, Mongameli. "Black People and White Worship." In *The Challenge of Black Theology in South Africa*. Edited by Basil Moore, pp. 104-8. Atlanta, Ga.: John Knox Press, 1973.

MacArthur, Terry. "Towards Global Worship: Beyond the Headlines." In *The Ministries of Christian Worship*. Library of Christian Worship 7. Nashville: Star Song, 1994.

Maduro, Otto. "Directions for a Reassessment of Latina/o Religion." In *Enigmatic Powers: Syncretism with African and Indigenous Peoples' Religions Among Latinos*. Edited by Anthony M. Stevens-Arroyo and Andrés I. Pérez y Mena, pp. 47-68. New York: Bildner Center for Western Hemisphere Studies, 1995.

Mannion, M. Francis. "Liturgy and Culture: Four Paradigms." In *The Ministries of Christian Worship*. Library of Christian Worship 7. Nashville: Star Song, 1994.

Mapson, J. Wendell Jr. *The Ministry of Music in the Black Church*. Valley Forge, Penn.: Judson Press, 1984.

Marshall, Michael. *Renewal in Worship*. Wilton, Conn.: Morehouse-Barlow, 1985.

Martin, Ralph P. *Worship in the Early Church*. Grand Rapids, Mich.: Eerdmans, 1975.

————. "History of Israelite and Jewish Worship." In *The Ministries of Christian Worship*. Library of Christian Worship 1. Nashville: Star Song, 1994.

Martinez, Jill. "Worship and the Search for Community in the Presbyterian Church (USA): The Hispanic Experience." *Church and Society* 76 (March-April 1986):42-46.

Matovina, Timothy. "Liturgy, Popular Rites and Popular Spirituality." *Worship* 63 (July 1989):351-61.

Maultsby, Portia K. "The Use and Performance of Hymnody, Spirituals and Gospels in the Black Church." In *The Black Christian Worship Experience*. Black Church Scholar 4. Edited by Melva Wilson Costen and Darius L. Swann, pp. 141-59. Atlanta: ITC Press, 1992.

Maynard-Reid, Pedrito U. "Poor and Rich in the Epistle of James." Th.D. diss.,

Andrews University, 1981.

———. *Poverty and Wealth in James*. Maryknoll, N.Y.: Orbis, 1987.

———. "Caribbean Worship." In *The Ministries of Christian Worship*. Library of Christian Worship 7. Nashville: Star Song, 1994.

———. "African-American Worship." In *The Ministries of Christian Worship*. Library of Christian Worship 7. Nashville: Star Song, 1994. Incorrectly attributed to Melva Costen.

———. *James: True Religion in Suffering*. Abundant Life Bible Amplifier. Boise, Idaho: Pacific, 1996.

———. *Complete Evangelism*. Scottdale, Penn.: Herald, 1997.

McClain, William B. "The Black Religious Experiences in the United States." In *This Far by Faith: American Black Worship and the African Roots*, pp. 28-37. Washington, D.C.: National Office for Black Catholics and the Liturgical Conference, 1977.

———. *The Soul of Black Worship*. Madison, N.J.: Multiethnic Center, Drew University, 1980.

———. Preface to *Songs of Zion*. Nashville: Abingdon, 1981.

McNamara, Patrick. "Assumptions, Theories and Methods in the Study of Latino Religion After Twenty-five Years." In *Old Masks, New Faces: Religion and Latino Identities*. Edited by Anthony M. Stevens-Arroyo and Gilbert R. Cadena, pp. 23-32. New York: Bildner Center for Western Hemisphere Studies, 1995.

Mirande, Alfredo. *The Chicano Experience: An Alternative Perspective*. Notre Dame, Ind.: University of Notre Dame Press, 1985.

Mitchell, Henry H. "The Continuity of African Culture." In *This Far by Faith: American Black Worship and the African Roots*, pp. 8-19. Washington, D.C.: National Office for Black Catholics and the Liturgical Conference, 1977. Pp. 8-19.

———. *Celebration and Experience in Preaching*. Nashville: Abingdon, 1990.

Montoya, Alex D. "Worship in Evangelical Hispanic Churches." In *The Ministries of Christian Worship*. Library of Christian Worship 7. Nashville: Star Song, 1994.

———. "Music in Evangelical and Pentecostal Hispanic Churches." In *The Ministries of Christian Worship*. Library of Christian Worship 7. Nashville: Star Song, 1994.

Moore, Joan. "The Social Fabric of the Hispanic Community Since 1965." In *Hispanic Catholic Culture in the U.S.: Issues and Concerns*. Edited by Jay P. Dolan and Allan Figueroa Deck, pp. 6-49. Notre Dame, Ind.: University of Notre Dame Press, 1994.

Moore, Joseph G. "Music and Dance as Expressions of Religious Worship in Jamaica." In *African Religious Groups and Beliefs: Prayers in Honor of William R. Bascom*. Edited by Simon Ottenberg. Merrut, India: Folklore Institute, 1982.

Morales, Beatriz. "Latino Religion, Ritual and Culture." In *Handbook of Hispanic Cultures in the United States: Anthropology*. Edited by Thomas Weaver, pp. 191-208. Houston: Arte Publico, 1994.

Moule, C. F. D. *Worship in the New Testament*. Richmond, Va.: John Knox Press, 1961.

Murphy, Joseph M. *Working the Spirit: Ceremonies of the African Diaspora*. Boston: Bean, 1994.

Niebuhr, H. Richard. *Christ and Culture*. New York: Harper & Row, 1951.

Nketia, J. H. Kwabena. "African Roots of Music in the Americas." *Jamaica Journal* 43 (1980):12-17.

Noble, Beverly B. "A Development of Liturgical Tradition Since 1962: A Study of the Anglican Church in Jamaica." Paper presented at the United Theological College of the West Indies, Jamaica, 1985.

O'Gorman, Pamela. *Caribbean Church Music: Some Problems*. Kingston, Jamaica: University of the West Indies, Mona Campus, 1975.

———. "The Introduction of Jamaican Music into the Established Churches." *Jamaica Journal* 9, no. 1 (1975):40-44, 47.

Ofori-atta-Thomas, George. "The African Inheritance in the Black Church Worship." In *The Black Christian Worship Experience*. Black Church Scholar 4. Edited by Melva Wilson Costen and Darius L. Swann, pp. 41-74. Atlanta: ITC Press, 1992.

Oliver, Paul. "Spirituals." In *The New Grove Gospel, Blues and Jazz*. Edited by Paul Oliver, William Bolcom, and Max Harrison, pp. 1-22. New York: W. W. Norton, 1986.

———. "Gospel." In *The New Grove Gospel, Blues and Jazz*. Edited by Paul Oliver, William Bolcom, and Max Harrison, pp. 189-222. New York: W. W. Norton, 1986.

Ostling, Richard N. "Strains on the Heart." *Time*, November 19, 1990, pp. 88-90.

Palackdrarrysing, Raymond Ray. "In Search of a Caribbean Theology." Paper presented at the United Theological College of the West Indies, Jamaica, 1976.

Pearson, Walter L. "Why I Have Hope." *Adventist Review*, February 1997, pp. 8-10.

Pena, Silva Novo. "Religion." In *The Hispanic American Almanac: a Reference Work on Hispanics in the United States*. Edited by Nicolas Kanellos, pp. 367-86. Detroit: Gale Research, 1993.

Pérez y Mena, Andres I. "Puerto Rican Spiritism as a Transfeature of Afro-Latin Religion." In *Enigmatic Powers: Syncretism with African and Indigenous Peoples' Religions Among Latinos*. Edited by Anthony M. Stevens-Arroyo and Andrés I. Pérez y Mena, pp. 137-55. New York: Bildner Center for Western Hemisphere Studies, 1995.

Pero, Albert. "Worship and Theology in the Black Context." In *Theology and the Black Experience*. Edited by A. Pero and A. Moro, pp. 227-48. Minneapolis: Augsburg, 1988.

Pitts, Walter F. Jr. *Old Ship of Zion: The Afro-Baptist Ritual in the African Diaspora*. New York: Oxford University Press, 1993.

Plant, Bob et al. *Worship Around the World*. Don Mills, Ontario: CANEC, 1980.

Pollak-Eltz, Angelina. "The Shango Cult and Other African Rituals in Trinidad, Grenada and Carriacou, and Their Possible Influence on the Spiritual Baptist Faith." *Caribbean Quarterly* 39 (September-December 1993):13-26.

Powell, Annie Ruth. "Hold onto your Dream: African-American Protestant Worship." In *Women at Worship: Interpretations of North American Diversity*. Edited by Marjorie Procter-Smith and Janet R. Walton, pp. 43-53. Louisville, Ky.: Westminster John Knox, 1993.

Prescod, Patrick, ed. *Sing a New Song*. Vol. 3. Barbados: Cedar, 1981.

Pressau, Jack Renard. "Songs of Salvation: Yesteryear's Music for Yesterday's Faith." *Duke Divinity School Review* 43 (winter 1978): 54-67.

Prince, Sister Donatine. "Music and Liturgy in the Roman Catholic Church in Jamaica." Paper presented at the University of the West Indies, Jamaica, 1979.

Quinn, Daniel. *Ishmael: An Adventure of the Mind and Spirit*. New York: Bantam Books, 1992.

Quintero-Rivera, Angel G. "The Camouflaged Drum: Melodization of Rhythms and Maroonaged Ethnicity in Caribbean Peasant Music." *Caribbean Quarterly* 40, no. 1

(March 1991):27-37.

Ramirez, Ricardo. "Liturgy from the Mexican American Perspective." *Worship* 57 (July 1977):293-98.

————. "The American Church and Hispanic Migration: An Historical Analysis— Part 1." *Migration Today* 6 (February 1978):16-20.

————. "The Challenge of Ecumenism to Hispanic Christians." *Ecumenical Trends* 21 (1992):117, 128-30.

————. "Reflections on the Hispanicization of the Liturgy." *Worship* 57 (January 1983):26-34.

Ramsey, Richard O. "The Relationship Between the Church Music and Songs Used in the Main-line Churches in Jamaica and the Jamaican Culture and Social Classes." Paper presented at the United Theological College of the West Indies, n.d.

Randoo, Mother Monica. Interview by author. Cocorite, Trinidad, July 3, 1997.

Reckord, Verena. "Rastafarian Music: An Introductory Study." *Jamaica Journal* 11, no. 1 (August 1977):2-13.

Rivera, Raymond. "The Political and Social Ramifications of Indigeneous Pentecostalism." *Prophets Denied Honor: An Anthology on the Hispano Church of the United States.* Edited by Antonio M. Stevens Arroyo, pp. 339-41. Maryknoll, N.Y.: Orbis, 1980.

Rivers, Clarence Joseph. *This Far by Faith: American Worship and Its African Roots.* Washington, D.C.: National Office for Black Catholics, 1977.

Roberts, Debbie. *Rejoice: A Biblical Study of the Dance.* Bedford, Tex.: Revival, 1982.

Rodriquez, José A. "Hispanic Hymns in the New Hymnal." *Reformed Liturgy and Music* 24 (spring 1990):82-83.

Rodriquez-Holguin, Jeanette Y. "Hispanics and the Sacred." *Chicago Studies* 29 (August 1990):137-52.

Rogers, Jefferson P. "Black Worship: Black Church." *Black Church* 1, no. 1 (1972):59-67.

Rosado, Caleb. "The Concept of Pueblo as a Paradigm for Explaining the Religious Experience of Latinos." In *Old Masks, New Faces: Religion and Latino Identities.* Edited by Anthony M. Stevens-Arroyo and Gilbert R. Cadena, pp. 77-91. New York: Bildner Center for Western Hemisphere Studies, 1995.

Rosas, Carlos. "Mexican Americans Sing Because They Feel Like Singing." *Pastoral Music* 1 (June-July 1977):14-17.

Rouse-Jones, Margaret D. "Changing Patterns of Denominational Affiliations in Trinidad and Tobago: An Exploratory Study." In *Social and Occupational Stratification in Contemporary Trinidad and Tobago.* Edited by Ryan Selway, pp. 350-74. St. Augustine, Trinidad and Tobago: Institute of Social and Economic Research, University of the West Indies, 1991.

————. Interview by author. University of the West Indies, St. Augustine, Trinidad, July 2, 1997.

Rowe, Cyprian Lamar. "The Case for a Distinctive Black Culture." In *This Far by Faith: American Black Worship and the African Roots*, pp. 20-27. Washington, D.C.: National Office for Black Catholics and the Liturgical Conference, 1977.

Ryan, Selwyn, ed. *Social and Occupational Stratification in Contemporary Trinidad and Tobago.* St. Augustine, Trinidad and Tobago: Institute of Social and Economic Research, University of the West Indies, 1991.

Salomon, Esaul. "The Role of Liturgy in Hispanic Lutheran Churches." *Lutheran*

Forum 25 (May 1991):30-31.

Sandoval, Mercedes Cros. "Afro-Cuban Religion in Perspective." In *Enigmatic Powers: Syncretism with African and Indigenous Peoples' Religions Among Latinos.* Edited by Anthony M. Stevens-Arroyo and Andrés I. Pérez y Mena, pp. 81-98. New York: Bildner Center for Western Hemisphere Studies, 1995.

Sandoval, Moises. "The Church Among the Hispanics in the United States." In *The Church in Latin America 1492-1992.* Maryknoll, N.Y.: Orbis, 1992.

Sauceda, Teresa Chávez. "Becoming a Mestizo Church." In *!Alabadle!: Hispanic Christian Worship.* Edited by Justo L. Gonzàlez, pp. 89-100. Nashville: Abingdon, 1996.

Schattauer, Thomas H. "How Does Worship Relate to Cultures in North America?" In *What Does "Multicultural" Worship Look Like?* Edited by Gordon Lathrop, pp. 6-15. Minneapolis: Augsburg Fortress, 1996.

Schineller, Peter. *A Handbook of Inculturation.* New York: Paulist, 1990.

———. "A Roman Catholic Approach to Liturgical Inculturation." In *The Ministries of Christian Worship.* Library of Christian Worship 7. Nashville: Star Song, 1994.

Senn, Frank C. *Christian Worship and Its Cultural Setting.* Philadelphia: Fortress, 1983.

Siewart, Alison. "Worship and Culture." In *Worship Team Handbook.* Edited by Alison Siewart, pp. 17-20. Downers Grove, Ill.: InterVarsity Press, 1998.

Siewart, Alison, ed. *Worship Team Handbook.* Downers Grove, Ill.: InterVarsity Press, 1998.

Silva-Gotay, Samuel. "The Ideological Dimensions of Popular Religiosity and Cultural Identity in Puerto Rico." In *An Enduring Flame: Studies on Latino Popular Religiosity.* Edited by Anthony M. Stevens-Arroyo and Ana María Diaz-Stevens, pp. 133-70. New York: Bildner Center for Western Hemisphere Studies, 1994.

Simpson, George Eaton. "Baptismal, 'Mourning' and 'Building' Ceremonies of the Shouters in Trinidad." *Journal of American Folklore* 79, no. 314 (October-December 1966):537-50.

———. *Religious Cults of the Caribbean: Trinidad, Jamaica and Haiti.* Puerto Rico: Institute of Caribbean Studies, University of Puerto Rico, 1970.

———. "The Acculturative Process in Trinidadian Shango." *Anthropological Quarterly* 37:16-27.

Slough, Rebecca. "Worship and Multicultural Diversity." In *The Ministries of Christian Worship.* Library of Christian Worship 7. Nashville: Star Song, 1994.

Smith, Ashley. "The Christian Minister as a Political Activist." *Caribbean Journal of Religious Studies* 2 (September 1979):24-35.

Smith, Russ. "The Soul of the Caribbean." *The Other Side* 28 (May-June 1992):40-42.

Solíván, Samuel. "Hispanic Pentecostal Worship." In *!Alabadle!: Hispanic Christian Worship.* Edited by Justo L. Gonzàlez, pp. 43-56. Nashville: Abingdon, 1996.

Sosa, Juan J. "Liturgy in Two Languages: Some Principles." *Pastoral Music* 5 (August-September 1981):36-38.

———. "Let Us Pray . . . en Espanol." *Liturgy (Washington)* 3 (spring 1983):63-67.

———. "Liturgy in Three Languages." *Pastoral Music* 7 (February-March 1983):13-15.

Southern, Eileen. *The Music of Black Americans: A History.* New York: W. W. Norton, 1971.

———. *The Music of Black Americans: A History.* 3rd ed. New York: W. W. Norton, 1997.

Spencer, Althea. "Caribbean Church Music: An Introduction." Paper presented at the

United Theological College of the West Indies, Jamaica, 1980-1981.

Spencer, Jon Michael. *Protest and Praise: Sacred Music of Black Religion.* Minneapolis: Fortress, 1990.

————. "African-American Song." In *Music and the Arts in Christian Worship.* Library of Christian Worship 4. bk. 1. Nashville: Star Song, 1994.

————. *Sing a New Song: Liberating Black Hymnody.* Minneapolis: Fortress, 1995.

Stevens, Anthony M. "Tomorrow's Parish: Culture and the Church Today." *Ave Maria* 106 (August 1967):16-17.

Stephens, Joanne. "The Changing Perspective of the Roman Catholic Church Towards Music Used in the Liturgy in Trinidad." Paper presented at the University of the West Indies, Jamaica, 1984.

Stevens-Arroyo, Anthony M. Introduction to *An Enduring Flame: Studies on Latino Popular Religiosity.* Edited by Anthony M Stevens-Arroyo and Ana Maria Diaz-Stevens, pp. 9-15. New York: Bildner Center for Western Hemisphere Studies, 1994.

Stevens-Arroyo, Anthony M. "Discovering Latino Religion." In *Discovering Latino Religion: A Comprehensive Social Science Bibliography.* Edited by Anthony M. Stevens-Arroyo and Segundo Pantoja, pp. 13-40. New York: Bildner Center for Western Hemisphere Studies, 1995.

Stevens-Arroyo, Antonio M., and Ana Maria Diaz-Ramirez. "The Hispano Model of Church: A People on the March." *New Catholic World,* July-August 1980, pp. 153-57.

————. "Religious Faith and Institutions in the Forging of Latino Identities." In *Handbook of Hispanic Cultures in the United States: Sociology.* Edited by Felix Padilla, pp. 257-91. Houston: Arte Publico, 1994.

Taiwo, Moses Oladele. "Victory over the Demons." *Ministry,* April 1991, pp. 25-26.

Tarango Yolanda. "The Church Struggling to Be Universal: A Mexican American Perspective." *International Review of Mission* 78 (April 1989):167-73.

Thomas, Eudora. *A History of the Shouter Baptist in Trinidad and Tobago.* Trinidad: Calalous, 1987.

Thomas, Frank A. *They Like to Never Quit Praisin' God: The Role of Celebration in Preaching.* Cleveland, Ohio: United Church Press, 1997.

Thorne, Janet E. "Factors Contributing to the Growth of Nonconventional Churches in St. Vincent." Paper presented at the Faculty of Arts and General Studies, University of the West Indies, Jamaica, 1986.

Trulear, Harold Dean. "The Lord Will Make a Way Somehow: Black Worship and the Afro-American Story." *Journal of the Interdenominational Theological Center* 13, no. 1 (fall 1985):87-104.

Turner, William C. "The Musicality of Black Preaching: A Phenomenology." *Journal of Black Sacred Music* 2, no. 1 (spring 1988):21-29.

Vasquez, Edmundo E. "Hispanic Urban Ministry Comes of Age." *The Christian Ministry* 20 (March-April 1989):20-21.

Vidal, James R. "Towards an Understanding of Synthesis in Iberian and Hispanic American Popular Religiosity." In *An Enduring Flame: Studies on Latino Popular Religiosity.* Edited by Anthony M. Stevens-Arroyo and Ana María Diaz-Stevens, pp. 69-95. New York: Bildner Center for Western Hemisphere Studies, 1994.

Villafáne, Eldin. *The Liberating Spirit: Toward an Hispanic American Pentecostal Social*